FIELDS of VISION

FIELDS of VISION

A Journey to Canada's Family Farms

Phil Jenkins

photographs by

Ken Ginn

M&S

Canadian Cataloguing in Publication Data

Jenkins, Phil, 1951–
   Fields of vision

ISBN 0–7710–4402–X

1. Family farms – Canada.   2. Agriculture – Canada.   3. Farm life – Canada.   I. Ginn, Ken, 1954–   .   II. Title.

S451.5.A1J46 1991   630'.971   C91–093373–1

Printed and bound in Canada. The paper used in this book is acid free.

McClelland & Stewart Inc.
The Canadian Publishers
481 University Avenue
Toronto, Ontario
M5G 2E9

To you, whichever field you are in.

And to our dear families as they reap and sow.

We depended, as we journeyed, on the kindness of strangers. The farm families of Canada treated us only as friends, giving us an afternoon or an evening, a meal and sometimes a bed for no other reason than that we had arrived on their doorstep. Many, many thanks, and you are all invited to our place for dinner.

Thanks also to the people of Canada who pay tax. They, via the Canada Council and the Ontario Arts Council, partially funded the research and writing of this book. Thanks, too, to Dinah Forbes for her editorial efforts on our behalf.

And to Catherine and Liette.

If there can be such a thing as instinctual memory, the consciousness of land and water must lie deeper in the core of us than any knowledge of our fellow beings. We were bred of the earth before we were bred of our mothers. Once born we can live without our mothers or fathers, or any other kin, or any friend or any human love. We cannot live without the earth or part from it. And something is shrivelled in man's heart when he turns away from it and concerns himself only with the affairs of men.

– Marjorie Kinnan Rawlings

Once upon a time, all of Canada was land. And the day is coming when it will all be real estate.

– Phil Jenkins

Contents

Introduction

The fields of Canada. Imagine them all laid end to end. The cabbage field born from the bush of Newfoundland, a moose trampling and nibbling the rows under an eastern moon. The potato field in Prince Edward Island, neat as a golf green with the flag removed, rusted soil beneath. The cart moving across the freshly turned field near Lunenburg, filling slowly with stones. The feral meadow behind an abandoned farmhouse in New Brunswick. McIntosh apples the size of melons bending the branches of Ontario fruit trees. The bees pollinating a tight-knit field of alfalfa between Lake Manitoba and Lake Winnipeg. Antelope looking down from a butte in southern Saskatchewan onto a derelict grain elevator. The steers fattening in the feedlot across from the cupolas of a Ukrainian church in Alberta. A golden eagle tearing at the belly of a calf on the hills of British Columbia. Cucumbers sweet as apples heading for market in the belly of a boat on the Yukon River.

And in between them their almost endless cousins, defined in barbed wire, framed by ditches, surrounded by pole fences laced together like fingers. Fields holding the cities apart. Fields that have the seasons as their patrons, as they yield to the common task, to make food.

And working the fields, the landlovers and the landusers. Looking out through tractor and kitchen windows onto feast or famine, at reasons to stay or reasons to leave. All looking out upon their own fields of vision.

Birth of a Notion

On the night this book was born I was at the tenth birthday party of an Ottawa FM rock station. A farmer I know describes Ottawa as "Thirty square miles surrounded by reality."

The knot of people I found myself in at the party were all sipping free booze and swapping exaggerations and complaints. Ken, a photographer, appeared on the edge of this knot. He keeps his blond hair and clothes conservative, loves puns, talks to his mother at least once a day, and is very happily married to a lovely, understanding Frenchwoman.

A week earlier, Ken and his wife had been blessed with their first child. Freddie had taken forty-nine hours to make it into the world, leaving his mother completely exhausted. Ken was still high on the miracle and ready to love the whole world.

As we talked of babies and the future, people all around us were hatching schemes full of relevance and glory. Most of the schemes would go out with the wine bottles on Monday.

"Got any schemes?" Ken asked me.

"Well, I always wanted to do a book on farming," I said. "Go travelling from the farm farthest east in Canada to the farm farthest west, from the *A* back across to the *C* on the map. Talking to farmers along the way. Take a journey through my own misconceptions. If you want to find out how it feels to lay an egg, talk to the chicken, right?"

"That is," said Ken, "now that you say it, just about what I had in mind. Are you serious?"

That moment I decided that, yes, I was very serious. I wanted to know if farming would still be a career that Ken's newborn son could choose when he came of age.

A year later Ken and I left for Newfoundland. Although neither one of us could yet have said why, either with a specific photograph or a precise phrase, we knew ourselves to be rural romantics. Ken lived then on fifty verdant acres of southern Ontario. The walls of his house had been built a hundred years earlier, from logs of rock elm that had been cut, thrown in the pond for a year while the bark peeled off, hauled out, squared, and left to dry for another year. They had hardened to a toughness that scorned nails. He used an old tractor to shift the mashed-potato snow that would fill the half-mile dirt track to the hardtop. He liked to call out the names of old tractors he saw from his van window.

I had worked on a farm in England, as the son of the right-hand man of the millionaire who owned it. I had started there in my teens, skinny and nervous of the loose family of men that worked fifteen hundred acres of peat lying between the shore of the River Mersey and the Pennines. I had almost worked my way into their respect by the time I left ten years later. By then I had been run over by Black Angus bulls, had my rubber boots chewed by pigs, and had learned to back a free-axled hay wagon into a barn on the second try.

The drive from Ontario to Sydney, started two days after my thirty-seventh birthday, was a sort of platonic honeymoon for Ken and I. Getting ready for the trip had made us friends, but now we had to live together.

Ken, it would emerge, has a somewhat traditional diet: red meat followed by pie and ice cream. I lean towards green rather than red food, and consider a banana dessert. The red vinyl booths of truck stops across Canada, in what we came to call by the collective name the "Clone Restaurant," became nutritional battlegrounds, with the ammunition favouring Ken. The summer of 1988 was spent meeting our meals at both ends of the chain.

"The French word for farm and closed are almost the same," I told Ken on our first day of travel, as we rolled along the southern shore of the St. Lawrence, past a stretched necklace of barns and silos. I had decided that erudition might be a way of passing the time. Getting from here to there takes a while in Canada.

Every now and then a thought would intrude on the landscape, and I'd jot it down. Looking at them now, I read "the ghosts of those who have lost their farms sit like Banquo's ghost at the banquet in *Macbeth*"; I wrote that the day we counted over fifty Orchard For Sale signs in the Okanagan Valley. And as we sat on the Nanaimo ferry, having crossed the country and pivoted back towards home, I noted that "I'd like to meet some inhospitable, lazy, mean-tempered farmers, just for a change." We never did.

The cassette player in the blue Dodge van seemed to develop a sixth sense as we journeyed east. It would frequently play just the right mood or phrase to accompany a milestone in the journey. Jennifer Warnes sang lines from a Leonard Cohen song about fields being under lock and key as we passed our first Farm For Sale sign.

"The fields are under lock and key
Though the sun and the rain still shine through."

Some of the prettiest country in Canada, around Baddeck in Cape Breton, was hidden by darkness as we reeled off the hours to Sydney and the ferry to Newfoundland. The window lights provided little framed theatres to break the boredom. In the Clone Motel, the night before we boarded the ferry, the television was full of the Group of Seven Economic Summit. Seven very powerful people, none of whom were raised on farms, were in Toronto to pillow-fight politics. In a preliminary interview the prime minister actually said the phrase "farm families." That was the first and last time it was mentioned, although the journalists there worked their way, for free, through a stack of farm produce.

Far below the Summit, down in the fields of Canada, Ken and

I were free to ask those same farm families about their tiny pieces of the world. Every ten minutes of every day we travelled, a Canadian farmer somewhere ahead of, or behind us, was giving up that piece of the world. The farmers of the eighties, so we believed then, were a blighted crop.

The next day we awoke to rain drumming on the Clone Motel windows. Excitement about going to Newfoundland, my first time, overwhelmed the weather.

As we drove onto the ferry, an elf of a man with the smile of a baby asked, "Where to, boy?"

"Argentia," I said. (Argentia is the ferry stop on the east side of Newfoundland, nineteen hours distant from Sydney. The first building you see pulling in there is an American naval base. A spy was caught stealing "secrets" from there shortly after we passed through.)

"Some calls it Argentina," the elf said, with that eager, rushed way Newfoundlanders have of getting to the end of their sentences. "What do you think of that?"

I said I thought it was wrong.

"Well, thank you," said the elf, as though I had shared a secret with him. "Have a real pleasant time of it now."

I thanked him back. A day and a half ahead of us the farm farthest east in Canada awaited our footprints.

THE
ATLANTIC
FIELDS

1

CLOSE TO
THE EDGE

The most easterly field in Canada, and in North America, is a few minutes' drive northeast of St. John's. It lies thinly on the ancient rock beneath. As the sun rises out of the Atlantic, the first cows it warms on the continent are in this field. These most easterly cows can look up from their pasture and see the tops of the cliffs of Logy Bay, a rough-hewn V in the side of Newfoundland. Whales crossing the mouth of Logy Bay have Ireland and Canada as their fences.

One of these cows is called Valerie. Valerie has a habit of visiting children who stop at the fence. If this makes her late for milking, one of her owners, Kevin Powers, will call her by name, and she will come.

Kevin and his brother Charlie, both with identical bushy eyebrows are, on this bright sunny day, milking by hand the forty-odd Holstein cows they collaborate with on their farm. Milking all the cows by hand takes them about four hours. They do it twice a day. Apart from a brief period when they had automatic milking, ten years ago, they have always done it this way. They prefer it.

"Since I could see over the pail," says Charlie, when he is asked how long he has been milking. They are, quite simply, milkmen.

In the well-used, bleached red barn I can hear the sound of warm milk hitting the sides of buckets. Kevin and Charlie stay on their milking stools and listen silently to my stumbling explanation. They suppose that, yes, this is the farm farthest east in Canada – now that Newfoundland is in Canada.

Charlie is quiet for a moment, looking off through the barn window at the radio tower on the cliff top, an American-built relic of the Second World War. Charlie's wife, Mary, in a blue workout suit, is mowing the grass around their modern bungalow. Most of Mary's friends married Americans and went off the island to live mainland lives. One skipped clear across as far as Hawaii.

Kevin and his wife live on the other side of the lane, close enough for the brothers to decide, calling from window to window, who will go and see what is disturbing the cattle on a foggy morning – mornings foggy enough to give the sea gulls a hard time finding their nests.

Kevin joins his brother and they walk towards an odd-sized building, too small to be a useful barn, too big for a shed. Just outside the doorway there is a small leafless tree with rubber boots jammed on the end of branches. The rain washes the boots clean, free of charge.

Kevin talks about his sister, the second of his ten siblings, who died. The setting has caused Kevin's voice to drop to a church-like whisper. It's a voice, gilded with an Irish accent, that could be talking to you in the quiet corner of a Dublin bar.

"As a matter of fact, she died right there in the corner," Kevin Powers says, pointing to a corner of the building from the door-way. "Forty-two years dead yesterday, the longest day of summer. It was a long day for us, I'll tell you." The hay-filled building, on that death day and for two hundred years before that, had been the family home. The stairs that the brothers tumbled down towards the kitchen stove, their clothes the same summer and winter, are still there.

The Powers brothers begin, one talking, the other nodding, to weave a spell. It is a spell to wind back time, until the planes flying overhead, sliding down their flight paths into St. John's, seem like intruders from another era. Kevin, his big teat-pulling hands resting in his armpits, talks of a grandmother who said her prayers in Irish.

"And she would stuff a bit of bread in our coats," he says, "to give to the fairies. If it was raisins, mind, well we'd have it ourselves and take our chances with the fairies."

Charlie, the more pragmatic of the two, begins to add cross-threads of day-by-day detail to Kevin's weft of mischief.

"No plumbing, of course, it was the buckets then. And boys wouldn't be in school, and the teacher would ask, 'Now where's this fella?' and name him by name, and we'd tell her, 'Gone to the ice, Miss,' meaning he'd gone ice fishing."

And into the background threads the brothers stitch moments of colour – "Father turned his cows loose on the cliffs, though there was more grass on the ceiling than there was out there." – and respect, respect that had let Father do it his way, until he was gone, and then the hills had been cleared of stones and stumps. As well, in go the bright hues of the special days – "And sure, we'd clean out the chimney for Christmas, so that Santa Claus could go back to the North Pole with no marks of his trade on him." – And ordinary days stood on end – "Father would have the beggarmen in. There'd be a drop of liquor on the go, and soon there'd be dancing and scablashing round the floor. We'd have a grand time of it, looking at them."

They are happily rooted in the acres they were born on and will die on. "No, I've never left the island," Kevin says cheerfully. "And I don't intend to." Charlie admits to a wish to travel, some day, to Prince Edward Island, "To see the farms up there." Even on brief holidays, they take the farm with them. Charlie went to a son's wedding in central Newfoundland. "And at six in the morning I heard a cow bellowing," he says, "and I got up to see what kind it was. The wife nearly hanged me."

Rooted as they are, money is a lever that has been used more than once to try and pry them off. A developer came out from St. John's, fifteen minutes down the road, and offered them $2.5 million. The brothers had easily refused. "What would we do?" says Kevin, simply and irrefutably. It is not real estate that they and their herd live on – it is land.

But their children have all chosen other lives, and so the farm will, most probably, die with Kevin and Charlie and become real estate. The view will be sold by the lot. And people who have travelled far more than the Powers will live along Powers' Farm Road, and soon not know who gave the road its name.

Talking to the Powers brothers, there is a sense of having retrieved something before it falls from sight behind the horizon of history. They have chosen to stand in one spot and learn much about a little, rather than a little about much; and who is to say who ends up knowing more?

2

FARTHER ON
DOWN THE ROAD

I t is easy to fall in love with Newfoundland if mystery and humour are what you like in a lover. On the radio in the van, the day before visiting Kevin and Charlie, driving from the ferry to St. John's, the local CBC informed us of a telephone number that fishermen could dial for help if a whale got caught in their nets. This message was delivered matter-of-factly. After hearing this, trying to get our eyes on a whale becomes a mission second only to finding farmers.

And talking one day to a strong contender for the farm farthest east in Canada, I suddenly realize that I have been repeatedly calling the man a Newfie. "Do you mind me calling you a Newfie?" I ask sheepishly.

"Call us anything you like, boy," the farmer tells me. "We won't come." And then he laughs and rubs my arm to show no harm was taken.

The farmers of Newfoundland work and play with equal dedication, like voltmeters banging over into the red no matter which way the current flows. Mostly, they work. The rawness of the land demands it. One couple we visited had, twelve years ago, said to hell with Toronto, and loaded the truck for the land of the husband's grandparents. After a series of self-imposed plagues, most of them the result of ignorance of the character of the Newfoundland bush, and a Christmas Eve fire that had reduced to ashes everything they owned, they had discovered greenhouses and strawberries. Their enthusiasm for the island, unlike their hands, has remained unscratched.

One misconception we carried with us from Ottawa, but left on the ferry, was the extent of farming in Newfoundland. A farmer who had written a book on the farm crisis had guessed that there were three or four farms there at the most. There are four hundred, ranging in size from pregnant gardens to spreads like that of Joey Smallwood Junior. Nevertheless, the island earns more, as the deputy minister of agriculture (and tourism) commented, from moose-hunting licences than it does from agriculture. This fact is weighed when priorities are drawn up in the legislature.

I repeated for the deputy minister a conversation I'd had with one of his flock, Betty Parsons. I had called her up from Ottawa to ask if we could visit.

"What's the biggest problem facing farmers out there, Betty?"

"Well, with us, it's the moose," Betty had said. "Your moose can do ten thousand dollars of damage in one night."

"Must be a bloody big moose," I had laughed down fifteen hundred miles of phone line. Betty, with astonishing politeness, had actually given this rancid joke a brief chuckle.

The Parsons live in Lethbridge, a hundred miles up the highway from St. John's. Driving there, we pass icebergs the size of shopping malls, a road with the magical name of Horse Chops Lane, and the Come by Chance oil refinery. The first we see of the isolated refinery is a thin metal candle a hundred feet tall, topped by a windsock of flame, as though the whole refinery were only capable of this one small, constant, inflammable belch.

The hotel nearest to the Parsons's farm is called the Dunrovin.

This translates roughly as the "Ain't Going No Farther." The two people in the lounge, when we come through the door, appear to have decided to do just that on the day the hotel opened. Although they are the only ones there, they sit at separate tables behind bottles of Blue. Behind a screen at the rear of the hotel, in a vast dart–and–dance room, the local Rural Development Committee is battling its way through an agenda.

"Do you have rooms in the hotel?" I ask the bartender.

"Yes, yes we do."

"How much for two people?" I ask.

"For what?"

"For a room."

"We don't rent the rooms in the hotel, mind," she says. "We rent cabins. You just asked if the hotel had rooms."

"So I did," I say, and we are away, both of us in the same conversation, heading in the same direction.

3

BREAKING
NEW GROUND

The Parsons live just a mile back down the highway from the Dunrovin Hotel. The farm is midway along a peninsula, shaped like a farmer's fat finger, that sticks out into the Atlantic.

By the back porch, a gang of kids are listening to heavy metal on a boom box in the back of a half-ton. One of them is Donny, the Parsons's son. The Parsons, he says, have "taken the greens to market. Back soon." The half-ton starts up and fishtails down the gravel and onto the hardtop, leaving us alone with a collie puppy doing furry tumbles at the end of a rope.

The sun is big and red behind the scrubby bush as another pickup comes up the drive. The two small people in it are visible only as heads topped by baseball caps. They are sitting right by the doors like teenagers on a first date. Wilf and Betty Parsons hop out, grubby from a day's work.

"We'll shower, boys," says Wilf, after handshakes. "So why don't you walk the farm," and he points past the jumbled buildings.

We walk and walk and walk, past field after field of red oxide soil, each neat as a tablecloth. The fields fly off the path like flags on a crooked mast. There is hardly any machinery, just a middle-aged tractor and a old pickup with a back wheel off to provide the belt drive for a small sawmill. The sheer hard labour that has stolen this farm from the stumpy, swampy bush must have been enormous.

A moose head sits over the freezer in the hallway to the Parsons's kitchen, with a sprig of lilacs resting between its antlers. Coffee and pineapple balls quickly appear. Wilf, scrubbed clean in green overalls, rests his behind on the kitchen counter. He is about fifty, wiry and weather-beaten brown, small enough to knock over with a bad joke. Tonight he looks tired.

Betty, her short brown hair and glasses jiggling to the speed of her voice, begins to tell of a remarkable adventure. Wilf, an accomplished storyteller, joins her. Their thick accents and turns of phrase are entrancing. Some tales grow with the telling, adding stories to their architecture till they are tall tales indeed. But the tale of Betty and Wilf will get relayed across Canada, at other tables laden with cakes and coffee, almost intact.

Betty and Wilf met in the fitting room of a church. Betty was trying on caps for the choir she had just joined. She was having trouble finding one small enough. Deciding to leave, she was faced with three doors. She asked the gentleman in the room with her which door did not go into the church; there were people in it she didn't want to disturb. "You goes through that door," said the gentleman. Betty took his advice – and stepped into the church.

Betty and the gentleman, who was Wilf, began going through other doors together. They told each other about themselves. Wilf told her that he was the son of a schooner captain. The schooner was called the *Milly Ford*. Wilf's parents had six kids, which, perhaps not by coincidence, is the number of crew it takes to run a schooner. Wilf worked as a steward in his early teens with his father and uncles on the *Milly Ford*, but his stomach was clearly happier with land underneath it, not water.

Wilf established at an early age that he was not a lad to

consider the odds. While his father was discussing a standing bet with a farmer that no one could get in the pen with a killer bull, Wilf's cap blew into that very pen. Wilf was over the fence and back on the other side in no time, with the cap back on his head. "That bull never blinked an eye to me, mind," says Wilf.

Betty's people are from the northern side of Bonavista Bay, around Shambler's Cove, Newtown, up that way. "The breeding ground of the world," Wilf calls it. "There's neither a country in the world doesn't have someone from 'round there in it. They're artists, educated people. Those people are it."

"On May 24, 1961," says Betty, "we started for to build the farm." Create would be a better word than build. Wilf and Betty have made their farm from bush – bush that had never felt a farmer's foot. The soil they needed to level and reveal was clogged with the rock of Newfoundland and the stubborn pines that dressed it. "'Tis a pretty poggy-natured soil," says Wilf. The soil, stained red by the oxide in it, has the consistency of Plasticine. "If you were five feet eight when you went in," he says, "you'd be five feet ten by the time you comes out." The land they fought was not even theirs. Leased from the government, it would only become Parsons' land when a quarter of the eighty-five acres had been cleared. Most years they cleared five; the best year they had they cleared ten.

In those first struggling days Wilf would work elsewhere in land clearance, and at night he would join Betty, driving the pickup along the wooden slats she had laid leading to their rudimentary home. The flies were ferocious, at least for Betty.

"I likes to work when it rains," says Betty, "when them flies are not so bad. But I can be going down a row, blood all on my face, and there's Wilf next to me with neither a one on him."

"I puts her out as bait," says Wilf, with a not unkind laugh.

Wilf and Betty Parsons are pioneers. Go back two hundred years and nobody worked any harder. If the soil on their farm was analysed, a few parts per million of every sample would be Parsons'.

Betty calls Wilf "Dad," and Wilf occasionally calls Betty "Mum." They will call people visiting them "My darling" or

"Boy" or "Lovey" or "My son." Their accent, although they live only half a day's drive from the Powers brothers at Logy Bay, is West Country English. When Wilf talks of "wit soil," he is saying "wet soil." *Ee*s have become *eye*s, and *aa*s have become *oh*s.

"Wilf's fother said 'Who's you?' the first time we met," Betty says. That these coastal people have remnants of the accent of the breeding ground of England's sailors is altogether sensible.

Betty now looks up and moves her lips as she counts. "Thirty-three," she says, then "thirty-nine." She is adding up her children. She looks back down, smiles, and pronounces the total to be "forty-five."

"Well," she says, explaining this enormous number, "we had two of our own, see, adopted one, and reared up two more, and reared up another young girl. Every kid we had, we built on a piece to the house. And then we fostered some. We comes home one day, mind, and there was three more than when we'd left that morning." Another foster home had broken up, creating an emergency, and the Parsons had been the logical choice to receive the homeless trio. They have hearts that would topple wheelbarrows. The children that have graced this farm are as much its crop as the cabbage and the broccoli.

Today is the day, with cruel luck, that the last boy, Donny, an adopted son, is leaving home. He has found work in an Ontario steel mill, where a friend is already at work, making a steady wage – indoors. Betty has a tear permanently waiting to roll out of the corner of her eye. She sneaks glances, as she talks, into the house, past her doll collection, to the bookshelves where her photo albums, all sixteen of them, are stacked.

"You can't expect 'em to stay, my son," says Wilf. "'Tis pure hardship."

"I can do without it," says Donny, of farming. A picture of Donny in a playpen, in Betty's photo album, shows he hasn't changed much in nineteen years: rotund, coal black hair, wide-open face. Donny doesn't say this of farming in a cruel way. Rather he has watched his parents do battle with a series of enemies, and he has come to wonder why they continue to fight.

He will have to leave home, as Betty knows, to find that out. And when he does know why, it may not be enough to bring him back.

As their children have come and gone, the constant enemy for the Parsons has been the moose Betty spoke of on the phone. Almost from the day they staked claim to the bush, the moose have declared a dumb war of attrition. The moose's weapons have been its numbers, the cover of night, the size of its feet, and its appetite. "I can't win for losing," says Wilf, "with that damn moose nibbling at me."

Let there be no underestimating the damage moose can wreak. For twenty-five years the moose have been like a slow-motion hurricane passing through the Parsons's farm. In 1964 alone, Wilf estimates that they trampled or nibbled $25,000 worth of vegetables. "They gots feet the size of dinner plates," he says. Wilf talks of "crews" of moose coming into his fields at night, as in "wrecking crews."

Betty has a war story of her own, a tragic one. "I had one field, oh gash, I was proud of it. I don't know how many hours I put into it. There was neither a weed or a stone in it; it was beautiful. Well, I sets out to see how it is doing one morning, and the farmhand tells me, 'I don't think you should go out there, Betty. Just don't.' The moose had ruined it. Ten thousand dollars of cabbage destroyed in one night."

To try and defeat this relentless and unwitting enemy, Wilf and Betty have done what all beleaguered nations have done before them – turned to technology. First it was an electric fence. Most animals, when they come up against a wire that hits them with electricity, go backwards. Not a moose. The moose, electrified wire pulsing across its massive chest, goes forward like a runner breasting a tape that won't break. The result of all this is a frenetically trampled field and an electric fence that needs to be dragged back across the damage and reset.

Phase two of the Parsons' arms race was a propane cannon. A buildup of gas in a chamber is ignited at intervals, anywhere from three times a minute to five minutes apart. The noise, Betty says, was enough to bring her to her knees. For a while this worked, but then two moose brain cells got together and realized that the cannon was not a deterrent – it was a dinner bell.

Finally Wilf got a permit to kill any moose that he caught crushing cabbage. He can't keep the meat (a man from the Wildlife Service comes and hauls it off and dresses it), but he can make an occasional example for other moose. Some farmers have managed without permits. They have found a way of scaring marauding moose directly into the freezer.

There is, of course, a story to the moose head that hangs over the freezer in the hall – the one with the lilacs in its antlers. Wilf knows that there is a tragic and comic duality to all this moose talk, and he plays this story for its humour, which is abundant.

The moose met its end the day of a family barbecue. The Parsons rarely have the chance to get festive. Betty and Wilf do a little weekend dancing at the Dunrovin, and there is the annual Farmers' Field Day. There was even a holiday in Nova Scotia twenty-four years ago, but they take most of their hours and put them into the fields. When they do get festive, it's like a cork coming out of a bottle. Things were going fine until Alvin, the hired hand, came roaring in a truck up the path from the fields.

"There's a m-m-m-m . . .!" Alvin shouted to Wilf. Alvin has a stutter when he gets excited. He also has a crewcut head that resembles a bullet. On top of the bullet sits a cap. Alvin sweats when he's excited, and that lubricates the cap, which wobbles in time to his stutter.

"There's a m-m-m-m . . .!" Alvin shouted again, the vibrating cap Geiger-counting his excitement. Wilf got his gun.

The moose, amazingly, was right where Alvin had last seen it. Wilf admits that he is no marksman – he would have trouble hitting the water if he fell out of a boat – but he let go a shot. Either the noise or the bullet, he didn't know which, drove the moose into the reed canary grass. Reed canary grass grows taller than a moose, and Wilf couldn't track him. But he could hear him. "The living snorts was coming out of him, boys," Wilf says.

The next day Wilf had gone into the canary grass, and there was his moose, neatly shot in the jugular and bled to death. His head went up over a smaller freezer, but the lid had bonked his nose every time Betty opened it. He had come to rest over the large freezer.

But the occasional trophy has in no way levelled the score. Wilf will patrol his farm early in the morning, at three or four o'clock, and see nothing moosish. Later that day he'll return, and there is the damage – cabbage or turnips in decapitated rows.

In 1971, Wilf and Betty took on a new enemy. This one didn't look like an enemy at first – in fact, it helped them build a warehouse for the canker-free seed potatoes that Wilf grows. When it first started to get a little out of hand, they felt it might just be a phase it was going through. But since the early eighties it has gotten away from them. The enemy that, more than any crew of moose, may finally defeat them is the bank.

Wilf knew the bank was his enemy the day he went in to ask for a $4,000 operating loan. It's standard practice in farming, especially among potato farmers, to borrow the money to plant and fertilize a crop and to pay it back when the crop is sold. The difference between the loan, plus interest, and the money you get from the harvest keeps you alive – if everything else, the market and the machinery, stays calm.

Wilf had just finished paying off a $12,000 loan at 24 per cent – in two years. Twenty-four per cent is financial rape. The bank said they would give Wilf his $4,000 loan. But first he would have to renegotiate his other loans, the ones still outstanding that he had taken prior to the $12,000 loan, at the current interest rate. The current rate was not quite as violent, but it was still rape.

All banks do a very simple thing: they sell money for more than they bought it for. Farmers all across the country had bought money from them at a good price in the late seventies. The banks had encouraged them, as they were encouraging Wilf, to buy it.

But banks do something with money that no other retailer does. When the price goes up, they ask you to pay the new price on the old money you bought. And because you can only buy money from a bank, you agree. And they ask you, if you can't pay the new price, to let them sell bits of your life until you have paid. Sometimes the bits add up to everything you have.

"I'd never owed nor jingle till I took out my first loan in '71," says Wilf, "and paid them straight after that. But when they tried that I told them, 'If you can't work with people better than that, there's something wrong to you.'" And he swears, "Blood of a bitch."

"Oh, Dad," says Betty.

"Everyone knows what it means," says Wilf. And he adds, more to himself than anyone, "You goes for a loan, and then they owns you." Wilf and Betty have never learned the steps of the business dance, and no one has offered to teach them. They have never, for instance, incorporated the farm.

"So this may be our last year," says Betty. A dentist in nearby Clarenville has shown interest in buying the farm, but he is still looking for a partner before he makes an offer. Betty has worked off the farm for several years to help out. But the loan, like the moose, feeds and grows while no one is looking.

The bubbles rising up the side of an aquarium are, for a while, the only noise in the room. Wilf goes on to say that the dentist won't work it himself if he does take the farm, and that perhaps Wilf might stay on as manager. Nothing in his voice indicates that this is what he wants.

It is now late into the night.

"Oh no, my darling," says Betty. "You're not keeping us up. We haven't seen the bed under twelve-thirty these last ten years." But Wilf is tired. He still hasn't sat down.

"I used to say he had a button on his ass," says Betty with a smile, Wilf behind her in the doorway. "Soon as he sat down, his eyelids would starts to droop." My sympathetic laugh travels the night air, past Wilf's fine warehouse, past the rusted baler that Wilf can't afford to replace, and, perhaps, into the ears of a moose that is just about to step into a field of greens, lit grey by the moon.

4

THE MILKY WAY

T he fog in Sydney, Cape Breton Island, has lifted just high enough for the ferry to see its way into harbour. Coming out of the ferry's mouth and onto the road, we are at the beginning of a strip of asphalt that runs unbroken from the Atlantic Ocean to the Pacific. The Trans-Canada Highway. The final *A* in Canada printed across our highway map is just below us.

As we travel through the *D*, onto the *N* and into the *C*, most of the land the road bisects will be farmland. The Trans-Canada joins the dots of the major cities, but it only borders the vast acreage of food making. If we could pull all the farmland in Canada together, there would be a country the size of France, inhabited by less than a million people, not a padded shoulder amongst them. A country apart. There are another two solitudes beneath the pair created by our history: the two solitudes divided by the sign that says City Limits.

Nearly always damp, Cape Breton is still of a wild beauty. We fall in line with others who may or may not be crossing the country with us.

Transing. A new verb struck for the journey. I write this at the top of my notebook. To "trans," to travel the Trans-Canada. "We are transers," I tell Ken. "This guy in front, with the bumper sticker that reads 'How's My Driving? Call 1-800-TUF-LUCK,' is a bad transer."

The little aprons on the roadside overlooking points of beauty in Nova Scotia are marked with signs labelled Look Off. After several Look Offs, we come to Baddeck Bridge.

The hard times of Betty and Wilf Parsons in Newfoundland have left us heavy-hearted. Some of the weight is lifted by meeting Wendell and Joan MacPhee, dairy farmers, just along the road from the bridge in Baddeck Bridge. We are in the heart of Tarabish country. Tarabish is an indigenous card game, incomprehensible to outsiders, that occupies the evenings of Cape Breton farmers the way contract bridge does in the cities.

The MacPhees' is one of the many Nova Scotia farms that make the province seem like a storybook (with taxes) – farms of classic outline set in fields that roll and thrive. Nova Scotia fosters dreams of early retirement for the smooth-handed urbanites who drive through it.

The MacPhee visit is a three-cupper. The rounds of coffee divide the interviews into acts. The first cup is the prologue, usually coming within minutes of crossing the doorstep, and acceptance of us, of the likelihood that we are benign, is as quick.

In the first act, the MacPhees talk of milk. A child once told me that you make milk by putting fields into cows. Four stomachs later, the field emerges white and warm, thick with butterfat. Unable to wean ourselves from the first food at our mother's breast, we have conquered the cow to give us its surrogate so that we never entirely leave home.

Because milk so lubricates our days, the MacPhees can look forward, in twenty years, to a good retirement. There is no trace of greed in their lives, just the wisdom to know that enough is plenty. They work the farm unaided and live in a fine house set amid a fine view.

A dairy farm has two rush hours, twelve hours apart, when the cows, deprived of their calves, empty their udders into a cooled stainless-steel tank. (Some of the female calves are kept as replacement stock.) The MacPhee cows occupy the same stall at each milking, like schoolchildren at their desks.

A bulk tanker from the dairy connects every other day to the cooled tank, drains it, and in the MacPhees' case, hauls it to Sydney. There it is divided into two types, called fluid and blend. Fluid is rebagged in plastic udders or in cartons and sold. Blend becomes the basis of the rest of the family of dairy products. The MacPhees get about sixty cents a litre for fluid, forty for blend, although they are the same thing when they leave the cow.

Much of the MacPhees' life is spent making sure that the amount of milk that goes into the tank every day is consistent. Once dairy farmers got more from their cows in the summer, when the fields were green with protein, and less in winter. There are, however, no seasons in the supermarket dairy section. The dairies therefore asked the farmers to make the flow of milk from the farm a steady thing, so many litres a day come sun or snow. In return they agreed to guarantee a market and a steady price. The amount of milk the MacPhees have guaranteed their cows will produce each day is called the quota.

When the quota system first started (and the milk cans on the little stage at the farm gate disappeared), quota was not a commodity, like a stock or a share, it was just a number. The dairy would pick three months of your year (you didn't know which three) and lower or raise your quota for the next year, depending on what sort of a showing you made in those three months. You try not to lose a cow in a month you suspect is a quota month. If you wanted to raise your quota and expand your farm, you could apply to the dairy to have some of the extra quota that would come available if a farm went udders up or closed due to death in the family.

Quota thus became a thing to be bought and sold. To raise your quota by a litre a day, you wrote a cheque to another farmer or an auctioneer. To buy a litre of the MacPhee quota the cheque would have to read over $400. To buy all of the MacPhee quota, the fifty cows to make it, and the equipment to milk the cows, the cheque would be around $250,000. Which is why the

MacPhees can look forward to retirement. "Somewhere around fifty-five, when the jobs start taking a little too long to do." The farm is their pension.

Act Two is about the city, a place the MacPhees would not retire to. "I hate the city," Wendell says, landing a verbal jab. Wendell is a sharp-featured man, given to considering every word before he releases it, in an accent that turns Cape Breton into "Cup Breton" and butcher into "boocher." He stirs his coffee longer than physics dictates is necessary. He chuckles; Joan laughs outright, uses a laugh as punctuation when she talks. She was training as a nurse in Sydney when they met. They are in their mid-forties. They are calmly happy at the heart of themselves.

"It's too slow," Joan adds, of the city, as though describing a machine. "A faster pace, but everything takes longer. A to B out here is five minutes. It's five hours in there. Twenty minutes to park. I can be through Baddeck and halfway to Sydney by then."

"We were in Boston once," Wendell says, "near Harvard, and walking down a street. I had the feeling, if I'd fallen down, they'd have walked right over me. I couldn't even see myself living in Sydney."

There are less farms around the MacPhees than there were not so long ago. In their place have come more trees and more retreating city people. They bring, Wendell says, their city clocks. "Life even around this community has got geared to the nine to five. Some of my neighbours know as much about farming as people in the centre of Halifax. I can tell that by the questions they ask me."

Alaskans tell newcomers that they can call themselves real Alaskans when they die there. A little of that sentiment creeps in when the MacPhees talk of expatriate city dwellers who, their eyes clogged with romanticism, buy two of each animal, rototill half an acre, and call it farming.

"It's not farming, it's playing," says Wendell, jiggling his foot a little. "My respect comes for more work than that. Farming is a business."

"And the scenery," Joan adds, "is just the setting we do our business in."

Is there a little fear of competition here? Wendell quickly swats that suggestion, although he doesn't deny that farmers are competitive. "Farmer builds a silo, farmer down the road will build one a foot higher, you can be sure. But in dairy we have our marketing system; competition doesn't enter into it. In farming, it's your own when you sit back and look at it. I still do that. You start and finish something, and it may not put a cent in your pocket, but it was fun doing it. Just building up the farm."

The shadow of many family trees these days points towards the city. The MacPhees' grown son has watched them work, watched them take as many holidays in his lifetime as his city friends take in a year. He likes farming, but he doesn't see independence when he sees his father crossing the yard in the morning moonlight. He is training to be an electrician.

The third act is about sex. This is my fault. When I set out to do a book on farming, I knew the chances of catching the torn-nightgown crowd were slim. There is reproduction aplenty on most farms, both for business and pleasure, but it isn't the kind that heats up the pages of a best seller. There are, however, times when anything is better than nothing.

For several years Wendell was the area's artificial insemination technician. He took up the craft, by local request, when the previous man left the area. A week's course at Truro, then trial and gradual reduction of error. His area of service has shrunk to his own herd, forty servings or so a year, a proud 70 per cent conception on the first serving. The semen is stored in capilliary-thin glass straws in thermoses of liquid nitrogen. It resembles frozen yoghurt. Breaking off the end of the straw, when it is in position, imitates ejacualtion.

Wendell explains the process with doctoral detachment. "You go in through the rectum. And then once you get your arm in the cow, the technique of getting hold of the cervix and inserting the rod through the cervix, there's the skill. The cervix is made up of, like, three doughnuts in a line. You've got to know when you are all the way through. And you're doing all this one-handed."

The real thing – real bull entering real cow – is no longer logistically or financially feasible for small farms. A thermos full of straws is more portable than a ton and up of horny Holstein. An occasional coupling with both animals present still took place on the farm I worked on in my teens.

Excalibur, our fertile Fresian, would perform with gargantuan haste, nostrils foaming, his aim errant, and sometimes hand-assisted to the target so that we could get on to the next chore. Once in situ, there were a handful of massive thrusts, a tightening of his buttocks, and then he slid off, snorting triumph and conquest to the bored men nearby in rubber boots.

A single straw of semen can cost anywhere from $15 to $200 dollars, depending, like malt whisky, on its potency. There are catalogues of bulls: Playbulls with portraits of champion breeders and splendid, almost poetic, descriptions of virility, full of phrases like, "Living proof of the way he transmits," "A strikingly stylish individual, he has the rare combination of superior size and stature, feet and legs which approach perfection," and "For all these reasons and more, Hanover Hills Starbuck is very deserving as a focal point for this year's cover."

There is nothing left in the third cup of coffee. Joan begins dinner, moving aside the farm accounts she had put down on the counter. Wendell has an hour before milking, a field of Nova Scotian grass to fertilize. At the next gate down the road several heavy horses have gathered to watch the occasional car splash by. As I stand in mud, happily stroking a wet muzzle, the muzzle suddenly opens and two rows of grindstone teeth nip at my arm.

5

WISE ACRES

In 1840 the English Colonel Butler died on his estate near Windsor, Nova Scotia. He had been granted fifteen square miles of land there as payment for his military service. The land was divided up amongst the immediate servants.

In 1860 Mike Oulton's great-grandfather started raising some of the first Hereford cattle in Nova Scotia. The cattle had swum to him from a shipwreck off the Nova Scotia coast. The serendipitous herd was put to pasture near Amherst.

When his time came, Mike Oulton's grandfather left Amherst in search of his own land. In 1914 he bought 125 acres of the now subdivided Butler estate. The next year he built a barn. He finished it on October 13, 1915, and wrote the date with his finger in the cement cornerstone.

Standing in front of that same barn, over seventy years later, I am surrounded by activity. The Oulton family swirls around the farmyard. Mike Oulton is backing a tractor out of the tractor shed. His wife, Dianne, and her eldest son, Victor, are in the chilly slaughterhouse, tidying up the day's butchering. Wayne and Robert, fourteen and eleven, are attending to their two hundred turkeys in great-grandfather's barn. Eighteen-year-old Mary is carrying a pheasant taken from an outdoor pen over to the slaughterhouse. There she ties its feet to a rope hanging from the ceiling and expertly kills and bleeds it.

For the family farm to succeed, through the generations, both of its nouns – family and farm – have to prosper and multiply. The Oultons, despite the many sirens beckoning modern farmers, are too able a crew to shipwreck. Their collective enterprise is thriving now, but it has been hard work.

In 1963 Mike Oulton came home from agricultural college. "I was about the only farmer around not drawing old-age pension, and willing to try it. The rest of the circle I'd run with headed off to steady Friday night cheques."

Farming and competitive climbing have much in common. The weather can knock you off. Both involve inordinate risk and work for the return involved. "Because it's there" seems a fair reason for doing it in both cases. And the trick to both is to keep looking up.

His father had moved sideways into chickens, so Oulton reached up to his grandfather for support. They incorporated the farm in the grandfather's name, and Mike bought all but one of the shares. He now had his grandfather's credit rating for a handhold. The old man worked alongside Mike, not sitting back to rest until he was eighty-five. He died looking down from the great height of ninety-seven years.

Before tackling anything too steep, Mike Oulton rehearsed on a gentler slope. He borrowed $3,500 from Farm Credit (they baulked at the smallness of the loan twice before agreeing) and bought a parcel of land between himself and the river. When he owned it, he felt strong enough to get serious. Over the next decade he bought five farms.

"In each one, we rented before we bought, and we bought in such a way that it was worked into the price of the farm that they stayed in their home. The last one moved out only last summer, and we bought that farm in 1967." The Oultons now work 1,400 acres.

Like many Nova Scotian farmers, the Oultons have diversified: beef, an orchard, pulp wood, the slaughterhouse. Divided
they have conquered. When bad times have tipped down one
side of the business, they have moved over to another and waited
for things to level out. When hefty loan payments on the beef
cattle started to bite, they went into the woods and cut pulp for
ten years. To keep money coming up the drive, they market their
own production. Two thousand animals a year go through the
slaughterhouse, a third of them their own, the rest from neighbours that "grow cattle for us."

Slaughterhouses have their own macabre fascination. I
worked in one for six months and emerged a couple of years
older and still carnivorous. It was a big place, much like a car-
assembly plant in reverse, in that the animals started intact and
were then gradually disassembled with knives and chain saws,
down to something a little bigger than plate size.

I got the job by walking through this bloody factory without
fainting, something I later saw several applicants do. I started
with a broom, working under the line, sweeping piles of tails,
udders, penises, fat, and trimmings into a chute. At the bottom
of the chute, a floor below, enormous barrels on wheels gradually filled. I ran down to replace them with an empty one every
hour or so, and to load them once a day onto the back of the pet-
food truck when it arrived. I was thrown down the chute, on my
second day, as the first in a series of initiations.

The men who worked the line (there were no women) were
loud and cheerful, most of them with overdeveloped forearms
from dragging the skins off calves and sheep. Their knives sat in
wooden holsters at their sides, some of the holsters handmade
and engraved.

To a regular rhythm, the oxymoronic "humane killer," a gun
that fired a three-inch retractable bolt, would bang off. (The
Oultons use the same device.) A steer would drop to its knees,
the hole in its forehead an exact replica of the bolt, twitch
dramatically until a flexible curtain rod had gone down the hole
and wrecked its motor centres. It was then hoisted up by a back
leg, blooded, and cranked down the line at a walking pace.

Steers in the morning, then calves (killed with a set of deadly, electric earmuffs so as not to damage the hide), pigs (a hammer), and sheep (the same). There was water and blood everywhere, running over yellowing tiles into drains that needed constant unclotting. Start at six, finish by two.

I graduated from the broom to a hose, a promotion that suited my distressing sense of cleanliness. Lunchtimes I helped the shop steward, who was illiterate, with the paperwork. As with anything strange, done on a daily basis, it all became boring, and I would suddenly wake from a daydream to find five or six pigs whirling around and around in front of me, in the big tumbler used to debristle them after they had soaked in hot water. (I ended up in there as well.)

I moved up to some basic knifework, better paid than hosing and brooming. A month of that and I had enough in the bank to allow me to quit. I left with a did–it–myself six-pound steak and a stolen leather apron. The cuts on my hands, which the constant water had never let heal, were gone within a week.

The Oulton slaughterhouse is a less mechanized, more hands-on operation, but it puts out steady money. It displays the Oulton willingness to try a new route when another starts to get slippy. This is a trait Mike and Dianne have instilled in the kids. It would have been easy to leave ready-made handholds for the four children, but they have had to make the climb on their own.

"The biggest thing for us that I can see is to be able to sit back and let them make the decisions. Even if they might be wrong. The two young ones are growing a bunch of geese and turkeys. They had to go to the bank and get the loan to feed them." Neither of these debtors is yet fifteen. "They operate on sure speculation like everyone else. Learn to do it when they are young. They can't learn when they are fifty."

We wander down, during this wise soliloquy, to feed some of the cattle that will soon wander back up the path into the abattoir. The wind is drying the sweat on Mike's face, swirling around the grainy smell of the mash in his bucket. He has an air of earthy competence. He generally rises to the top of organizations he joins: president of the provincial cattle association, director of the Federation of Agriculture. There is no chance that the Herefords he is calling will rebel and run off to the other end of the field. He is the sort of father children measure themselves against.

"Come on! Come on then!" The command moves slowly through the herd and the cows turn out of the wind they have been using to unsettle the flies. "No fun being a cow," Mike says, concern on his face. "You get your tits pulled twice a day and your skin only once a year," and he switches his face to a grin.

Mike plugs the wait for the cows to get to the gate with a story. On the wall of his study is an eight-by-ten photograph of a horse – Gypsy. Gypsy and Mike, on a college summer break before Mike turned twenty, had gone on a ten-day horse roundup in Newfoundland. Summer of 1959. Gypsy was not there as romantic transport. There was no other way overland into the coastal fishing villages Mike visited. "No roads, no fences." The villagers hunted seal and traded fish to the monthly coastal trading ship.

"One community I was in, twenty-five men came over to sit around and try and figure me out. One guy spoke up and said, 'Ask any of us, I made more this year than anyone else in the community.' He'd made $120 the whole year, from sealing. When I bought horses, most of them signed the bill of sale with an X."

We have moved over to stroke a bull through a five-bar gate. "When we get back to the house," Mike says, scratching the bull's ear as though it is one of the new kittens in the barn, "I'll show you a picture of a team of big horses pulling a mower through one of our fields. The picture looks old, but it isn't. It was taken just a couple of years ago."

The Brueghel-like activity in the farmyard has drawn nearer the kitchen. Almost suppertime. The geese and the turkeys, competing sections of the barnyard orchestra, have caught the smell of meat pie.

In Mike's office, under the picture of Gypsy, the talk turns to farm financing. "Well, all those guys were over twenty-one when they borrowed," Mike says, meaning the victims of bank loans that proved fatal to the farms they were meant to improve. "It was traumatic for both sides of the industry. I personally know a lot of good bank managers who simply didn't have the heart to pull the pin, so they quit. It affected them for the rest of their lives. I don't agree that everyone in it has a God-given right to go on farming. If they can't make a living, and they aren't efficient, why stay in? Commit yourself to it, and you are committed to a forced saving plan."

This Darwinian statement is probably the key to Oulton survival. They could even, Mike hopes, swallow their obvious pride, if that's what is needed to keep the farm.

"Pride is the biggest killer when the loan gets pulled. If a guy can swallow his pride and say, 'Shit, I'm as well off as I was twenty-five years ago,' he will probably make it." This talk of survival suddenly strikes Mike as pessimistic, and he hastens to affirm his choice of living: "I can't think of anything I'd rather be doing, mind. I love what I'm doing. Had it over again, isn't one thing I'd do any different."

The family assemble in the softening sunlight for a portrait. The photograph will not record the young lamb in the background bleating its heart out. Dianne, a chicken farmer's daughter, realizes she is holding an egg basket, and she puts it down out of sight. When Ken asks for a proud look, no one has to alter a muscle.

I've got my hand on the tailgate to shut it down on the chaos inside the van when Mike appears at my shoulder, without his hat; his washed hands seem like a fresh pair he has slotted on for the dinner table. He is standing close to me. "You know, the bank tried to pull my loan three times."

No, I couldn't have suspected it. He is smiling as he drops this revelation. Passing my eyes over his face, I realize he has held this back on purpose.

"This guy came back to town. He'd been in Toronto twenty years. I grew up with him. I was no angel at school, like most normal people. The first thing out of his mouth when he had me in his office was, 'Where do you get off owing us so much money? You never were nothing.' He told me he was going to shut me down. Gave it his best shot. In the two years he was there, he shut down 80 per cent of the farm accounts in that bank."

The tailgate slowly hisses down as I let it go. The bank realized their mistake. Mike waved the threat of litigation at head office and used a little third-party pressure from the contacts he'd built up, deliberately, in the organizations he'd joined. As he says, "It's who you know."

A pregnant ginger cat walks slowly out of our way as we throw up some dust on the path out to Windsor. There is just enough light left to drive the back roads to the roadside fruit stands of the Annapolis Valley and pick up some peaches. I feel like biting something soft and sweet.

6

COUNTRY LIMITS

F arming smells. It rejoices in the aromatic facts of life, of digestion, perspiration, and decomposition. Its only deodorants are wind and time. Odours are the fifth dimension on a farm: the smell that comes from the spring thaw of the manure pile; the lifting of the first forkful when mucking out the calf pens; the cutting and trimming of a cow's toenail; the plastic sheet peeling back off the silage clamp and releasing the acidic breath of the steaming grass; wet bales from the bottom of the stack; ragwort milk on your hands after weeding; diesel spilling on the tractor cowling; fresh earth liberated by the harrows; the interior of a rubber boot as it lets go of your foot; the warm, damp antidote of the barn in winter.

There is, behind the smells, a hierarchy of manures. The hermetic marbles of horse and sheep, the sticky splashings of cattle, the ammoniacal cologne of chickens and turkeys, and the pungent cocktail of pigs. These are dropped, voided, sluiced, and deluged at will, without so much as a glance rearward, unfettered by genteel considerations of privacy and space.

The farmyard and its sibling fields are a society of smells. The farm nose grows up in them, exercised to its full range, unmuzzled. Its urban, puritan cousin lives in a smell-by-numbers nasal landscape, the facts of life camouflaged and domesticated.

The atmosphere about us now is of soil and sweat. I unbend my knees and a substantial rock comes up in my hands through gravity. Two wobbly steps and the rock drops onto a cairn of stones on the back of a middle-aged trailer. Ken puts the tractor, a '65 Abraham, in low first and it bumps forward along the field. The cairn shakes and settles down.

Puffing, I stop and look into the view. A gull sits on a single piling half a mile off, and behind the bird are the masts of the wooden ships in Lunenburg harbour. Down the hill and across the creek is a hundred-year-old red barn with its shoulder to us, a forlorn, modern breeze-block barn next to it and in between a fair-sized farmhouse, a collection of boots and a vegetable patch at its back door.

The tanned, easy-breathing man with us, who has taken off his shirt, carries on heaving stones onto the trailer. They are his stones, his trailer. He moves in a puppyish way, but there is strength behind it. You could easily be ten years under when guessing his age.

Vance Daurie and his wife, Beulah, live here, in a village called Front Centre, a little more than a stone's throw behind Lunenburg. Back down the road a little are Centre and then Back Centre.

Vance is comfortable with this venerable Nova Scotian task, getting the stones out of the field to renovate it into pasture. He is not shy here, though he says he is a shy man. In 1986, in the Supreme Court of Nova Scotia in Halifax, he was shy and nervous as he awaited the judgement of three men.

The three men decided, according to Vance, "that we was right, we had the right to farm on our farm." That was not the exact legal phrasing, but what Vance says is the truth of the matter.

Vance and Beulah's sad and absurd story begins with a letter Vance got from his father in 1978. The Dauries were in British

Columbia when the letter arrived. They had left Nova Scotia a couple of years earlier. "Things had got a little tight in the kitchen," Vance says. His mother, who was never keen on farming, and his pregnant wife had rubbed against each other. Truth to tell, Vance had not been that interested in farming either. As a teenager he preferred a steady wage and the time to go out hot-rodding.

In his letter, Vance's dad mentioned that he was thinking of selling the farm. It was hardly still a farm – a pair of calves and a pig, the acreage turning fallow. A switch in Vance went back on. He left his construction job, Beulah her receptionist position, the Datsun camper was sold, and they went back to the Maritimes.

Once back on the family farm, the Dauries embroiled themselves in meat and cash flows. Beulah got a job in the post office, and Vance threw all the hours he had at making the farm work. He didn't have enough cleared land for cattle, so he took to fattening smaller, more static animals – ducks, geese, rabbits.

Nothing fattens, though, like a pig. They can go from the weight of a football helmet to that of a quarterback in six months. They eat anything. Pig farmers often have chunks out of the tops of their rubber boots, nibbled off while they are in the pens dispensing feed. Horror stories of farmers slipping, knocking themselves out, and being chewed down to the wedding ring are part of rural folklore.

As well as getting fat fast, pigs breed with profitable haste. A six-month-old boar can successfully mate with a six-month-old sow. The sow can manage two litters a year and average ten piglets at each farrowing. The piglets are not so much born as ejected, skidding and squealing across the slippery concrete floor of the hog barn.

Mother pig will sometimes eat or accidentally crush the piglets, so they need watching as they siphon off a gallon of milk a day from their mothers. They mature quickly and they outstrip dogs in intelligence. They can come when called, learn tricks rapidly, and they like toys. They are one of the few animals that will not overeat if they are put in front of too much food.

And when pigs go to market, their grunt is about the only part of them you can't sell. If it weren't for their susceptibility to getting sick, and the cost of preventing them from doing so, hog farming would be like growing money.

Vance took a correspondance course on swine management then enrolled in a hog health program. And he chased money from desk to desk. He can recite a litany of men with suits and titles whose offices he haunted, looking to pry loose some of the grant money that was there – provided you knew the magic words, "cash-flow projections."

Bit by bit the money was assembled, second mortgages taken out. Vance and his father, who had moved off the farm in a vain attempt to hold his marriage together, built the breeze-block pig barn, levelling concrete by tractor light after midnight. The building was "A-one hurricane proof" in its solidity, double welds on the pens, bolts instead of nails. A building built to last.

Vance is the first to admit that pig manure "has a density that hangs a little more." Beulah, who had to scrape out the pigpens while Vance was laid up in hospital for four months in 1986 with an injured leg, agrees. On most pig farms the manure is scraped into a lagoon at the back of the barn. While the lagoon is stagnant, it is inoffensive. Disturbed with a good wind behind it, the odour is unpleasant. As unpleasant, say, as the smell of a soiled diaper to a bachelor. A stream of official and expert noses visited the Daurie farm and approved of Vance's efforts to quell the smell.

The Dauries had two immediate neighbours, one opposite and one adjacent. Both ate bacon. Neither were farmers. The neighbours opposite kept pretty much to themselves. The neighbour next door and Vance had played together as kids. "We used to have cowpattie fights with each other. He planted a garden every year that went over into my land. That was A-one with me. No problem."

Beulah, as an inside worker in a small post office, often handled and brought home her own mail. On April 17, 1984 she brought a letter home from a lawyer that read:

Recently [your neighbours] were in my office discussing a perennial complaint pertaining to the odours being emitted by your piggery operation. For over two years now they have been putting up with this smell and hesitate to make an issue of the matter due to the fact that Mr— lives across the street from you, Mr— on the same side of the street one property away. The smells continue to come from your property and something must be done to alleviate the problem. If you are to stop the operation of the piggery entirely I am sure that would end all problems. The reason I suggest you may wish to discontinue the operation of the piggery is that we seem to have some indication that it is not profitable. Should the operation continue and should changes not be made to prevent the continuation of the odours my advice to [your neighbours] is to take the necessary legal action for nuisance.

Let me emphasize that both [your neighbours] are hesitant to take action but I feel that they must to protect their quiet enjoyment of their properties as well as the valuation.

Although he didn't know it as he read the letter, Vance was being threatened with a truly ancient law. It was invented by the English in the thirteenth century to deal with the intrusion of country folk into city life. They brought the country with them, livestock and all, and were disruptive and frictional. They were, said the city dwellers, a nuisance, and a whole volume of nuisance laws grew out of those primal clashes. The right to prosecute thy neighbour was entrenched.

The law of nuisance was being used against the Dauries, only in reverse from its original intent. Seven hundred years later the city had gone to the country and didn't like the way it smelled. The complaining neighbours had already appealed their property tax assessments and had them lowered. The Dauries were caught, given that all is fair in love and property values, in a historical inevitability.

They weren't the first. The manure had hit the fan in several other provinces and in over thirty states in the U.S.A. The hanging density of manure had provoked a rash of legal clashes, with workers of the land in one corner and more delicate enjoyers of it in the other. Most cases had gone in favour of the farmer's right to farm in agricultural zones, but some had gone against.

A hog farmer called Sullivan in western New Brunswick had been hit with $30,000 in damages, which he was refusing to pay. The Dauries, and potentially many other Nova Scotian farmers, were being besieged by people quite prepared to pull the land out from underneath them, in defence of their property values.

Vance Daurie is a man without cunning. There is no hint of it in his laugh, which is loud and untainted. His sense of sarcasm is naïve, since he has no motive for it, no need of disguising what he means. He took the lawyer's letter and went next door to ask what it meant.

"He just said to me, 'You can read.' 'Okay,' I told him, 'there's no garden this year. The fence is going back up.' I was hurt. I'm soft, and I can take someone shitting on me, but I was hurt." They got a similar cold shoulder from the opposite neighbour, when they met her hanging out the washing: "Talk to a lawyer."

Reaching for a lawyer, Vance was told not to worry, to hang on. The lawyer started the meter running, and they waited for the discovery to reveal the depth of things.

The discovery was a revelation, a catalogue of spoiled barbecues, tainted laundry, and sealed windows, dates and durations carefully noted. The familiar campaign of a nuisance suit now took hold – the assembling of a posse of witnesses on both sides, the media attention, the suspended animation of the legal system. The other nineteen neighbours on Front Centre Road were petitioned for evidence, and they voted for Vance by going to court in his defence.

Vance won the first court case and partied on the back porch. Then came the appeal. Vance had by now taken a job off the farm as an electrician to cover mounting legal costs. He didn't even take the day off for the appeal. He lost it. It went to the Supreme Court for the final decision.

Vance and Beulah talk of these two years as do patients of a long illness. The file of legal correspondence grew like a compost heap. Vance posed for the cameras at six in the morning, walking back and forth from the house to the pig barn.

"It was the only time I could fit them in. I had about fifteen minutes in the morning to feed them, a one-man chain gang of five-gallon buckets. 'Legs,' I'd say, 'do your duty.'"

A farmers' fund was started for him; it reached $20,000. A mushroom farmer in B.C. called to wish him Godspeed. Their nerves started to twang like the rigging on the *Bluenose* in Lunenburg harbour.

Despite himself, the pigs became the object of Vance's frustration. "I'd run through the barn, seeing things that would normally have me reaching for the penicillin. I'd ignore them. I was close to the last straw. I sat out on the patio one night and thought, Well, maybe we should hang out the For Sale sign. I walked that off in the woods on the back forty, but it was close." It was not A-one.

The Supreme Court left open the chance of a new trial, but ruled that the initial decision was correct. Costs were divided. The night of the decision one of the neighbours sold his house. Both had moved by the end of the year. A few months later the Nova Scotia legislature passed a bill, nicknamed the "Daurie Bill," that removed the nuisance for farmers of the nuisance act being applied to their daily living. The Dauries were home safe, too exhausted for joy – and broke. It came too late to save Vance's pigs. He sold them to pay the lawyer's bills. There is no smell now from the lagoon. It's empty.

"The deputy sheriff came down with an execution act our lawyer had put on his bill. The sheriff's office charged us 3 per cent of the bill just for bringing it down here – $700. I sold most of the pigs, the '79 Dodge, then the rest of the pigs. The lawyer even rang the farmers' fund to see how much we had in it. Lawyers ain't nothing but legalized criminals."

I pull off my shirt in the rock field. I can see the beginning of a farmer's tan on my arms, a red-white border on my biceps. "If I had a nickel for every one of these, I'd be clear and in the black,"

Vance says, throwing a rock into the trailer. He stops for a cigarette.

"So, why me?" His smile is wrapped in smoke for a second. He asked the same question last night as we left for the Clone Restaurant, followed by another restless, broody night in the Clone Motel.

"Well," Ken says, "I knew a farmer in Perth had a run of bad luck. Ralph. His tractor caught fire the day before harvest, and then it rained a flood anyway. He broke a leg the next week falling off the silo, and mastitis got into half his herd. One rainy night, the other side of a bourbon bottle, he staggered out into the farmyard, fell in mud, looked up and cried out, 'Why me?' A dark cloud opened up, a lightning bolt hit the rooster on the weather vane, and a voice like Pavarotti's boomed out, 'I dunno, Ralph. There's just something about you that pisses me off.'"

The Dauries' dog, Lady, mostly sheepdog, comes to meet us when we've crossed the creek. Vance bends down to check the splint on Lady's leg, broken in a rabbit hole. "Good girl," he says, lifting her ears to shake them. "Good girl. Healing nicely, aren't we."

7

SEEING RED

I t has been raining for ten days straight when we get to Prince
Edward Island on the midday ferry. The famous red soil,
rusty with oxides, forms the shore along the back end of
Charlottetown, probably the ugliest part of the island. Driving
into town, the red of the maple leaf in the flags lining the street
takes over. It is Canada Day.

Maps of Canada showing the distribution of agricultural land
depict Prince Edward Island as solidly devoted to farming. As
you tour it, the Island seems to be one large farm, populated
either by cows or potatoes, surrounded by water, and divided by
reddish lanes lined with lupins. The mood of the soil shifts to
swampy in the western Acadian county of Princes. The
wealthier farms in Queens and Kings counties are as neat as
freshly ironed laundry. There are outcrops of tourism, particularly around Cavendish, where the Japanese turnstile in and out
of the home of Lucy Maud Montgomery to consummate their
fascination with Anne of Green Gables.

In fact, in the last twenty years, the number of farms on Prince

Edward Island has halved from 5,000 to the 2,400 there are now. Fewer farmers own more land, a trend that has gone on for most of the century. Potatoes have been hot since the mid–seventies, when there was a boom in their acreage. Today fifty farmers grow 50 per cent of the Island's annual crop.

Base camp is a bed and breakfast near Charlottetown called Just Folks. The owners, Mr. and Mrs. Woods, have divided the labour at breakfast into entertainment and catering. While Mrs. Woods piles basket after basket of muffins and scones on the table, Mr. Woods winds up his rocking chair near the head of the table and relates tales of the Island. His is a true Island accent: "wersh" for "wash" and an *s* added to first-person verbs. "I loves it here."

Mr. Woods, a retired agriculture inspector, knows many of the Island's farmers. He learned to visit them on rainy days so he stood some chance of getting the figures he needed, and laughed at their honest cunning, like the time a farmer offered a crop of undersized turnips as "just fine for older people." He is proud of them, and for a history primer he directs us just along the road to the Farquharsons, a farm family of six generations. "She is the best cook on the island, too." The moment we meet Russell and his wife, Isabel, I'm captivated by his hands.

We look to faces to find similarities in the generations, a repeated nose, recurrent eyes, but what story would a lineage of hands tell? How much different are Russell Farquharson's hands from those of his great-grandfather, John, who a century and more ago built the house Russell and Isabel live in. "You could count the stars through the roof when he built it," Russell says. The odds are even if he is joking or serious. "I can't remember which room I was born in. Might have been outside for all I know."

Russell's hands are works of heart. The lines of the palms have become gorges, carved down by sweat. The foothills of his knuckles have swelled to mountains, from which the fingers run in bony ridges to the deltas of his fingertips. They are seventy-one years old, and in their time they have served, slaved, stroked, and spoken. They are his biography. Linked with Isabel's hands, they still work the farm, milking cows and growing grain.

Isabel and Russell married in the forties. "I'm from a farm just a couple of miles away," Isabel says. "We met at church and I was one and a half years younger than Russell."

"She still is," says Russell.

His grandson, Stephen Farquharson, who lives across the road, is five. Stephen can look back through the generations on this land as though through a series of open windows. His father gets up at four in the morning and leaves the barn at seven for his day job. His grandfather is then milking in the gleaming white dairy. "Four generations around here usually dies them all up," Russell says cheerfully, "but we're still going."

The past for Russell and Isabel is something they talk about as they might a holiday they once took to a place of cheap prices and exotic customs. Russell, the tale teller, says, "My grandfather, you could give him all the pencils in the world and they was no good to him. No written arithmetic. But mental, you couldn't beat him that way. He always had milk cows, and he never milked a cow in his life. There was always men around. They would get their board and tobacco and that would be their pay. The lot you get now, well, they are not much force. A milk cow then, mind, was twenty-five dollars and now they are upwards of a thousand, so it's not all as bad as it looks."

"You used to get a lot of sailors walking," Isabel says, the strain in her voice showing a little of the disease that has recently begun spreading inside her. "One stayed in the barn and spliced the broken hay rope. I remember the beautiful job he did of it. He knew the ropes."

Soon the last generation to work the farm with horses, as the Farquharsons did, will be gone. Gifted with idiosyncrasy, horses differed from tractors in several vital areas. The cost of parts for them was nil, but no tractor ever took off across a field in swift panic. Russell's father collected a scar from one such stampede in the midst of haymaking, with all the family gradually drawn in to the drama. "He could have been off when the horse took to run," Russell says, "but he'd hardening of the arteries, makes you slow to think, and he'd too much speed on then to bail out. Eighteen stitches from hitting a telegraph pole."

"Meanwhile," says Isabel, "Russell and my brother was building the stack, and I had another horse driving the fork. When the two went he thought he should go, too. They went right across the fields over to Russell's aunt's. Aunt Jessie was out on the doorstep. She thought they were going to come right in the door, but they turned down the lane and came right on home. My brother had a stake ready to give it to them, but they slowed themselves down."

"And last thing in the fall," Russell pops in, "we'd fill four wagons with hay as high as they'd go and drive them into the barn and block the wheels up. You knew that soon after that it would be the first of winter." The arrival of a granddaughter, her hands pudgy versions of her grandmother's, nudges the talk back to contemporary concerns.

"You couldn't start from scratch today," Russell says briskly, "and that's all there is to it. It's the city for them. This family farm, though, you may not make a lot of money, but it takes a while to starve you out. In the city you're living out of a paper bag from one meal to the next."

It is time to take a photograph. Isabel compiles the family collection of four aerial photographs of the farm, the first a black and white that has been hand-coloured. The farm buildings jump and grow from one bird's-eye view to the next. Isabel and Russell pose, stiff as fence posts, till Ken thanks them. Russell stands up, his arms and legs rusted bolts turning slowly in their sockets.

"Yes, I'm pretty crippled up now," he says, an observation, not a complaint. Then he tap-dances towards the door. The best cook on the Island moves into her kitchen to make lunch.

8

DEFENSIVE PLAY

The driveway to the MacPhail home runs straight for a couple of hundred yards. It isn't treed, so nothing hides a clear view to the farmhouse and the large potato storage barns. Squeals and grunts drift over from the piggery. The dogs make a fine set of country doorbells.

The kitchen stretches a fair way from the rubber boots by the door to the calendar, "MacPhail Farms – Seed and Table Potatoes," turned to July on the back wall by the table. Betty MacPhail's wide, cheerful face is below the calendar, as she sits at the kitchen table. The diary she kept of the events in the fall of 1984 lies under her arms. Les MacPhail stands next to her, hovering between staying to talk and getting on with his nightly chores. Les looks, with his reddish complexion and sad eyes, like a man who has long carried a weight he can't put down. Betty and Les lift and carry their story between them, a full pail slung on a pole that rests on their shoulders.

"Thirty-three years ago I borrowed the money to buy this farm," Les says. "Seventy-five hundred dollars for eighty-four acres. Listen, all these buildings wasn't there, just that one, and that one, and the house. I farmed around home, and then worked on a milk farm, milking in the morning and delivering it during the day. I done everything, pretty near, after that, but I come back to farming."

"Farming's your love," Betty tells him. Then she says to us: "We married in '51. I knew what it was like to milk cows, do all the chores, grade potatoes, from my dad's farm. We've got six kids. Three boys and three girls. Three were born in the winter. The house then was something. I'd come home from the hospital and the oilskin on the floor was buckled with the cold. You'd go out to the barn to get warm. Milk to keep your hands warm. All the family is married. The boys all farm. None of the girls married farmers."

Les decides he does want to talk about it all again and sits down with us. "Everything's done from here, eh. This is the main, and the boys live on farms themselves. Alan, Kenneth, and Wayne. There's two halves on one farm over the road, and one has the dad's farm."

"It wasn't a gift," Betty assures us. "We had to purchase the land from him."

Les nods agreement. "When the boys came onto the scene, then we had to have more to produce more. That's when we had to start building. You couldn't hire help, so we went the machinery way to make it go."

Two of the boys appear at the door. A heifer may be calving and they'll check her. Les also has one milk cow that he jokes keeps him in the dairy business. They used to have a dairy herd, but potatoes and milk don't mix. The one remaining cow feeds the family their daily milk. She is due for milking now. But Les will talk a little longer.

"We have all the land required for our whole establishment. About twelve hundred acres between four families, with renting and all. Plus we have all our animals and machinery, for our hogs and potatoes and beef. All we need now is the prices. That's the big one."

The story starts to teeter-totter back and forth between the couple, sometimes in mid-sentence, other times after a reflective pause or a rest to get calm again. Betty takes over. "There was land being sold all around, so we bought it. Thousand dollars an acre. Right after that the interest rates jumped. But with the advice of the bankers, that was the right thing to do. Same as putting money in the bank, they said, when you purchased property. We thought they should know what's right, so that was the choice to do. There was really one individual, the assistant manager with the agricultural field, he offered this money. He'd call Les up and ask him come in for a chat."

Confronted with the name of the bank, the Royal Bank, Les's laugh is almost that of a family secret revealed, and Betty says, "Why not?" as if a skeleton has at last been dragged from the closet.

"He used to come out to the house. He was a Newfoundandler, and I always think they're very good people," says Les. "I don't blame him. Then we were making and turning over good money, things looking not too bad. Then the big crunch came, things doubling and tripling. How are you to know? Plus land prices dropped, so we didn't have enough security for what we had borrowed. That was the real thing right there. Simple as that."

Betty takes the weight now: the numbers are her domain. "That was the big number. Everything just leaped. Some of the loans were locked in, others weren't. Twenty-one per cent at one time, on two or three hundred thousand, on our operating loan. You could figure on one hundred thousand for your sprays and fertilizer."

Turning even redder in the face, Les says: "We got money taken on us in the spring of 1982. We lost fifty, sixty thousand. A potato broker skipped out on us. We'd dealt with him five, six years. He used to stay here with us some. He'd come in the fall, leave in the spring. He took the Island for about seven hundred thousand. We spent another thousand the next year looking for him. Private detective."

"The bank looked on that as being a bad management score,"

Betty says, in a can-you-believe-it? tone. "We were lucky that year to pay the interest without paying the payments."

Now Les says: "I dealt with that bank thirty-five years. All my business was in there. I'd pay in and they'd take it out to pay the notes, whatever they thought I could stand. Every week we put money in. Then, after I'd already put the seed in, they cut our operating loan by half. Potatoes was six dollars a hundred-weight then. Three the year before.

"It really was the head ag [agriculture] rep for the Maritimes. He was American. He worked in with the government first when he come. He never got along with anybody in here. However he got into the Royal Bank I don't know, but he was there a few years. He come out here with our fella once in the fall. He knew it all, eh. He was the one."

Betty is anxious to take a poke at this fella. "We're not making any progress, he said, in our farming, especially with the hogs. He said they were a losing battle, so that you might as well get rid of them. The next spring they were the highest they ever were since we came here. Now, what do you call that for a judgement? His crystal ball wasn't working too good.

"The deal was they got 60 per cent and we got 40. We had to sell all the marketable animals. So I had to go to the bank every Friday with a cheque. Sometimes there might be twenty thousand. And they got 60 per cent and we lived off the 40."

There is a break for coffee and cakes. Betty opens her diary to the first page. The mood of the storytelling changes, as the mood of a piece of wood changes when the nail is driven in. The two halves of the long-married couple juggle the story between them now, passing it from Les to Betty and back, until it doesn't matter who is talking.

"They called at seven o'clock in the morning. The phone by the bed. I was still on the bed. October 24, 1984. We'd just finished harvesting the crop. It was still in the dryers. One day we'd finished and the next the manager called. We had no idea it was going to be anything as cruel as this.

"He said he wanted to see me. I said okay. He said, 'The Royal Bank doesn't want to finance your farming operation any more.'

I said, 'That's fine.' I didn't know whether I was supposed to go in there or they were coming out, I didn't know nothing. If I had known as much as I do now, there wouldn't have been a thing around this place when they landed. Because they didn't land out till half past nine, ten o'clock. We'd done all our chores by then. I was going to go and phone them, and here they arrived."

Les is repeatedly lifting his arms, clasped together at the fingers, and bringing them down onto the table. He's not aware that he is doing it.

"They all come in. The receiver for the Royal Bank, the lawyers. Five of them, in two cars, the receiver in his car, a black one. Middle-aged, all in suits, very finely dressed, with their big valises. It was just like where you're put on the judgement stand, for a crime committed. I knew right away to head to the bedroom, to make a phone call to my accountant.

"We used them good, I didn't say nothing. We gave them comfort, a little coffee, a little lunch, around this table. The Newfoundlander, he was gone a couple of years before this. This was a new assistant manager fella, and I could never make head nor tail of him. When we'd go in to see him, he'd tell me all his troubles. I never could get to tell him my troubles. After an hour I'd kind of get tired and I'd get up and leave. At the last I couldn't be bothered.

"They passed everybody a dated memorandum of what was happening. They read it out to us then, what they wanted. Les and the boys all had to sign one. They wanted $650,000 in fifteen days. It was a great shock. What does go through your mind? Our lawyer was away, so they sent out a woman lawyer from his office.

"I met her, took her in the patio way. When she went in she said, 'My soul, what a fine looking bunch of men! All new suits on! And what would you people want? Why would you do such actions to people at this time, just after they've just completed their potato harvest?' We went in the family room away from them and she shook her head. They were here till about dinnertime with our accountant.

"When they were talking they said, 'Les, does anyone owe

you money?' And I said, 'Yah, that fella there,' pointing at the assistant manager of the bank. I'd sold him a halfside of beef for four hundred dollars, and I never got paid for it. They were all saying 'Collect! Collect!' but I said, 'No, just leave it there, I may need it some day.' He never said two words, he just sat there like a gombie. I never said nothing while they were talking, I let them do it all. I think they took us for being a little soft. Then they all left and the receiver said they'd all be back in the afternoon to do a – whatyacallit – inventory. The assistant manager came back that night and paid me for the side of beef.

"The receiver came back with a bunch, three or four young fellas. They took an inventory, counted the cattle and the machinery, and all the Joes he had with him were writing things down. They were in jeans and sneakers, and kind of timid around the animals. When they came to count the cattle, they just banged on the wall of the cattle shed, driving them out and counting them as they came through the door. They didn't realize the back door was open, so half the cattle walked around, went in the back door, ran out the front, and got counted again. They also put the receiver's car on the inventory, that's the truth. A 1984 Oldsmobile.

"We had a great chuckle on that one. I call them all cowboys. So the receiver comes in after it was done and he says to me, 'You have to keep a check on what's moved and sold every day, and here's some new cheques you might need for to make your payments. And each week, when it comes Friday morning, you must call me and tell me what's happened. And if you've any problems, I'll be only too glad to help.' Now, he'd be the last person I'd ask to help me.

"To top it all, they had a man down at the gate twenty-four hours watching us, two at night, in eight-hour shifts. He appeared that afternoon. They told us we would be watched, under surveillance. I said, 'What the hell for?' and they said, 'Well, the last place we never put anybody there and all that was there when we went back was a broken chair.'

"I stayed up late watching the good fellas at the gate with binoculars. We had a lot of people give them a hard time. It wasn't our fault, people just wanted to protect us. We've always been good to our neighbours.

"The next day we had to meet with them downtown, ten o'clock, at our lawyer's place, the same crew pretty well. Our lawyer had reappeared. He has a massive room, pretty near as long as this one, and a long, long table.

"He was a bad number, our lawyer, as it turned out. We had worked with him three years. He told us this is a very grave thing and that we'll have to just sit down and listen to what they had to say. They are going to have the floor and whatever they says, that goes. He really had us all baffled up. He was also just down the street from the good Royal Bank crew, and they had been giving him work. I think if we'd had the money I could have taken them buggers to court and fought the cursed thing. But lawyers run into a pack of money. They're not cheap.

"At that meeting the next day, we had a statement our accountant had made of what was around, what it was worth and that. We went to one of our fertilizer suppliers, and he put us in touch with some good fellas. One was an accountant, a Newfoundlander, called Fudge – 'Like the candy,' he says. He got in with us and it was a whole new ball game."

Betty's brother, Sid Hurry, lives a few miles away on the outskirts of Charlottetown. Sid is the chairman of the Farm Crisis Committee for Prince Edward Island. The committees were established, like MASH units in the field, when the rate in foreclosures began to haemorrhage. The National Farmers' Union was figuring then in 1984 that for every bankruptcy declared, seven other farmers left farming against their will. Sid alerted the National Farmers' Union, who by good fortune were in Charlottetown in large numbers for a conference.

"The people from the conference began turning up. There was some here every day, twenty, twenty-five sometimes, from Alberta, all over. When they really set up, put the roadblock up, was when them Joes came from the receiver's to price the machinery, a couple of weeks later. We knew they were coming. There was all kinds of machinery here that wasn't ours, to confuse the buggers.

"One of our neighbours put his camper right down to the gate. Wayne Easter, the president of the union, has his farm about five miles from here, and he was phoning away pretty near all day. He can talk. He could be prime minister. I've often said that's where he should be setting right now. He's a super fella.

"When they set up the roadblock, the receiver phoned and said, 'What's going on up there?' I said, 'I don't know. I have nothing to do with the road down there.' The bank told us to keep our friends at bay.

"There was, oh, seventy-five men in the lane, with vehicles and machinery. I wasn't in on it at all, so to speak, so they could pin nothing on me. And see, after a while nobody could get up the lane unless they knew who was coming. They had a catering truck, Joe's Catering Service; he lives just down the road. The lane was like an obstacle course, just no room to get by. They let the woman from the television through, and they let the newspaper fella walk up."

Les laughs with real pleasure at this, his mind clearly back at the window, watching the farmers defending his gate in a sort of reverse siege. Betty has turned to a page in her diary and wants to read something out loud.

"We had a letter written to us, just a little note, from the bank manager we'd dealt with for quite a few years, before all this. He wrote: 'Dear Les and Betty, Just a note to let you know that you are in my thoughts. I sincerely hope that it all works out with you and that you all go on to bigger and greater things. Don't give up. Have a Merry Christmas and many good fortunes in '85. In friendship, Wayne.'

"One neighbour said we should walk away from it. I said, 'Yes sure, leave after thirty years of working and slaving the land of your own farm. Why would I walk away? He was looking for the land. He was the only one. In the first month over a hundred people took their accounts out of the bank.

"They took a run up here one night, the hired security men, with some kind of a light circulating on the top of a car. Now they were really invading our privacy. So the next day some of our neighbours got the young fella cornered down there, one went either side of the car, and they announced, 'We will escort you out to the King's byway down here, and you be gone.' So one went ahead of him and one back, and they escorted him and said, 'Never show no hair or hide again,' and he didn't.

"Garden of the Gulf Security was the name of them. Honest to cripes. They must have had trouble hiring after that. They'd been coming one day, gone the next. Shots were fired, I hear, in the air.

"The first fifteen days went past. And the next. And the next. We went to the lending people; they wanted a plan. Well that took a couple of weeks. And they turned it down. The day we fired our lawyer, and the new one come on, that was the day it all turned around. He came out here, we never had to go to him. He come in on a Thursday, and Friday evening we had them going the other way. And the next Friday it was all settled. He's some man, I'm telling you. A young fella, but he don't take the back seat.

"He was just starting up new. We were kind of wondering, well, should we or shouldn't we? He said to this neighbour, 'I'd like to help those people if they want any help.' He's from the city originally, Toronto.

"Towards the end of third fifteen days, coming into the last, the bank called us in, down to town, and then they wouldn't see us. Our lawyer pretty near threw a fit. He's a big man, near three hundred pounds, solid. Big handed, and he gets them going on the table, like this – bang, bang.

"The bank wouldn't come to an agreement till the Union had cleared away, so our lawyer he called them and asked them. We went down and apologized and explained we had to do it for the bank. They moved off. I think the biggest thing the bank was scared of was one of the men blocking the lane. He has a bit of a reputation. He owns a big road maintainer. He threatened to just dig a big hole at the end of the road. He shot the lights right off a Mountie car one time.

"The day it ended was December 8 – the day our son Alan had his daughter Sarah. That was our good news. A Friday. Now we lease the farm and have a mortgage elsewhere. Saturday they moved the machinery away from the lane. Our boys had been in a kind of shock. Our granddaughter had said, 'They can't take our farm. If they take our furnace, we'll freeze.' We said we'd have a party, but I don't know, I guess we never did. We had a lot to do. To get things going again, reassembling it all.

"We was beat. Played right out. We had lost the big contracts with our potatoes, real good money. The potatoes hadn't been graded because they had told us to hold shipment. We were without a bank for six months, we did everything by cash. There are good people left in this world, and they helped us. Some suppliers didn't mind what had happened; they said they had no trouble dealing with us.

"The last we had to do with them was sell all our beef, our feeder lot, the next August. Les went with one tractor trailer, seventy-five animals on it. I never cried in my life till then, taking the animals away. It was a bitter thing.

"Last fall they sent out a statement here that we still had $5.35 left in the bank. They said if it didn't come out by the end of October, it would cost $7.00 to close out the account. I said, 'Betty, no way they're getting that.' Get a Royal Bank cheque and get her out of there. That was the end. No more, no more.

"It's an awful cruel thing to say, but I call a lot of this sort of thing the evil part of the world, where they are just searching for money, money all the time. Money is the crop they look for now, whereas they should be looking at it in this respect – we're looking at providing food for the table. Farmers aren't selfish people. We're looking at helping everyone to have a good life. A farmer is a happy person, normally. Some said we were crazy to fight to stay here, but I didn't care what kind of fight I had to put on. There is always hope. Keep the faith.

"We've had one good year since, 1987, but this was a bad year. The price of potatoes is fairly sickening – $1.85 a hundred-weight. You need six cents a pound to break even. It's pretty crazy when you sell 60,000 pounds of potatoes and get about $1,100, and the year before for the same amount you got close to $5,000. There's no sense to that at all. You just don't get any adding up at all to make things go.

"That's why there is not too many young farmers taking over. Listen, anyone asked me today to take up farming, I'd say, don't." There is a cruel joke about how to make a million dollars in farming – start with two million.

It has been a hard story to carry, and Betty and Les slip it from their shoulders and put it down, all drops spilled.

At the end of June the MacPhails' potatoes will blossom, the fields of fresh white flowers ignorant of their troubled ancestry. In October they will harvest another crop and the price per pound will arrive like a rumour, or a joke, started who knows where. Seed becomes money, money buys seed. The seasons compound themselves into years.

This day is not over. The family milk cow has made her way to the fence, looking for relief from a distended udder. As Les slips on his boots, Betty points at six trophies they won over the years for best cream producers on Prince Edward Island. They were awarded by the Royal Bank.

It is a quiet, clear twilight on the way to the fence. The lights are on in the potato barns. Machinery hulks beside sliding doors. The beef herd at the far end of the field sound off like wheezy bellows. The milk glows in the darkening air as it fills the bucket and Les, perched on a two-legged stool, talks of his son's success as a stock-car driver.

In the piggery two calves enjoy the fresh milk. Les leaves his finger in the mouth of one while it strains its neck and drinks, the only way it will suckle. We walk past a pen and Les tells of the time he nearly died in it. A 1,600-pound Holstein bull cornered him. Les still doesn't know why the bull let him go. The things that saved him were the horns. The massive forehead couldn't quite flatten him him against the wall.

"I kicked him in the throat, and he backed up and give it to me worse. I heard things breaking. I figured if he hit me again the third time I was gone. He lifted his head and I grabbed a horn, shoved him aside, and struggled past him down to where a cow was tied. I went over her chain. He backed up with me and put his head under her and lifted her to the ceiling. There was a little hole into a box stall just barely bigger than me. I went through that headfirst. An hour later I couldn't move. I was smashed to hell. For three weeks I never moved. Everything was all jammed up."

That was twenty years ago, well before the bank lowered its horns and charged.

9

TURNING BROWN

I t isn't hard to imagine a trendy little store in Toronto, not too many years from now, selling old family farm signs. They would make marvellous swing doors into the galley kitchen of a Harbourfront condo, or restaurant wall fixtures, or coffee tables to support coffee-table books about old farm signs. The store would call itself Signs of the Times.

The sign at the entrance to the Ling farm announces Fair Acres. Written beneath that is, A Women's Institute Member Lives Here. The "Fair" does not apply to the appearance of the fields. Rather it describes the attitude the Lings have to their fields, the way in which they wish to treat them. The Lings are organic farmers. David Ling prefers the word "ecological."

He isn't splitting hairs. The health-food store label "organically grown" on a packet of carrots might only be telling you that the soil the carrot was reared in was nourished by compost from questionable sources, such as a commercial feedlot. Labelling the carrots "ecologically grown" would tell you that the farmer that grew them for you was concerned with organic relationships: the relationship of the compost to the soil, of the soil to the crops put in it, the crops to the weeds that colonize them, the crops and weeds to the winged hordes of insects, birds and bees that visit them, the animals to the crops they eat and then favour with their manure. Some farmers call this "Old Farming." Something old, something new.

The Lings are still in the fields when I arrive. The evening sun is turning the colour of the dirt path leading into some two-foot-high barley. The Lings' backs straighten long enough to say hello, and then they dip back to pulling mustard weed from between the barley stalks. The mustard hasn't gone to seed yet, and it is in insufficient numbers to call it a full-scale invasion. Just the odd terrorist clump here and there.

Stooping to pull my first clump, a mosquito with an attitude bites me squarely on the bottom lip. My lip swells immediately to the size of a pickle. I work on in forced silence while David Ling identifies this strain of barley as Charlottetown-80. It is a strain largely abandoned by Island farmers in favour of newer hybrids. David found a neighbour still unfashionably growing a patch of it and tried some.

"When you use chemicals, they've got you changing crop strains like cars," he says, putting a hand to his black hair to shield the setting sun. "The head on the Charlottetown-80 is two row instead of six, so there is less bulk per acre, but this has a bigger kernel. It's better quality, a better yielder." David strokes his hand absentmindedly over his adolescent crop.

"I can tell its quality because my beef cattle feeding on it go off to market months earlier and heavier. Before they were averaging 1,200 pounds, now they go out at 1,400 after eighteen months." (The 1,400 pounds is live weight. The dressed weight of beef is roughly half that.)

Another half hour of pulling and the ten-acre field is clear of weed. I've learned the first lesson of organic farming: Reduce the chemicals and you have to increase the elbow grease. Edith Ling's strong, calm face looks out from under a vintage field hat. "Nice bite on your lip," she says. "Let's go in."

David walks me over to the pig barn. An enormous sow

greets us with some Niagara-like urination. "You are really brainwashed," David Ling says with a laugh. By "you" he means chemical farmers. He farmed intensively for twenty years using chemicals. He was an old dog, and the trick of abandoning the chemical crutch did not come easily.

"I just started to feel that something was wrong. Like when I'd go through the barley with pin harrows after it was up. The field would be like powder, like flour, gullies eroded down into it in the spring. That leads to compaction. Then the fields were more like roadbeds, eating horsepower as I tried to pull implements through them.

"You have to realize what soil is, what humus is. It is not just something to hold up roots. A lot of farmers treat the soil like dirt; they burn the soil out."

Ling's conversion began with an over-the-fence conversation with a neighbour about four miles to the south. They got to comparing yields. Ling's had dropped over the last two years. The neighbour's had held steady. "How much you spend an acre on fertilizer?" the neighbour asked, setting the mousetrap. Ling, a man with a joy for farm statistics the equal of a baseball fan, answered, "Fifty-four dollars." The neighbour countered with his total, "Zero."

"The next year I went to an organic farm in Lindsay, Ontario, run by a Swede émigré. What I saw intrigued me. That spring I had bad soil erosion, and I thought, Okay, let's try it, I may be farming my farm away anyway."

A rueful smile comes onto Ling's serious face. "I went cold turkey. I wouldn't recommend that. It should be done gradual. That was four years ago, just before I turned forty. The first two years the yield went down, the third my average was back, and now I'm up to previous yields."

Farmers are not easy people to make generalizations about. Two common denominators do emerge, however, in an unscientific kitchen-table survey. Most of them have aquariums, and most don't like using chemicals, but they do anyway.

The reason for the first is unclear, but the second is the invention of a perceived necessity. The necessity was to make an acre grow as much produce as it could. Driving every acre on the farm as hard as you can is a business decision. If the cost of farming is going up like fireworks, but you are still coming back from the market with the same old income, there is only one thing you can do. Take more crop to market.

In the nature of things, the acres become exhausted. To keep the right-hand side of the growing equation up, you have to replenish the variables on the left. If you can buy the variables in a bag or a can, then why not use them? And if some bug, some evil weevil, starts attacking your wallet, there is a can of chemicals to take care of that as well.

Farmers such as David Ling consider this sort of farming myopic. They feel the huge chemical farms to be roofless factories, their whole bottom-line attitude a betrayal of the soil, a shortcut that may end, literally, in quicksand. While many farmers in their hearts may agree with them, they cannot afford to give up chemicals and stay the size they are. Ecological farming on a large scale is not really possible; it works best on a family farm of modest acreage. And so the factory farmers ask the fields to carry more and more weight, and offer them Ciba-Geigy and Dow soil-steroids to help them do it.

The underlying reason for the growth of chemical farming is written on the receipt the cashier throws on top of your groceries at the supermarket checkout – cheap food. If we were willing to drive to the nearest farm gate and buy our produce direct, the supermarket walls would begin to shudder. But farm gates have been getting steadily farther and farther away. An act of agricultural *perestroika* that led to farmers everywhere pouring chemicals down the drain would work, but only if everyone agreed to pour at the same time. It would be a process as tricky as getting everyone to agree to drive on the other side of the road.

The likely future of ecological farming lies within a sort of environmental class system, ranging from white bread in plastic bags to organic wholewheat in recycled brown paper. There will be farmers ready to cater to each.

There was a moment in the mid-seventies when David Ling almost took the carrot the government was dangling and went into potatoes in a big way. The money was there in neat little bales of $100,000 ready to be loaned to Island farmers who would buy land and potato-ize it. It crossed David's mind more than once to go out one day and come back with two hundred acres and a fleet of potato machinery.

"That would have set me back three-quarters of a million dollars. Everything I owned at the time was worth about a quarter of that. Now, you can clear a thousand dollars an acre on potatoes in a good year. Four good years and I'd have been clear."

But the odds of four good years in a row, David knew, were about the same as drawing four aces – with Nature dealing. Still, he'd have tried it, but his partner steered him clear.

"I grew up on a small mixed farm," Edith Ling says, "so I'm not the type to delve into anything too fast too soon. After our first girl, David talked of potatoes, but there is no sign of a market board on the Island for them."

And the decision to go ecological?

"I can't take much credit for that decision, I guess; I was more a follower than a leader in that one. He came home and just started to do it. It's nice to grow crops without chemicals because I don't like eating chemicals. It is common sense to me, our way of farming, at this size – doing without things that we can't pay for till we can – but I guess our sense is not that common at the moment."

If you hitched a ride from the nearby Summerville air force base, and flew over the Lings' Fair Acres, you would pick it out without a map. Fair Acres is turning brown, dark brown, as the humus, the decaying organic matter, builds up. Brown is healthy in soil constitutions. "Your soil isn't red any more!" was the first thing out of the minister of agriculture's mouth when he visited.

As a believer in what he is doing, Ling preaches what he practises. Visits are arranged, twenty or so potential converts at a time. Come spring, the phone gets as frisky as a lamb. "He'll have to learn to say no to some of those," says Edith, a little world-weary. "Running away from dinner four times a meal."

Getting soil back "in the brown" is something like

physiotherapy. Ling composts his manure instead of applying it straight from the livestock. This breaks it down and makes the nutrients easier to digest. Chemical soil is incontinent, in that it can't hold water. "My soil is drought resistant; it can hold its moisture," Ling says, rhyming "drought" with "truth."

He has worked out an exercise regime, a crop rotation, that doesn't strain the soil back into ill health. One year is alfalfa, its deep roots will haul up nutrients from the subsoil and capture airborne nitrogen and plant it in the ground. And he has learned to watch for symptoms, weeds that show something is wrong with the soil. "Goldenrod, for instance, means it's low in calcium. Thistles show a lack of trace elements. Adjusting your rotation can correct that. One of the real signs of a problem, though, is earthworms – a lack of them. When you don't have earthworms in your soil, you have a problem."

Other doubting Thomases are lined up along the fence, waiting to see if the Lings make a go of it. There is, so far, no reason to suppose they won't. Edith Ling likes to tell a departing visitor, "If we can leave the farm better than we got it, regardless of who gets it, that will mean a lot to us."

The earthworms have returned to Fair Acres, like villagers returning after an earthquake. Thirty-five of them were counted in a single spadeful this spring. "Hey, you've got earthworms!" a post digger recently called out in mid-dig. "Back home I could dig all day and not get enough to go fishing."

ROADSIDE
ATTRACTIONS

W eaving along the Canaan River in southern New Brunswick, the corner of my eye is caught by an abandoned farmhouse. The other side of the Bay of Fundy, due south of here, is the Annapolis Valley, picturesque and lush, but the road we are on now is poor and sparse. Abandoned farmhouses stare back at us in a mournful parade from both sides of the highway. This one is peculiar in that its blue paint is hardly faded, the level of the grass still below the porch, the For Sale sign free of bullet holes.

The door is open. Directly inside are some bookshelves. The décor is traditional farmhouse: sheet panelling, big rooms, the kitchen the biggest, double sink, dirty boot marks engrained in the linoleum by the back door. There is a clean rectangle on the dining-room wall, the ghost, probably, of the aerial photograph of the farm.

The wood stove is still here, too massive to bother taking, perhaps a sign that whoever lived here was headed for the city. What had forced them off? From the look of the barns they were

beef farmers, probably grew some vegetables as well. Did they
run aground on the bank? Or was it some disease in the cattle?
Or a final, crippling leap in the price of feed moving the whole
damn business out of reach?

Perhaps, I find myself thinking, my hands resting on the
kitchen sink, a death. A day like any other, like this one, then a
shotgun blast in the barn. "Turn that TV off!" and then sprint
along a wet path in stockinged feet, wrench open the barn door,
and stand before an eternal vision. He has walked out to meet his
father and grandfather standing waiting in the barn, to die as
they died, still a farmer. Not so unlikely either. In the early
eighties, one in three adult male deaths in farm families were
suicides.

My imagination drives me outside for some fresh air. A robin
feels its nest under threat and it chatters a soprano warning at me
and I head back for the van. I take note of the estate agent's
number in town from the For Sale sign, and wish them, the
family, to wherever gone, a better fate than my daydream gave
them.

In Fredericton, after loading up in the Clone Restaurant, we
make an appointment with the estate agent. He has the Dicken-
sian name of Chippens. Supposing we are interested in the farm,
he has the plans ready.

"Hello, Chippens here. Well, there it is" – he stabs a finger
into the drawing – "It's thirty acres, $55,000. Great ground for
vegetables. It's a German owns it, going back to Germany in
two weeks. I sold his house, $300,000. The farm manager lived
in the house you saw. He moved into the city. Fifty-five thousand dollars written there, but I would say right now it would
go off cheaper, oh yes. Anywhere's handy, you'd own the farm,
that's the story."

I wonder if many other farms have been sold around there.
"Well, it's holiday camping 'round there, you see. Some are
turning to that." Mr. Chippens does not need to clean his glasses
to see I'm not a farmer. I let go I'm a writer.

"A writer? Oh, it would be ideal for you, the birds and trees.
Heaven."

★　★　★

Mr. Hubert Harvey, a coal miner turned farmer, is astride his tractor when we descend on him. The sun has caught his face; when he takes off his hat his forehead is neatly divided, like a block of Neopolitan ice cream, into red-and-white stripes, topped off by short brown hair.

"Thirteen years old, I went down the Minto mine. Lost my father in there. Brother-in-law, too. Took to farming, oh, thirty years ago. Don't know why. I farmed for another man seven years before I bought this one. Down here to Arthur Day's. I still consider him the best farmer in the country. He's eighty years old today. Some kind of a good farmer. He's retired. Still a great feller. Yes, yes. Lots of people try to farm, but oh boy, my gracious. The government took his farm for the Burton Bridge."

Hubert Harvey's vegetable stand is alongside the Fredericton road. Inside it is shady, tables and baskets stacked and empty. The first cucumbers and lettuce will appear in a matter of weeks.

The growing of vegetables along this stretch of the Saint John River, among the islands of the river's delta with the Bay of Fundy, is lucrative. The little pressboard huts, with their flaps at the front that envelope open and shade the fruit, are dotted like sentry boxes along the roadside.

"I had a stand down home where I live, for, what, fifteen years. The traffic moved us. Too dangerous hauling. The traffic today is outstanding. Outstanding. Scary in fact. I sell everything right through here now. Right off the press as you need it. If I run low, go to the field, get new stuff. Oh my gracious, yes."

Though shady, the temperature inside the hut is getting sauna-ish, and Hubert is glancing away, through the walls to his untended fields. He moves an extended finger in a windscreen-wiper motion across the sweat on his brow, flicks it onto his trouser leg. The presence just down the road of Arthur Day, "the best farmer seen in this country," beckons.

"I saw him walking around yesterday. He could talk to you forever. Think the world of the man, oh boy, guess I do. Best ever there was. These other fellers, they live on fertilizer, now don't they. Arthur Day. His woman's a great talker. Yes, oh my, yes."

"Don't holler!" Arthur Day, his hearing aid on full to hear my questions, is asking his wife to keep it down.

"That's deafness," Greta Day tells herself. "I'll go get my hearing aid." She disappears into the kitchen, bangs a drawer open and slams it shut. She reappears, without the hearing aid, but with a book, thick as a brick, with metal filigree corners. A book of spells? Greta slams the book onto the table.

Looking down from the wall is a framed newspaper picture of the Dionne quints. They share the wall with a varnished jigsaw landscape. A television in the corner has a tiny Japanese "belly telly" television sitting on top of it.

Greta turns to the first page of the book of spells, and it becomes obvious that the book is a photo album. But it is full of tintypes, not the modern celluloid snaps. The positive was made directly in the camera, on a rectangle of tin. The process precluded copies being made. Each of the portraits in the book is an original and at least a hundred years old. A 100-watt smile on his face, Ken leans into the book, immersed in photographic archaeology.

With that end of the table occupied, Arthur is free to recount a life on the bank of the Saint John River. Almost empty now of boats, it was a river choked with bustle in Arthur's early years. Fall was the rush season, when the fields set aside for shipment to Saint John were harvested. Loaded into barrels and bags, the vegetables were hauled to the nearest wharf. The wharves came in twins, low water and a high water, at four mile intervals. I had taken a swim that morning off the high-water wharf nearest the Days' house, and felt the strength of the current that had borne the ships to the warehouses of Saint John. I could have lain on my back and floated without a stroke to the Bay of Fundy.

During the spring thaw the river used to scorn its banks, winning through at least once a decade to flood the fields. "Hay land was better after that," Arthur assures me. "Flood leaves a silt, just like fertilizer. Soil is the very best because of the flooding. It's less compact as you go down. Push a pole in it, and it gets easier to push in the further down it goes." The dam at Oromocto has corralled the river somewhat and cut off the soil from its natural cycle of rejuvenation.

It is on this floodplain that Arthur's family established their pedigree. His grandmother came into land after her father divided the farm among six children, the prime lot nearest the river being the smallest, the biggest lot back in the bush. Arthur's father married the daughter with the riverbank lot.

"One of the best," Arthur says of his father's skill in the field. "He grew good stuff and never sold poor stuff. One farmer told him, 'I was down your place and you were throwing out better than I was selling.' That was his system."

Arthur took over the farm when his father died in 1957. He isn't sure how old he was then, so he asks Greta.

"You were fifty!" Greta says in a bird-stunning voice. The tintypes have been shoved down the table and the photographic revue has moved into the twentieth century. There seems to be quite a few snaps of things Greta has either fished or hunted.

"That's the sturgeon I caught. One hundred pounds!" she exclaims, rattling Ken's glasses back on his nose. "They had to shoot it in the net so we could get it out!"

Beneath this heavy barrage of reminiscence from Greta, Arthur lets off a light memory or two. As he does so he has only to look up towards Greta for her to fill in the blank date or number he is stumbling on. They seem to share, after fifty years of marriage, a collective memory pool, with Greta having the clearer view of the bottom. A little of the air has gone out of Arthur, but Greta mocks her eighty-two years. Greta was born in the house directly opposite Arthur's, on the other side of the river. They looked at each other over the water as children from their second-storey bedroom windows.

Arthur, meanwhile, is on a delightful sidetrack to the Prairies. He went there twice as a young man on the harvest excursions in the twenties. "Twenty-five dollars to Winnipeg, a cent a mile after that to wherever there was work. Hundreds of fellows went from here."

"That's the salmon I caught," Greta announces, spearing a snapshot. "Thirty pounds!"

"I worked in one field that was a mile long and two miles wide. They cut with two teams on reapers and a tractor on another. The first cut the horses made in that field was six miles long."

"Now here's the freshet in '36." Greta again. What's a freshet? A deer? "No!" Greta scolds me. "A flood."

"What's the difference between a flood and a freshet?"

"Nothing," says Arthur.

The freshet of 1936 was wicked. It coincided with the breakup of the ice, and invading slabs of ice crossed the Fredericton road and scared the cattle out of the barn and up onto the highest thing in the farmyard – the manure heap. In a later freshet, Arthur had to row down to the Harvey house and rescue the kids. "The house was slanted over. There was a television in the middle of the bed in the room the kids had fled to."

I'm anxious to hear Arthur's opinion of his own skill, to test Hubert Harvey's claims for him. "Are you, ha-ha, outstanding in your field?" I rehearse this in my mind. Perhaps not. Instead, I remind Arthur we've met Harvey, and report to him Harvey's estimate of him. Was the best farmer in the country sad to leave farming?

"Well, I wasn't too keen about farming at any time. One old feller up here said to me, 'You're married to the farm,' and I said, 'No I'm not, I could quit farming, wouldn't bother me a bit in the world.'"

This is the agricultural equivalent of Graham Greene casually mentioning in mid-interview that he would just as soon have sold cars. Arthur found himself the recipient of a duty historically donated, and he pursued it. But he didn't enjoy it! When the need for a bridge over the river that had bordered his life gave him the chance to leave the farm, he took it.

"And here are the letters for our fiftieth anniversary." They are tucked at the back of Greta's most recent album. She gathers them up and deals herself a hand of form–letter congratulations from the Governor General, the prime minister, the premier of her province.

A phone call interrupts the Days as they pose for a portrait. Greta has built a wall on the table in front of her of family portraits between herself and Ken's lens, her plum–red hair the only thing visible above it. Arthur has relieved himself of his hearing aid, so Greta reaches across him to pull the phone from its cradle.

"Hello. Hello? Oh, to hell with you!" Arthur doesn't blink, just continues to stare down the lens. Click.

11

WAITING FOR
THE MAIL

The road from Fredericton north to Quebec is an asphalt shelf on the side of the Saint John River Valley, Maine to the left and almost nothing but provincial park to the right. The variety of vegetables grown in the river delta has narrowed down to one as we climb north to Quebec. This is the potato belt. Potatoes dominate to such a degree here that the fall harvest in September is an official school holiday. The books are shut till the potato houses are full.

An osprey with a fish in one talon disappears from sight into a wooded hill. We are lured by a sign saying Old Farm House, tucked down at the side of the road. The sign looks official, county-made rather than family-made. We bump up the path into a herd of small cars, a pickup or two standing bull-like among them, outside a whiteboard old farmhouse.

Just the other side of the lace curtains a province-wide meeting of the Farm Vacation Association is underway. Margaret McCarthy opens the screen door and invites us into her home. On a ring of chairs sit a dozen or so older farm couples in skirts and jeans. The bedrooms of their large farmhouses dotted about New Brunswick are now empty of children. Rather than sit perched in memory at the end of long kitchen tables, they have recast themselves as hosts in the bed-and-breakfast business.

Their hospitality is immediate and the agenda is happily put on hold. The Acadian gentleman nearest the door turns his firm chin towards us. "You work for the government? I'm allergic to government agencies."

"No, we are funded by the Canada Council. Do you pay taxes?"

"Well, yes."

"Then you are paying for our research. All of you."

Cleared by security, our Acadian interrogator delivers his message to the distant masters of his fate, whom he hopes will read our book. "Quebec potato farmers," he tells us, "have a guaranteed price for their potatoes. Not so the New Brunswicker." His English has a poetic simplicity.

"No stabilization. Have to pay even for inspection. Quebecer get that free. If the price drops way below, they don't mind. Big shed, they wait, survive. Little feller, little shed, gone. On my road, from home to the highway, forty years ago, we have eleven farmers. Now just my family. My neighbours get further away. Farming is in a coma, like those people who are sick. When they get into a coma, it's too late."

The others in the circle laugh in agreement. Lunch is decided on as the appropriate next step. A feast of plain food covers two tables; the desserts outnumber the salads. Teapots and coffee-pots the size of watering cans circulate. The men take to one table beneath a reproduction of *The Last Supper*. Of the six men at the table, four have half a finger missing. Farm long enough and the odd digital sacrifice is demanded.

Eugene McCarthy, pressing another heaping of trifle on us, has someone he wants us to meet, someone not here at the meeting: an older farm family, the Toners, successful enough to have paid $28,000 tax in 1978 and who lost the farm "when the eighties struck." The neatest farmer hereabouts, it wasn't booze that felled Toner, "for he never took a drink of rum in his life. He would go to the wedding, but not the party." Despite that, his land was gone, and he had had to put up quite a fight to keep his house. He may be in now, since it is noon. Do we want to go look?

There is a tone to Eugene's little tale of the Toner tragedy that is becoming familiar. It is the tone of betrayal, of something right being overwhelmed by something wrong. It is not the tone of conspiracy. Losing the farm is grounds for temporary insanity, when the comforting nightmare of a cabal of bankers high above Toronto gives the mind something to hang onto, but that nightmare passes. Some farmers in the American heartland have found the insanity easier to bear than an unforgiving reality. They have stayed there, a shotgun resting in their folded arms. Canadian farmers have yet to point the gun at anyone but themselves.

Joyner Toner is heard before he is seen. He rounds the garage on a tiny tractor, disconnected from the tiller he has been using to work part of the five acres left to him. He drives right up to us and puts out a hand without dismounting. His shorts and pastel shirt, topped with a straw hat and a warm grin, give him the air of a Sunday golfer stopping to chat between tees. Stan Rogers is singing a slow folk song on the garage radio.

"The birds have a radio in there," Joyner tells us. "They like it. I tried to stop them nesting in there, but they hounded me. They said, 'You kept your house, we want to keep ours.' So I said, 'Go to 'er.'

"The upper corner of what's left of our land is up there," he says in a rich voice that drags a little on the esses, a grandfather's voice. "Six hundred and ninety feet by 390 – 5.07 acres – and I figure I was lucky to hang on to that."

"How did you manage to keep the house?"

Joyner's chuckle is an infectious thing. "A lot of hard dickering, boy. Took us a gone while. I met the Agricultural Development Board on the first day of June last year, and I never got the legal documents till February 18, this year."

The Toners spent those seven months waiting for the other boot to drop. Good land, hard work, and a houseful of children had not been enough to keep the farm theirs. One son put in ten years before the future came into sight farther down the valley. "We weren't extravagant. My last car had 221,300 miles on it," Joyner chuckles. "The wife got a little frightened of it, never knew if she'd get back."

In the spring of 1981 Joyner had enough in his seed–potato house to pay off his debt to the bank – $40,000. He offered the bank the chance of complete repayment. They declined, and counter–offered to raise his operating loan. "I'd have been better to go fishing, but I took it. What the hell else would I do?"

"How do you feel driving through your old fields?"

"I feel sad. My son gave me a worry stone for Christmas. This is it, Irish Connemara marble. Where my people are from. That will bring you peace and contentment. Rub harder." Joyner's fields are gone to a big farmer, who supplies the McCain's corporation, the Maritime dukes of potatodom. "A big farmer would sooner have his neighbour's farm than his neighbour," Joyner tells us. "What's going to happen when you're not with the land?"

Joyner is determined to catch the conversation each time it threatens to hit the ground. He uses his infectious laugh like an alarm, to rouse himself up from the bed of sadness within him.

"I don't have anything against a big woman," he suddenly says. "In fact, I prefer a big woman to a small woman. I'll tell you why: A big woman is warmth in the winter and shade in the summer."

"How big is yours?"

"She's big. I told her we'd never have to leave here. Took a lot of courage, yes sir. Lot of trust."

Despite himself, Joyner is pulled back to the battle to keep his home. Tragedy is magnetic.

"Yes sir, when I saw the mailman for the documents, I knew that's what they were, when he put them in the mailbox, February 18, 1988. And I had told my daughter, when I had the documents for this house I was going to quit smoking. I haven't smoked since." Joyner bought his house back by cashing in his life insurance.

Eugene McCarthy, a silent bystander so far, though his face has not been quiet, feels the need to defend his friend.

"You rizzed a lot of nice crops," he tells Joyner. "Joyner could plant potatoes better than any man along the road. The rows would be just as even on the in where he riz his planter and where he set it."

The radio gives the two o'clock signal. "How come I've got ten to?" Ken asks, shaking his wrist and putting his watch to his ear.

"You're from Ottawa," Eugene reminds him. "They're always a little slow there."

Eugene leaves to resume his Farm Holiday meeting. Joyner conducts a tour of the garden, of his shrunken world within which he now proves his worth in flowers. "Come see my weigela. Just planted it. That birch tree there we planted as a twig when we come here, thirty-four years ago. Those are French lilacs. Nice quiet place, isn't it? Seven-tenths of a mile from the Trans-Canada. Would have been hard to leave here. It would have killed us, I think, maybe."

Joyner disappears into the garage and emerges with what looks like the bottom piece of a hat-and-coat rack. "The premier of the province has one of these. A Christmas tree support, see. I can't make enough of those. They all want them." He turns it in his hand, and rubs a little at a grease spot on the bright green paint.

"Well, I'm back on my tractor, boys," he announces. The tractor is small enough that he can just step over the seat. The engine starts first time.

12

TALKING BACK

W e are driving back down the valley towards Fredericton. The journey is temporarily rewinding to take
advantage of a windfall. Two young potato farmers,
Darrell and Floranne McLaughlin, have steered us towards a
banker. Although it is the same countryside we drove through
two days ago, I am looking at it with different eyes. Before it was
simply a landscape, a painting on the windscreen. Now the
McLaughlins have interpreted it for us.

"People coming out from the city see only the greens, the
pastorals," Floranne had said. "They can't see the crisis for the
beauty. They can't feel the chill for the air-conditioning. Three-
quarters of the houses they call farmhouses probably aren't;
they're just homes outside the city."

The passion in her voice was close to anger. When she had
moved from the kitchen to the small dining room to join us, she
hadn't merely sat in a chair, she had taken possession of it, a leg
folded under and both elbows spiked into the table.

Her husband, Darrell, his face softened by a full beard, was of an equal passion. We had caught a flash of it when he and his son had posed for a photograph in the barn where we first found them. Realizing his son had a cap on advertising a chemical company, Darrell reached over and hauled it off like it was on fire.

"My father had to quit spraying the fields, so my brother took over when he was fifteen. They had films back then put out by the chemical companies, showing a guy drinking a glass of water with a dash of pesticide in it." Potatoes are a pesticide-heavy thing to grow. "Now he can't do it any more, so I do the spraying. We're backing away from them, but it still costs $10,000 a year. I'm damned if I'm going to advertise for them."

He had pulled on his own reins for most of our conversation, anxious that some understanding get through, but he had dropped the reins and let it gallop when describing the big farmers Joyner had caught in that phrase about them preferring land to neighbours.

"They buy out twelve others to get to the level of success they think they want, and then when they go broke, they take half the county with them. No family farm can afford to buy them out, so they have to sell up to the corporations. The year I was born, 1949, there were more than twenty thousand farmers growing potatoes in New Brunswick. All over the province. Now there are about four hundred full-time, no more than a dozen of them outside these three counties. Same acreage, though. Our historical cycles have been broken by specialization: pigs up by St-François, potatoes here, dairy down in Sussex County."

Almost annoyed with himself for lapsing into cold statistics, he pokes the embers of his own argument. The flame is still there.

"They build these big farms like kids clamping together some modular toy. They suck hole around the trade, looking for the best deals. A slap on the back and a joke for you, and they think everything's just fine. They are, well, they are a miserable beast.

"The big question is, though, who does all this change serve? Is getting a strawberry intact from Mexico to Toronto what it's all about? A few years ago we organized a potato giveaway for people near here in the Miramichi. It was coming up to Christmas. People had lined up for two hours when we got there. We loaded off 600 fifty-pound sacks in half an hour." Darrell's shoulders move with the recalled labour.

"Two little girls rolled their sack onto a sled and, laughing, set off back home. Two groups of people, separated by seventy miles of woods; one hungry, the other dumping food year after year." Another sigh. "We're a disappearing lot. The people that like the land."

There are about a quarter of a million farm families, take a few, in Canada. In the Depression, a third of Canadians were farmers. Now they struggle to make up a twentieth. If all those families called it quits and founded a city, they would only create a metropolis a third the size of Toronto. (They would gain, mind, a whole bunch of political representation.)

But the true farmers, the landlovers, are separated only by distance. Darrell has more in common with a Prairie farmer, or a Russian potato farmer, than his fellow Canadians in Vancouver or Montreal or Toronto. The bookends of our journey, the farmers on the Atlantic and Pacific coasts of Canada, are probably closer neighbours in spirit than any two condo-dwellers separated by the length of a corridor.

The strongest sense of community I have ever felt was when I worked the land with people who liked the land. It was not a romantic's notion, a false fraternity of shared sweat. I knew the men and women I worked with for what they were. Indeed, the worst human I have ever met was one of them, a Scottish herdsman who redefined cowardice. But I never felt less than one of them, and they forgave me more than the city ever has. By and by, when I had learned to enjoy and return their kindness rather than take it for granted, they silently awarded me the status of "Good Neighbour."

Good Neighbour. You can hear the capital G and N when a farmer says it. It is an earned title, a code for life as much as a description. It is the erosion of this code that is at the heart of the McLaughlins' anger.

"Farmers around here often say, 'Well, things around here will just have to get a little bit worse, and then they'll break, and we'll fight back, and then they'll get better after that,' " Darrell says. "Well, I was in Bolivia in the seventies, looking at farm projects, and what I saw there showed me that people can be pushed an awful long way and still not break. A lot further than we've been pushed here."

Darrell, like many of the potato-belt farmers, is of Irish stock. Floranne is Acadian. (Her father is the plain-talking man who checked our credentials at the Old Farm House.) Acadians were the French-speaking thorn in the side of English colonization of the eastern seaboard. Claiming neutrality after the English had conquered Acadia and renamed it Nova Scotia, the Acadians were pulled out with rough tweezers and flicked to the south in 1755. Some found their way back, and the generic name Acadian was also given to the many thousands of Québécois farmers who drifted south and joined them in New Brunswick.

The Irish have Napoleon to thank for their prescence here. Cut off from Scandanavia by the Napoleonic Wars, the English went west across the Atlantic to Nova Scotia for the timber for their ships. (New Brunswick was then merely a county of Nova Scotia.) This required colonial labour, and the Irish obliged by plunging into a potato famine. The poorest of them, caught in a simple choice of death in Ireland or life elsewhere, crossed the Atlantic to fell trees. They planted potatoes as a sideline, a sideline held at subsistence level by the English who preferred they swing axes than push ploughs.

Darrell and Floranne have a history, then, of being pushed, but now the enemy is as much within as without. In a sense, they see the farmers who choose the corporation over the community, agribusiness over agriculture, as collaborators. The occupying forces come disguised as mercenary bank managers and divisions of multinationals.

As members of the resistance, reactionaries unwilling to discard the virtues of the farm community for the vices of growth for its own sake and no one else's, Darrell and Floranne push back in differing ways. Darrell has published essays – "not

because I can write; because no one else is telling the story" –
and he has embarked on a law degree. (His first degree in plant
science technology is, in his estimate, in relation to the times, a
paper airplane.) Floranne has served on the board of the
National Farmers' Union.

It was while chewing over Darrell's remark that no bank has a
dispossessed farmer on its advisory board that the McLaughlins'
sympathy came out for a bank manager they had had. "He
wasn't a bad sort," Floranne had told us. "They are human, too.
He didn't like all he was asked to do."

"Can you recall his name?"

"Elwood Zwicker. He's been promoted. Works in Fredericton. His wife is still here actually, while the kids finish school."

Mr. Zwicker, in a phone call that night from the Clone Motel,
had been brave enough to agree to an interview, the next day, at
the bank. And so the van was pointed back the way we had
come. This was not a chance to be missed.

There is a brass band playing on the bandstand in Fredericton,
and the citizenry have filled the park to hear it. The sun catches
the brass curves, the same sun that bounces off the glass of the
pale blue Bank of Montreal.

We're a little early. I drop down into a blue-grey couch, by a
potted Dieffenbachia that is shedding a little natural oxygen into
the air-conditioning and, with its curves and variegated leaves,
taking the sting out of the straight lines and theatrical grandeur
of bank architecture.

"Mr. Jenkins?"

Elwood Zwicker is an unassuming, dark-haired man, kindly
of face, whose batteries seem a little overcharged. As we take our
seats in a interview cubicle, he defuses some of his extra voltage
by clicking the end of his pen in and out. If it is true that our
faces, as they age, become a bulletin of our inner selves, Mr.
Zwicker seems to carry no special burden of sin.

The anticipated disclaimer comes immediately. "I can't speak
on behalf of the bank, in regards to farming, without their

approval; that's policy, simple as that. If you submit a list of questions, I can submit it and get approval and . . ." He realizes the point is made. "We have a public relations department that does that. I think that's pretty standard in a lot of companies." Of course it is. Public relations and television makeup are, to my mind, equivalent skills.

In the next hour in the cubicle, no one learns anything new about banking or farming in general. Zwicker, it emerges, was raised on a small farm and worked on farms while he was in high school. When it rained, he wasn't paid. He never considered taking it up as a living. He has respect for the many people he came to know that do it, that "get up and work from daylight till dark. We're lucky to have people that still want to do that."

He worked eight years in the Grand Falls area as the local bank manager of farmers like Joyner Toner, Eugene McCarthy, and Darrell McLaughlin. The troubled years. "Looking back, nobody expected what happened. Farming is unpredictable. You can put the numbers on a wheel and spin them."

To find out more about those spinning numbers, I later called Harry Fraser in Prince Edward Island. Since 1967, Harry has put out *Fraser's Potato Newsletter*, four or five pages weekly, packed with potato prices and potato gossip, such as the fact that the potato chip was invented in Saratoga Springs by a chef called Crumb. Harry confirmed the roller-coaster prices Maritime farmers have received over the years. Prices were actually better for the farmer in 1937 than they are this year, and in April 1917 they were getting nine dollars a hundredweight bag for export, three times what they get now.

Elwood Zwicker never had to foreclose on any of the bank's Grand Falls farming clients. "I preferred them to sell off, or sell out, before things got to there. They had to recognize that they were in trouble. Getting better begins when you admit you are sick."

Talking farmer to banker, some farmers told him that they were the last ones to realize they were in trouble. Others confessed that they could have taken the troubles they were having when they were thirty, but now they were older they were going to sell. "I'd see them a few months after the sale; they looked ten years younger, like the world had come off their shoulders."

To bear the weight of modern farming, Zwicker explains, modern farmers have pumped up their skills. After a day's ditch-clearing they can project a cash flow related to debt–equity ratio and pop it into a laser-printed business plan stuffed with power verbs. Their pencils are as sharp as their baler-twine knives.

The farmers of Grand Falls now have a new manager. Zwicker has moved into the city. A change of bank managers makes the needle jump for farmers using that bank. Many of them reported to us that the phone call announcing that the loan was being called in came soon after a change of name on the manager's door.

The clicking of the pen has stopped, replaced by jiggling a handful of small change. "There's some beautiful farms up there. If you want some beautiful scenes, go to New Denmark, Sissons Ridge, when the leaves change. If I were a photographer . . ."

Outside, the brass band has finished. A reconstructed paddle steamer wheels down the river, tourists shoulder to shoulder at the rails, cameras aloft. The meeting with Zwicker is, was always going to be, a teacup in a storm. In an outpost of the empire, he applied humanity where he could. Back in Rome, the numbers for the wheels were fashioned and programmed in and networked afar to the interfaces of Main Street.

A year later, armed with many a sad kitchen-table tale of banks and farms, I followed Zwicker's instructions. A letter was drafted to the Bank of Montreal's head office.

In the letter I put the questions I supposed farmers would ask if they could sit across from a banker responsible for agricultural policy. Some were asked out of curiosity: How many foreclosures against farm accounts had the bank made in the eighties? Was that better or worse than other decades? Other banks?

In asking other questions I wanted to get inside the bank's brain: Would the bank ever contemplate a separate interest rate for farmers? Was getting as much of the money back they had handed over in the seventies boom while they could, as fast as they could, a priority in the eighties? Was there a dispossessed farmer on any of their advisory boards? Did superb farmers who were inept businessmen still have any place in agriculture?

A phone call to the Bank of Montreal's customer InfoService directed me to write to a Mr. Charron at head office in Old Montreal. I posted the letter, waited a week, and on a slushy, snow-beaten day followed it down to the city of spiral staircases, festivals, and the world's ugliest baseball stadium.

The edifice that is the Bank of Montreal head office is one side of a square called the Place des Armes. Its design makes the traditional connection between high finance and classical architecture. A pediment atop the entrance centrepieces the bank's motto around a shield – *Concordia Salus* – Prosperity through Harmony.

Just off to the left of the lobby is the tiny Bank of Montreal Museum. On a table sits a collection of antique tin money boxes. One depicts a farmer on a stool milking a cow. When the money is dropped in the cow's back, the farmer begins milking vigorously. In the visitors' book I wrote, "Once upon a time all of Canada was land, and the day is coming when it will all be real estate."

A talkative guard, a retired butcher, directed me to the third floor. Mr. Charron appeared within a minute, a trim, bespectacled man with receding hair, in a blue suit, who clicked his expensive pen while he informed me he was not the person I should be talking to. Although this was the head office building, the actual headquarters were in Toronto. He handed me my letter back.

I reposted the letter to a Mr. Zilkey at First Canadian Place, a white building of great height and spectacular ordinariness in downtown Toronto on one of Bay Street's mercantile corners. It is the metaphor of modern money, money without history or imagination, a stack of money a hundred stories tall.

First Canadian Place rubs its steel-and-glass shoulders with the towers of the Toronto-Dominion, Canadian Imperial, and Nova Scotia banks. Twenty-two thousand people go to work in this hive every day, one for every farm family in Manitoba.

Mr. Zilkey, senior manager of agricultural policy, called me within two days and promised a written reply within a week. True to his word, a three-page letter arrived replying to my questions in a style of decaffeinated English reminiscent of the architecture surrounding Mr. Zilkey when he wrote it, devoid of sentiment or flourish.

Mr. Zilkey explained that the bank didn't release foreclosure totals, but allowed that they were the highest they had been since the thirties. "The largest proportion of farm financial difficulties," he wrote, "can be found in the portfolios of direct government farm lending agencies," by which he mostly meant the Farm Credit Corporation. I've heard Farm Credit officials refer to farmers in danger of losing their farms as "distressed portfolios."

This is how he described the steps the bank takes before issuing a foreclosure notice: "They are unique to each situation and involve working with clients over an extended period of time to attempt to develop workable solutions through revision of loan terms and considering operational or structural changes that may assist. The bank will normally not undertake foreclosure actions unless the cooperation or communication from the customer deteriorates. . . . Each farm case is reviewed on its own merits. Nobody, including the bank, emerges positively from foreclosure procedures."

I had asked if the bank had built any of the experience it had gained in the boom and bust of the last fifteen years into its policy, and Mr. Zilkey informed me that they had "established a group of experienced bankers who manage financially problemed customer accounts in a more intensive manner. The mandate involves turning the farm business into a profitable position to the degree it is possible."

And did superb farmers who are inept businessmen still have any place in agriculture? "A superb farmer has to be an excellent businessman. There exists a percentage of farm businesses that are managed by people possessing skills second to no other comparably sized business in the country. These skills include technical production and financial management expertise including marketing and risk management."

Mr. Zilkey ended his explanations with this thought: "Customer situations that involve financial difficulty require very careful and, to the degree possible, empathetic management. This apples [*sic*] whether the situation involves a farm, a commercial business, or a personal banking relationship."

It is said that 85 per cent of the best farmland in Ontario is visible from the CN Tower, and no doubt from the roof of First Canadian Place. Unfortunately, Toronto is sitting on it.

THE
CENTRAL
FIELDS

13

AVEC UN ACCENT

"And the word for barn is?" I can't remember. Ken looks at the page in the French dictionary and then at me, the smugness of he-who-knows on his face. I look out of the Café Clone window, hoping one of the passersby on the Rue Ste-Anne will suddenly hold up a card with the answer. No help there.

"*Grange*. Try this one: tractor."

Ah. More than half of English is born in French; add a little accent and cross your fingers. "*Tracteur?*"

"Correct – and lucky." And on it goes. Field, *champ*. Harvest, not so easy; a harvest of corn, *moisson*; of fruit, *récolte*. To plough, *labourer*. Crop – interesting – it's *culture*."

The clock on the café wall, an American beer ad, gives us half an hour till we leave Quebec City and drive over to Ile d'Orléans, twenty minutes away, to meet a chicken farmer. Rooster, *coq*. Like spies about to go behind the lines, we are preparing a functional vocabulary. We have discovered in ourselves, two anglophones, each with a French-speaking partner, enough

French to let us interview without a translator, we hope. The point is to try without being too trying.

The French were the first colonial farmers in Canada. The first years of the seventeenth century saw ground broken in Acadia (at Port-Royal) and around Quebec City. Since colonization is essentially the exportation of systems, the French *seigneurial* or feudal system was applied to New France agriculture. There were lords, *seigneurs*, and tenant farmers, *habitants*. *Seigneuries*, roughly two hundred of them, were handed out to the haves (the church and the military) and then divided up to be worked by the have-nots.

The bones of the seigneurial system are visible still in satellite photographs, in which the St. Lawrence River appears like a magnet with iron filings lined up at right angles to it along both shores. Each filing was called a rang, or river lot. Each narrow strip was pinned to the arterial river. Neighbours, at home on the rang nearby, were easy to find.

The seigneur, in return for his concern for the well-being of his habitants, was paid by them. Then as now, a variety of extractions taxed the peasants. The *dîme* was a tithe, a payment for the right to be subjugated. The *rente* was a straight handing over of cash and the delightfully named *banalités* were taxes on grain.

The system was abolished in 1854. The notion of the township had gained ground, and the feudalness of the old way was a millstone around the neck of economic development for the province. Although abolished, it was ingrained enough to keep Quebec a rural-thinking province for another century.

Like any system that lingers past its time, the seigneurial mentality postponed the changes Quebec farming needed to make. It clung to wheat production long after the land had proved itself unsuitable. The delay and the Catholic dutiful enjoyment of large families were a recipe for poverty and exodus. Between 1850 and 1930 a million Québécois left the province, half of them for New England and industrial feudalism in the mills.

Today only 3 per cent of Quebecers are farmers. Their land is protected by law against the virus of subdivision, and with the provincial government as their modern seigneur they have begun to prosper again.

The café clock is pushing us out the door. Shortly, after leaving the grey stone maze of Old Quebec, we will cross to Ile d'Orléans. It is, the tourism book has told us, a history lesson come to life.

The bridge across to Ile d'Orléans, a concrete rainbow, was built in 1935. When the ferry yielded to the car, the ferryman docked his memories, and three hundred years of detachment ended. The island sits like a swallowed marble in the throat of the St. Lawrence. The explorer Cartier stood on the northern end of the island in 1535, looking out past the wild vines to the brackish meeting point of the fresh- and salt-water currents in the St. Lawrence. Tourists now catch much the same view through car windows. Along the southern shore, the island gradually abandons the historical monument and Norman-style churches for the tourist trap – pink-and-blue wooden emporiums of fast taste. The farm lots run in rangs back from the shoreline, stone houses and wrinkled barns at the roadside.

Luc Turcotte's ancestors arrived here to begin farming in 1666, in the parish of Ste-Famille. Abel and Marie Giroux Turcault (the name has mutated with time) crossed over from the Poitou grain-growing region of western France in 1659, and settled briefly in Beaupré on the northern shore of the St. Lawrence. There were then around 3,500 French colonists along the river.

Abel and Marie must have looked over to the island and seen even cleaner and more fertile grounds than the ones around them. Despite the reports they had undoubtedly heard of the island's first farmers being killed by the Iroquois in 1656, they boated over and staked their claim a century before Wolfe arrived on the island to plan the campaign against Quebec. A family with the similar name of Turcot arrived in 1668. There are now fifty-four Turcots or Turcottes in the Ile d'Orléans' phone book. Luc's father, brother, sister, and uncle all live nearby. Family tournaments on the tennis court between the houses always have Turcotte versus Turcotte in the final.

Luc's chicken farm is ten minutes from the rang that Abel first moved onto. The drive out of Ste-Famille takes us past a line of diverse Turcotte farms and small, almost two-dimensional villages. A scale model on the roadside, the doll's house equivalent of a church, houses a flaking plaster of Paris figure of a Madonna and Child.

Luc comes out through the screen door of a modern bungalow as we pull into its drive. He incorporated the business with his father and expanded it greatly with his brother François. Of four chicken producers on the island, they are by far the largest.

Every fifteen days, ten thousand chickens, tiny bodybuilders, are collected from Luc's *poulaillers* (chicken coops). They each weigh around three kilos. They leave, as they arrived, alive. At the nearby slaughterhouse they are hung on a parade of hooks, hosed down, and electrocuted. A rotating cam slices the neck, the bled carcass is dipped into scalding water and re-emerges to be plucked and gutted.

Most of the Turcotte chickens end up in red-and-white boxes flanked by fries and coleslaw. Their brief mortal span, six and a half weeks at most, is merely one turn of a spinning wheel of life and death. The wheel turns endlessly, oblivious to seasons, rolling out over half a million Turcotte birds every year to the fast-food Clone Restaurant chains. As many generations of chickens go through the Turcotte coops in two years as there have been generations of Turcottes on the Ile d'Orléans since Abel arrived.

Luc himself is more like an owl than a chicken, steady rather than peckish, droll in his explanations, his voice monotonic, free of clucks and pukaws. A long scar on his forehead documents the time he was hit by a car when he was two, thirty-one years ago. He was two years in a cast. He went to school in the village till Grade Six, then crossed the bridge daily to the mainland for high school.

In winter, Luc quite often crosses to Beaupré on a skidoo. The basilica there, visible from Luc's living-room window, is a healing shrine. A million visitors a year go there, most of them sick or disabled. Two pillars inside the church doors are decorated with the cast-off crutches and braces of the miraculously cured.

A rising line of five *poulaillers* comprise the core of Luc's operation. Each is a little higher, larger, and newer the farther it is from the road. The *poulaillers* are Lilliputian chicken condominiums, three stories high, windowless, and set at an eternal dusk. Two of the coops are co-ed, roosters and hens. The other three are segregated, like an old-fashioned high-school dance, boys to the left and girls to the right.

A little card outside each room in the coop records the deaths, "flip overs" as the Turcottes call them. One or two a day is the norm, often from *rhume*. When Luc tells us this, I get a little confused, thinking he means rheumatism, when he only means the common chicken cold. He realizes I'm thinking in Franglais, and sneezes to show me what is meant. I promptly bless him in German, an English habit, and the whole multilingual mix-up gets everyone smiling awkwardly at each other.

Inside one of the rooms in the largest chicken coop, a crowd of adolescent roosters are racing around as though caught in an air raid. The ammonia smell is no worse than in a baseball stadium lavatory. The temperature is over twenty centigrade, and it's dimly lit, which encourages the young cocks to eat and sleep as much as possible – their assigned role in life. I've heard of classical music being used to soothe laying hens and boost production, and I'm working out the French for this, to see if Luc has contemplated letting his chickens gorge to Grieg and snooze to Strauss, when I catch sight of his taciturn face and decide against putting the question. I realize the patience he is showing as he is being asked things he has already explained, meanwhile having his own jokes ignored.

Instead, I ask him what he thinks of the movement towards "grain-fed," new-age chickens. The van that delivers his feed is parked outside, with "*mouture balancée*" written on the side. He snorts.

"What do you think is in the bought feed we use?" he says briskly. "It's mostly grain, no steroids. The only medication in bought feed is to prevent worms in chicken bowels. The mark-up on this so-called grain feeding is 15 per cent. It's just fashion."

I follow one young rooster as he runs on skinny yellow legs to the walled edge of the floor space, under the fan and then past my feet. The Swedes, I recall, actually have laws that dictate the amount of outdoor exercise space each chicken should have, like prisoners walking the yard. Would he appreciate the difference? Is he food or fowl? Perhaps the point is not whether he would feel himself a better rooster, but that we give him an even break. I vow to remember this burst of sentiment if we end up herding sheep somewhere down the road. The debate over which is the dumbest farm animal, which of them would win "Reach for the Bottom," usually comes down to chickens or sheep. Certainly both seem to have their brains in backwards.

Just as much as the pungent odour of chicken urine, the smell of free trade is very much in the air. Unlike his industrial compatriots, Luc is certain free trade will cost him business.

"The problems with the banks don't compare with the problems free trade will bring. I've done a course in administration, so when the talk is of credit and debit, I know what's being said. There's not a Canadian on earth who can compete with the Americans at any time." He unfolds his arms, tucked till now in his armpits, so he can add some manual emphasis to his argument. "They have the climate, the cheap manpower, the technology, everything. Take chickens. When we build a coop it needs a wall this thick. Good insulation. In the States they build coops with thin wood. They heat them just to say they have. A hundred thousand chickens a farm there on any given day, watched over for forty-two days by teams of women. Then they empty the farm completely, the women go on holiday, and another team comes in to clean the buildings. When the border taxes come off in the next ten years – look out."

We spend a half-hour manoeuvring a gas tank into the hole dug for it alongside part of the Turcotte apple orchard. The apples are sold in the market in Quebec City – Melba, Lobo, Cochrane, the white apples and the newer strains, Jersey Mac,

Istabella. The apples are a sideline, mostly handled by Luc's brother. Trimming them back in March and spraying them provides a welcome sense of seasons passing; working in the chicken coops, like working down a mine, is a linear series of identical months. The tank-lowering job gets done, as most jobs do on a farm, with a tractor parked at an odd angle, a chain, a plank of wood, and a couple of kicks with a rubber boot.

"Do you know," I ask Luc, as the tank finally settles into place, "of a recipe that calls for apple and chicken?" He can't think of one, and he anticipates my next question by saying that, yes, he does go out and eat fast-food chicken. Yes, probably some of his own; a carpenter buying his own chair in a store.

As a finale to the visit, we travel back down the road to see the monument dedicated to Abel Turcault. It is a rough-edged rectangle, facing the parish church, its back to the mainland. In the winter it is boxed over to prevent it from cracking. The wind makes a whistling noise around the edges of the monument. Despite a family tree whose canopy puts most Canadians in the shade, Luc is blasé when discussing his roots. The day of the reunion, he says, was no big deal, but "I admire that the land has always stayed in the family. I appreciate that."

When Luc Turcotte was twenty-three there was a massive reunion in Ste-Famille of the descendants of Abel and Marie Giroux Turcault. Over 3,500 lunches were served on that crowded day, June 17, 1979. There was a service in the red-roofed, stone parish church, and all three bell towers pealed. The monument was unveiled. The day, a year in the planning, ended in a dance, a whirling kaleidoscope of cousins.

14

OBJET PERDU

After leaving the Turcottes', we make a circle of the island. The thin, elongated fields provide a rapid test in crop identification, a sort of multiple-choice game we play out of the van window, like kids playing I Spy on a long car journey.

"Brussels sprouts."

"No, the right height and colour, but not that green sleigh-bell effect. Broccoli. But they're both varieties of cabbage. *Brocco* means 'sprout' in Italian."

"How the hell do you know that?"

"I read it in the dictionary, back in the Café Clone. Are those people picking it at the back of the field?"

The scene, when we get nearer to it, is a blend of ancient and modern. The motion is in an ancient rhythm, the field-workers' backs bent as they stoop to cut the green helmets of broccoli from the stalks; the clothing is modern, bright synthetics, rubber boots filling slowly with broccoli crumbs. There is only one white worker among the dozen of them; the rest are too dark to be Chinese but their faces are clearly Asian – just one woman.

French, at least our brand of it, doesn't work; when we switch to English, some of them point at the white man in the blue coat. Most don't look up.

"Yes, I speak English. Go ahead." He is small under the bulky field jacket, fortyish, and has a look of anger that has long ago boiled over and is now held at simmer. His delicate hands don't look as if they should be able to handle a knife as well as they do.

He doesn't wait for me to finish with the introductions, and butts in as a valve somewhere in him flies open. "Well, yes, the conditions here, I'm telling you, in Quebec, they are the worst. *Merde*. I've worked across the country. I was a teacher, I want to write an article about this."

"Would you be able to talk to us later on, when you finish?" Some of the others are watching, their knives idle.

"Cambodians – Kampucheans," the man says, as though they are behind soundproof glass, waving his knife at them. They are refugees, rich or smart or scared enough to get out of Asia, now making $5.25 an hour in a broccoli field in Quebec. "Yes, I'll talk, sure. My name is Majella. I'm a lonesome rider. Now? Let's go now. I'll come with you. I'm sick of this. Where is your van?"

He means it. To him we are an act of precognition, someone who has pulled over to offer a lift just before he decided to become a hitchhiker. We postpone the talk till the field is finished, just another hour, and he has had a chance to talk first to himself.

Four-thirty. The Cambodians leave the field in a crowded station wagon. Majella jumps down from the pile of broccoli and says, "Drive me to my trailer," as he lights the first of an unbroken chain of cigarettes. He settles some debt along the way at a grocery store, and back at the vegetable warehouse he showers. While we wait, the Cambodians leave in clusters in immaculate Toyotas.

Cleaner and calmer, Majella comes out waving goodbye to a South American with spectacles and a book under his arm. "He's a lawyer, this guy, from San Salvador," he explains from the back seat. His accent gives "lawyer" an Inspector Clouseau twist; it comes out as "liar." "A political refugee, like the

Cambodians from concentration camps." The voice from the back seat goes on, almost without punctuation, with the gusto of a man hauled off a raft in mid-ocean by a passing steamer.

"One year two months I'm on this cheap island. Cucumbers, broccoli, cauliflower, in the fields of one of the biggest producers on it. Before I was in Ontario, Dresden, picking tomatoes for the Heinz factory in Leamington. Altogether different. Ontario draws the best pickers. Fifty-three days straight picking, except for the two when there was lightning in the fields; there is a law to prevent going in during lightning. Here is the bridge." We roll off the Ile d'Orléans, the Montmorency Falls ahead, taller than the Horseshoe Falls at Niagara. In winter a cone of ice forms at the base, frozen spray the height of a church steeple.

"Two hundred boxes a day there, and I'm not a good picker. Thirty-two pounds a box, forty-six cents for each one. The best pick twice this, a thousand dollars a week, winter in Rio, own a Harley. A lot of Quebecers in those fields, so I'm useful to speak two languages."

Quebec, Majella wants us to understand, is trapped in its own history. By Quebec, I think he really means the small vegetable growers. The chain of father and son linking back to the seigneuries is rusty but still binds its farmers to tradition. The old men hand over the farm too late, when the new ideas are already long at work in the fields elsewhere. "Agriculture is evolution," he tells us, "but Quebec farmers don't want to *evolute*." He preaches, it is true, from a low pulpit, but that is real dirt under his fingernails.

The conversation needs lubrication. Majella leads us to a fake English pub in Old Quebec, near a McDonald's. He orders beer in twos, about fifteen minutes between rounds. Cigarettes, ashtray, and a slim gold lighter are set just so to his left; the distance between each is adjusted until it is equal.

Bartenders soon learn to their boredom that the people who should really be running the world are all warming bar stools and driving taxis. Majella seems to be another of those men, anxious to prove that working as a picker in, as he calls them,

"Salvation Army designer clothes" is where he has fallen, not where he belongs. But what did he trip on?

"So," I ask, leaning into his smokescreen, "what are you doing on that island?"

The lighter gets a minute adjustment. "I had to return home, personal things to finalize in the family. My father died. Legal things to do, a question of wives not to discuss here. He lived up at Lac St-Jean. After this, I want to be in Quebec a little, I phone a field agent for work. They always need people on the Ile d'Orléans, he tells me. A dangerous sentence; why do they always need people? I arrive, Salvadoreans, Latinos, Babel Tower."

Majella swears liberally, bilingual expletives, divided between the sex act (English) and the Catholic church (French). The most common English swear word is thrown at the Cambodians. Familiarity has bred contempt. His main objection is their refusal to learn French or English, unlike the East Europeans, whom he picked alongside in Ontario, or the Ivory Coast students from Laval, who worked with him last summer. His daily frustration with them has overwhelmed any sympathy for their history. I ask him for his own history.

Majella becomes more cautious. From what he says, I gather he was born, forty-three years ago, on the Fourth of July, in Gaspésie, but left as a boy when his father found work in the huge aluminium works in Hebertville on Lac St-Jean. Both his parents were from farms, and he worked in the summer fields as a boy and then as a student.

"A student of what?"

"Pure mathematics at McGill. Then fifteen years a teacher, some in Terre Neuve, Newfoundland. Then a shift is needed, I'm tired, so in 1985 I quit and worked in Ontario – back to the land and my knowing it."

No two strangers tell each other the complete truth. Hitch-hikers are free to be anybody they want while they are in the passenger seat. Clearly, Majella's life came apart somewhere – booze, drugs, love, one leading to the other in some tragic spiral – and, I think, he is gluing it back together with lies, starting again picking vegetables in fields like he did as a boy. A veteran of differential calculus, I set out to shovel aside the lies and strike metal.

But he is telling the truth. Either that or pure mathematics is his hobby. Unlikely. He discusses the topography of current abstract physics, the largest prime number found, $(2^{86243-1})$, the mathematical greats such as Gauss, and on a napkin, damp in one corner with beer, writes out a short proof from the *Principia*, the great work of Isaac Newton.

There is a fog of hops in our minds as we give Marcuse a dusting over. "He talked in Germany," Majella says, "and told them that the *campagne*, the country, abandoned by those people seduced by the city, will have a revenge. They will one day want to return, but it will be, how to say, *un étranger*, a stranger, to them." I cannot tell from his face if he realizes the self-profile in this. Perhaps so, because he changes subjects, moving, as many mathematicians do, to music. There is a swapping of Beatles' lyrics.

It's late. No, Majella doesn't need a lift, he will take a taxi. "This is a special night. Most of them I'm in my trailer, reading magazines of science, asleep by nine-thirty; I'm too old to use my hands for pleasure. And I'm writing a book on differential calculus for people without money to go to university. Three years on this book. Listen to Tom Waits, read Ginsberg poems." And he quotes one – "Do it!"

Majella is a foot soldier in an army without ranks, the army of the hired hand. There are no statistics for them in their camps strewn across the country, only the numbers of mailing boxes. From what he says, the fields are perhaps where true multi-culturalism is scattered, where the lowest common denominator survives. Cambodians, Salvadoreans, East Germans, Mexicans, Gypsies, lapsed professors, men from prison cells of all kinds, refugees from states of mind, side by side in the rows.

15

BEEF AND CHIPS

T he road rolls and dips north through a provincial park, the Parc des Laurentides. The conifers are gregarious, breaking ranks only for lakes and ridges. The lakes are negative images of the night sky, black constellations of ducks arranged on silver. The brief outcrops of humanity bear elemental names: Des Roches, Sept-Iles, La Passe, Portes-d'Enfer. (The Rocks, Seven Islands, The Pass, The Gates of Hell.)

Then, almost on a knife edge, the Canadian Shield yields to the floodplain of Lac St-Jean. The curves of worn granite and lakeshore are replaced by the right angles of fields. This is the heart of Quebec. The Alcan works where Majella's father worked falls away on our left. The lake itself blocks our path. On its far shore, a faint smudge on the horizon, is the blueberry capital of the country, where a fifth of the national crop is harvested between August and September. The harvest begins with a festival – blueberry pie washed down with white blueberry wine.

After a right turn at the lake, we parallel the Saguenay River, a sword stroke that cuts deep into the shield. Rolled bales of hay are wrapped in white plastic and stacked alongside barns like giant marshmallows ready for some campfire of the gods. We pass dairy farm after dairy farm, shoulder to shoulder, till we reach La Baie and the Bergeron brothers. They remind me of the Powers brothers in Newfoundland: weathered faces that camouflage their true age, outsized hands with knuckles like stones. They share too the same gentleness of pace. Their farm is five times the size of the Powers', but they are all of the fraternity of milkmen.

I fear there is nothing new to learn here until we all go in the office. Beneath a dusty map of the farm, with a roll call of names and photographs of their ancestors going back to their great-grandfather taped to the glass, there sits a scruffy, blue *ordinateur*, a computer. It must be at least five years old, but it still an anomaly, the equivalent of a hay bale on a banker's desk. The screen is on. It gives the dietary and production details of cow number eighty-five, in numbers and percentages that resemble a patient's chart.

The computer's role in the feeding system becomes clear when we cross to the barn, past a miniature street of ice-fishing huts that the brothers rent out in the winter. The straw bed in the barn has been fluffed up and the damp smell of manure climbs into our noses. One of the herd wheels away from us and pokes her head into a narrow trough on the wall, one of only two troughs in the room. As she does so, a helping of feed drops in front of her nose. The feeder, at the computer's instruction, has dished out just the right bovine blend for this particular cow, six months along in her gestation.

The feeder is able to discern the correct diet for this particular member of the herd because of the large plastic pendant dangling from her neck like a cow bell. In the pendant there is a coil that gives off a unique signal. When that pendant dangles in the trough, a reading device connected to the computer informs it who has arrived for dinner, and the proper meal is dispatched.

The oldest profession and the newest, agriculture and electronics, have been slowly merging. Heat sensors on cows can now inform the farmhouse, via small radio packs, when they come into heat. In the milking parlour, the milking machine will automatically disconnect when it detects a drained udder. Out in the field, in-board computers on tractors and combines absorb the reports of sensors slung underneath and adjust cutting heights and ploughing depths.

The future will be even tidier and faster. The micro-coil is an advance on the somewhat clumsy pendant the Bergeron cows are wearing. The size of a grain of rice, it is planted in the ear via a syringe, and has locked within it a unique number. It was originally designed for swine breeders to track animals in slaughterhouses. Knowing exactly which animals weighed in light or too fatty at slaughter has already helped Canadian breeders catch up with the kings of pork, the Danish.

The micro-coils may also make branding obsolete. Unbranded hides currently fetch seven dollars more per hide than branded ones, which more than covers the cost of the coil. Orwell, of course, would have shrugged knowingly at all this: Big Brother comes to Animal Farm.

The Bergeron brothers are the first generation of computer-literate farmers, who have happily allowed intuition and imprecision to stand aside for science. In the future, grandmothers will amuse grandsons with tales of shoe-box accounting, grandfathers will bore granddaughters with stories of mower blades clogged with grass, and the youngsters will peruse the latest prices of patented tomato seeds on the computer bulletin board. The electronic family farm.

A computer would also not forget the French word for bull. In mid-question, I realize that I have no idea what it is. I get involved in an absurd pantomime, more a request for the bathroom than the noun for a male cow, and I collapse into bad French: "*Une vache qui est un homme?*" René, the elder brother, catches on. "*Taureau!*" he shouts, with a click of his fingers. A pause, then everyone shouts "Olé!" and there is a bout of unilingual laughter.

16

THAT'LL BE
THE PHONE

Ottawa again, and a new regime of smells: chip wagons on the streets, office cocktails of aftershave and perfume, carbon monoxide traffic jams. Farmers on holiday taking snaps of the kids on Parliament Hill with the Peace Tower in the background. Parking spots as rare as lottery prizes. Clusters of fashion statements smoking cigarettes in the doorways of smoke-free government offices.

When I unclog the answering machine and the mail box, I find two cheerful messages from farm groups. One is from a group in Prince Edward Island inviting us, too late, to a meeting of Women for Survival in Agriculture. After some phone work, I discover that the founder of the group lives just outside Ottawa, in Winchester. The second is from Cor Rook, the chairman of a Farm Crisis Committee in the Ottawa Valley.

Cor lives near Cobden, an hour's drive from Ottawa, on the Ontario side of the river. The seventeenth-century astrolabe (a hand-held device for working out from the sun just where on the planet you are) at the entrance to the Museum of Civilization in Hull was found in a farmer's field at Cobden. Cobdenites claim that the astrolabe is litter from Samuel Champlain's exploration group, which passed through here in 1613.

The region is stiff with Irish history, and just about everyone in the Ottawa Valley is of temporary Irish descent on St. Patrick's Day. The Ottawa Valley twang is an Irish mutation. It is thick enough to cause confusion. When a request went out at one wake for "three more chairs," the Valley veterans in the crowd called out "hip hip hooray" three times.

Cor Rook, however, is Dutch. "It's '52 Dutch," he says, denoting the vintage of his accent and the year he came to the Valley. Holland has a fixed amount of farmland and an increasing number of farm sons and daughters. Much of the surplus comes to Canada to found tidy farms that run like clockwork.

An imposing man, Cor has a cigar smoker's gravelly voice, a face like an old cushion, and wrists like two by fours. He calls money "shmackers," and he had to work ten years off the farm in a foundry to make enough shmackers to save it, while his wife held the fort.

Cor is a twenty-year union man. In this he differs from most Ontario farmers, who are in the Ontario Federation of Agriculture. He uses quotes from the common handbook of unionism, phrases like "We have to live with each other, not off each other," but he is not parroting them; he does as he says. He has held various union positions, and he is currently the chairperson of the Farm Crisis Committee in his area. His informal caseload is light compared to that of his counterpart in southwestern Ontario, but he has four farms under threat currently on his mind.

"A shoulder to cry on, give advice, think straight for them when they can't" is how he describes his role. He worries with them, listens when, their minds working like eggbeaters, they kick away the sheets and reach for the bedside phone.

Some farmers, Cor readily admits, are the authors of their own misery – they are in the wrong business. They bought cheap and paid dearly, or they didn't look for information that could have saved them, or they tended the fields without tending the books. These farmers will come and go. But the margin of error in modern agriculture has narrowed down to a razor edge, ready to amputate the not yet strong or the still learning. You do not become an agronomist-cum-welder-cum-entrepreneur-cum-mechanic-cum-accountant overnight.

"We can't afford to lose these ones," Cor says, crossing over to the big double sink to refill his glass of iced water. We are all sweating in the July heat. The evening cicadas are sending out their piercing static.

"They are the young ones, the replacements for us old parts. Last fall, the wife and I, we went to the ploughing match, just south of Georgian Bay there. The average age of the crowd, well I would be in the younger half – at fifty-six!" The Rooks have no children; their farm will pass out of the family. There is doubtless some parental concern in Cor's crisis management. A fatherly tone filters into his explanation of the troubles of a nearby young farmer.

"Sloppy books. His, yes, but the bank's, too. I saw their ledgers. The interest rates changed so fast they couldn't hold the horse. They panicked and called the loan. The farmer sold his quota. Two years without a milk cheque, he makes some money from cash crops." The bank Cor is talking about is actually both the bank and a crown corporation, the Farm Credit Corporation.

In 1959, Diefenbaker, a man who had grown up in Saskatchewan, allowed the setting up of an alternative to the banks for farmers seeking loans – The Farm Credit Corporation. (Saskatchewan has always been the corporation's most frequent customer, way out of proportion to the other provinces.) The corporation's lending rate, achieved without the motive for profit, is always a little under the rate the banks enjoy. And the rates to farmers have always been nailed down, initially for a ten-year period. In 1984 the fixed rate was for five, ten, or twenty years, depending on the type of loan they took. Some loans have payments pegged to Bank of Canada interest rates, others to the prices crops and animals are fetching. Farmers can also form syndicates to buy equipment with FCC money and share it.

The FCC gets used. In the summer of 1988, almost a quarter of Canadian farm families were making payments, large and small, to it. Twenty-six hundred new loans were approved the same year, two-fifths of them in Saskatchewan. If, in an act of political suicide, it called in all its loans in arrears, the FCC would become the biggest landholder in the country. Many farmers feel that the FCC has shed several skins and emerged more or less indistinguishable from the banks. And they view it with the same healthy suspicion.

Like any creditor, the corporation has the power to foreclose. And it does, to such a degree that the government jammed a stick in its wheels in September 1985 with a moratorium that lasted a year and a half. Midway through the moratorium it set up the Farm Debt Review Board. According to the packaging, farmers could ask the board to mediate between them and a bank or the FCC, after they had received the terrifying fifteen-day notice that the Farm Debt Review Act requires creditors to send to farmers before they come after them.

Asking the board to step in stops the axe from falling for at least 30 days and up to 120. The board appoints a guardian for the farmer's assets, usually the farmer himself, although it can be anyone the board chooses. The trick to using the Farm Debt Review Board is to treat it like a stalling card and to play it at the right moment. Rushing to them as soon as you feel the first tug on the debt can lose you the farm.

As soon as you call in the board, you will get a visit from a review panel. There are farmers and FCC staff on the panel who judge the operation of the farmer who asked for review. The panel had made two visits to the farmer Cor Rook was helping. There wasn't an accountant on the panel Cor met, so the sloppy books never got an expert eye run over them. They visited two years after the dairy quota had been sold, so they pulled into a fairly sad-looking farmyard. A while later they made their report, in a motel meeting room overlooking the St. Lawrence.

They recommended that the farmer sell up. So far he has resisted this final solution.

Cor settles back to relight his cigar, which he has been too busy talking to draw on. I ask him a hard question, one I've wanted to ask someone since we started our journey two months earlier. He has seen farmers leave their land. What does he think goes with them? What does the land lose when a family leaves it?

"Loyalty," he answers, after a couple of puffs and some minor adjustment to his cap. It is the perfect answer. From loyalty comes concern and the wish to fight on the land's behalf, as David Ling does back on Prince Edward Island. When Cor spreads fertilizer on his land, he uses not fresh but what he calls "rotten" manure, broken down with a little liquid. He waits till the buds are on the poplars, until the ground has punched in for work, before he ploughs. He rests his fields. He does this out of loyalty.

When Cor adjusted his cap to make his head more comfortable for thinking with, he was fine-tuning the farmers' favourite piece of clothing. A cap is not a fashion accessory; it is a tool. It is a combination rag, shade maker, billboard, flyswatter, and baldness disguiser. Cor has a particularly fine collection, set like bone-china plates on a high shelf running around the summer porch. Funk Hardware, TransCanada PipeLines, National Farmers' Union, Super Sweet Feeds. There is one for John Deere, and I slip in the joke about the farmer's wife who ran off with the tractor salesman. "Two weeks later the farmer got a John Deere letter."

The tour of the caps is done with solemnity, Cor the concerned curator. They are subdived into winter and summer caps, and town and country caps, some of them identical twins. "This is a town cap," Cor tells us, pointing out an immaculate red-and-white model. "The dirty one goes on the chair, and I change into the clean one if I go into town."

I'm about to ask if there is a Rook cap when the phone rings. Cor has his hands full with caps, so it rings several times before he can cross to it. He is looking at us when he picks it up, but he turns in his chair when he realizes who it is. He listens for a while before he replies.

"Okay. I'll look out for that. I see. Well, time will tell." He hangs up; it's a moment before he remembers us. "That was the farmer we talked about. He has a party line, so he calls me. Mine is private. His lawyer from legal help, legal aid, has bought him some breathing time. I like to hear that. The newspaper is going to visit him in a few days to do a story."

"Will he make it, Cor?"

The cap gets a good rocking up and down. "Sometimes loyalty isn't enough. Time will tell."

17

ACTIVE PARTNERS

The road to Winchester, Ontario, starts almost directly opposite the Peace Tower on Parliament Hill. At this end, it is called Bank Street. It passes through downtown Ottawa, an asphalt canal running between silent skyscrapers and booming construction sites.

Gradually more of the sky becomes visible as the buildings shrink to a human scale, and the occasional cluster of high-rises stands out like a sore thumb. Brash malls and loud car dealerships, identikit suburbs, all slide by. The first graveyard appears, then Bank Street becomes Highway 31. The natural horizon is broken now only by roadhouses, a variety of brief Main streets, and then farms seize the majority. Thirty miles from the Peace Tower lies Harkhaven Farm. The name is nailed to the barn at the end of the drive.

Dianne Harkin made much the same journey, from the city to Winchester, in 1970, when she came out here with her husband, Dan. When he married her, Dan told Dianne that he wanted to work outside, with his hands, and own his own business. "I figured," Dianne says, "that he wanted to own a ski resort. I didn't know I had married a closet farmer."

Dianne's grandmother wept the day Dianne told her that Dan had quit his job and they were starting a farm. Though a farmer herself, her grandmother had warned Dianne never to marry one. "You'll be old before your time with work and poverty," she told Dianne.

Dianne does not look old before anybody's time. She is an engaging, attractive woman, now in her fifties, with wide-set eyes and a cat's grin and softness. She works on her image, dressing to suit the occasion and not leaving the mirror until she likes what she sees. You can tell she has been around the media and can see herself as the TV camera portrays her. The whole thing comes tumbling down, fortunately, when she laughs. Her laugh enjoys escaping, coming on loud and joyful. There is no severity beneath the polished veneer.

The Harkins started with a cow-calf operation, then pared that down to just a feedlot. Though neither of them had farmed before, and their parents hadn't either, there were farmers further down the family tree. Dan's family had farmed in the same area, though Dan didn't know it then, in the 1800s. Both of their families had simply missed a beat in the rhythm of generations on the land.

When it rains on the farm, it pours, and in 1972 the county cows were knee-deep in mud. As they were desperately moved from field to field in search of unflooded grass, they trampled and chewed their own winter feed into useless mulch. Dianne's phone rang one day, asking Dan to attend a village meeting to get the local agricultural rep to declare the state of affairs an emergency. When Dianne said that Dan was away, the farmer at the other end of the line invited her in his place.

"The rep shifted things to the town hall when he saw the size of the protest. In the hall there were 199 men – and me. I could see them nudging each other and saying 'What's she doing here?' That's when I decided, hey, this lady is going to be involved off the farm as well. I started to go to farm meetings where the only other woman was the secretary."

A woman at these meetings was off-limits, and it did cause friction. Dianne was told, by anonymous heroes in late-night phone calls, to go back where she had come from. Which, she felt, was exactly what she had done when she moved back to her grandmother's way of life.

Dianne saw herself as simply following the code her foremothers had set – to affect your community for the better. Having an effect had not been so easy for her foremothers who might rarely see another woman for weeks on end, and then only at church. The community was now defined by coasts instead of county lines – electronics and airlines had shrunk the scale of things.

Dianne began to infiltrate herself into the society of farm wives about her. "I quickly came to respect them. They were walking encyclopaedias! I didn't know hay from straw, and I was scared of big animals, and they'd say, 'Here, this is how you do it, this is what that is.' And yet they didn't respect themselves. I had a button I wore that said 'I'm proud to be a farmer' that I wore into the city. They'd point and say, 'You wore that!'"

It's hard to find a farm sign that reads John Smith and Daughter, or, for that matter, Joan Smith and Son. Of the thousands of farm gates we passed, only one mentioned the daughter by name. The flow of time in the country has hugged the male shore for centuries. Thinking back along our journey, I realize that despite the strength I have seen in the wives, the genuine half of the story that they are, most of the voices I've taped so far are male.

Feminism took to the streets long before it went through the farm gate. Dianne is sure that skipping a generation on the land made her a likely candidate for the role that she eventually took in guiding the women's movement to the fields. She knew, in a sense, where it was coming from.

A professional volunteer, Dianne often found herself in groups of farm women, discussing crafts and church functions. When she extolled the virtues of farming, there was silent agreement that her temperature was running a little high, and someone would assure her that she would soon get over that. When she talked of forming a farm women's group, eyes would head for the ceiling and wait for the cloud to pass.

Dan Harkin, meanwhile, had become a delegate for the Ontario Federation of Agriculture. At a Toronto conference in 1974, he heard a woman called Laura Heizer, from Michigan, talking about a movement in the States called Women for the Survival of Agriculture. "Gee, Dianne," he told her, "I wish you'd been there. She was talking about all the things you talk about."

"So I wrote to her. She sent back a brochure and a card in the shape of an apple – she was in apples. On the card she wrote, 'Start something in Canada, Dianne – and give 'em hell.' That's all. It was all I needed."

The first step in giving them hell was to find an ally. In early 1975, International Women's Year, Dianne and a neighbour were shooting the breeze. "I shared with her what I wanted to do. Ghislaine put down her weaving and said, 'I'm with you.' I said, 'Right, we've just formed the Canadian Women for the Survival of Agriculture.'"

A month later Dianne found herself addressing the dinner crowd at the annual federation dance in the local school gym, as a five-minute token gesture to Women's Year that Dan had cajoled the organizing committee into allowing.

"He waited and told me about two days before, so I had no choice. I had the passion by then, so the words were easy. Ghislaine had produced for the CBC, so she gave me the dramatics, where to smile, some hand language. My dinner stayed on the plate like a still life. My speech came right before the dancing." She made the speech and left, holding back the information that the total membership of Women for the Survival of Agriculture (WSA) was two. At the feed store the next day Dianne met one of the guys in the band. "You really shook 'em," he told her. "We played for twenty minutes and nobody danced." Twenty-five of the women there signed up as members that night. The clutch was out on the movement.

At the first meeting, they went past midnight, the younger ones jumping up and down, uncorked – "We want to be farmers!" It was not a plea for a simple shift in perception. There was law to be changed. When the third- and fourth-generation farm women started appearing, Ghislaine said, "Now, we need a grant."

Grantology is not an easy subject to master. Grants cannot be taken for granted. Like humour, the trick lies in the timing. "We made what we really wanted to be an agricultural issue into a feminist issue. That got us mislabelled. We wanted to work with the men, not opposite them." The proposal, an agricultural one dressed in feminist clothing, went down Highway 31 to the Secretary of State, where they were given fifteen minutes to make their pitch – to a woman.

"It was bombing," says Dianne, "so I said, 'You don't like farmers, do you?' 'No,' she snapped back, 'I'm from Hungary. I read of farmers killing calves and ploughing fields in protest. It makes me sick.' 'Can I tell you why?' I asked her. We were there three hours, her body language gradually unwinding. She even helped us with our budget. We got funded."

From there on in, Dianne was "a monomaniac on a mission." She and her fellow members were salmon swimming upstream, using sheer energy to overcome resistance and man-made obstacles. Several times, curiously, they struck a fellow salmon swimming the wrong way. The Women's Institute thought they were overlapping, even poaching. But WSA was more punkish, more a reminder of raw energy as a force for change.

A woman on the Food Review Board, with the ironic name of Plumtree, held a strong antagonism towards farmers. She was giving dairy farmers particular grief. WSA volunteered to survey the real cost of producing a litre of milk. Milk figures flooded in, because it was women who did the farm books.

Before they presented their figures to the Food Review Board, Dianne says, "We stood in a nearby restaurant holding hands. Then we went in to Plumtree's office, and they told us we weren't experts, we had figures from small farms, not the big corporate ones that they were interested in. Ghislaine told the man saying this, who had grown up on a dairy farm, that his poor mother must be so ashamed of him. They took our figures, and they never went after dairy farmers again. They went after chicken farmers instead."

The postmarks on the letters delivered to Harkhaven Farm began to prove that WSA had arrived nationally. One group in B.C., the Cattle Belles, wanted to get everyone together. Ilona, the Hungarian civil servant they had converted to get their first grant, now suggested that it was time for a national conference. "That," says Dianne, "sparked off the most stressful year of my life."

Over the summer, before the conference, Dianne directed teams of researchers in the preparation of background papers on farm women's issues. They had titles like "Equal Partner or Just a Wife?," "Credit Where Credit Is Due," and, "Old MacDonald Had a Farm, but Will his Son or Daughter?"

When the dust settled from months of vanquishing crises, minimizing the damage caused by saboteurs and pulling out-of-pocket expenses from empty pockets, much was accomplished at the First National Farm Women's Conference. A research paper by the Quebec women was endorsed by the conference and led to legislation that allowed farm women to draw wages and thus make pension payments. Eugene Whelan, the federal agriculture minister, came down and tipped his green stetson towards them by putting a woman on the advisory board of the Farm Credit Corporation.

"The wake was wide and subtle from that conference," Dianne says proudly. "Two names started appearing on cups and awards at farm shows. When the man was called up to get his award, he'd look back and wave his wife up to the spotlight too. College courses for farm women got out of the kitchen and under the tractor – and farm women were designing them." After taking a stab at the media with a paper called "The Invisible Pitchfork," Dianne noticed more microphones in women's faces when farming made the news.

Dianne is the first to admit that hers was not the only voice in the wilderness. There was a chorus of farm women's groups across the country, including the Cattle Belles, calling for change. The National Farmers' Union had published a report on employment practices of farm women in 1982 that had been heard loud and clear down on the farm, and the handbook *Weaving New Ways*, written by the union's women's vice-president, Nettie Wiebe, was and still is required reading for anyone joining the chorus.

At the core of WSA and its sister groups, the scattered embers that kept them glowing, were the gatherings of women across the country in farm living rooms. They avoided the love of process rather than progress that eventually incapacitates many organizations – procedures and motions, picking the lice from previous minutes, deferring till tomorrow that which should have been done long ago.

"Our minutes were the news clippings, our newsletter, the TV reports, and our letters to each other. It was coffee, doughnuts, and down to work. At one meeting, for the first time but not the last, the whole thing of wife abuse came out."

Harkhaven Farm had become the movement's headquarters. A letter sent simply to "The Funny Farm, R.R. 1, Winchester" by Dianne's daughter at university arrived within the week. The telephone became the daily alarm bell. But Harkhaven was also a farm, susceptible as any other to the vagaries of money. In 1981, with beef prices low and interest rates high, the bank called the Harkins' beef loan.

"The GD bank wanted us to consolidate everything into a long-term loan at 18 per cent," Dianne explains. GD (God damn) is the nearest she gets to swearing. "We told them to stick it in their left ear. We started to liquidate everything. I don't think I'll ever recover from that. Even the silo came down. The bank manager they'd sent to try and convince us to buy a combine was replaced by grim inspectors from Toronto. The first batch gave us a favourable report, so they sent in an even grimmer bunch. It was like a modern, sick fairy tale. They found no mismanagement. They simply found victims of the times."

They didn't capsize, but the Harkins were forced to trim a sail that had hardly begun to feel the wind. Dan got a job off the farm with Agriculture Canada. The herd was reduced. The pertinence of the name they had given their group – Women for the Survival of Agriculture – was driven home. Home was where Dianne, for the moment, had to concentrate her efforts.

The founders of popular movements often pass a point where they no longer run them – they become run by them. Dianne came close to this point, to running this red light. Nature intervened. In 1986, she flew into Ottawa airport from an out-of-town conference and was greeted by her kids, a signal that something was wrong with Dan. His heart had attacked him. He recovered, but seven months later Dianne was diagnosed as having breast cancer. She evicted the cancer through holistic means and it hasn't returned. It was time to gear down.

Dorothy Middleton's house now resembles Dianne's; mail addressed to The Funny Farm reaches either house, as Dorothy and Dianne now share the guidance of WSA into a second decade. Dorothy, a neighbour of Dianne's, is a farmer and a teacher, so members at meetings now sometimes find themselves called "kids" instead of Dianne's impolitic but affectionate "girls." Dorothy has no fear of delegation, and puts out the same voltage as Dianne. They resemble a twin wall socket jammed with plugs and wires leading to a national network of brightly lit farmhouses.

When they divided the WSA duties between them, in an attempt to improve Dianne's health and jeopardize Dorothy's, the work load promptly doubled. In 1987 they worked with a team of professionals to produce a study called "Cover Your Assets," a guide to taking wives as legal partners on the farm. Five thousand of these were requested and delivered.

Back down Highway 31, at the head of Bank Street, the government was drawing the decade of women to a close. The flag came down in 1988 when the oxymoronic Progressive Conservatives funded, for the first time, the group of traditionalists called REAL Women. A year later WSA, also for the first time, received no funding.

Dianne accepts this turn for the worse in the political climate with a farmer's philosophical sense of meteorology. WSA will go where it wants, blown by the times and shifts in personnel. "Some people draw nearer as the fire goes down," Dianne says.

She doesn't know what new fires will flare, but she knows herself and the women who joined her to be tempered and strengthened by the flames they faced. Her vision for Women for the Survival of Agriculture was that agriculture was ignoring a resource that could help it survive – a resource sitting just at the other end of the kitchen table. And she wanted to hand farm men, the myopic ones, a new pair of spectacles that would bring their partners into focus.

Harkhaven Farm, on this cloudless summer day, is in sharp focus. The cattle are gone; less demanding cash crops now stand in the fields they once grazed. Their barn has been converted to house Dianne's eldest son and his building company. A small cottage just away from the farmhouse is home to the eastern editor of *Farm and Country*, and the farmhouse itself now welcomes the bed–and–breakfast trade. The farm's true crop is people.

Upstairs in the office Dianne's humorous farm-life column, which goes regularly into a poultry magazine, is half finished. The plans for a book on the farm women's movement and the funny side of life on the farm are somewhere within the obese filing cabinets. Also in there are the letters notifying her that she has been awarded the Order of Ontario and has been given an honorary degree in agriculture.

Lucky, the dog, hops in the car with me, as he did when I arrived, cleans my chin in farewell, and hops out. At Highway 31, I turn south and drive into Winchester and pull up opposite a thirteen-room house, the double garage alongside converted to offices. This is the Naomi Family Resource Centre, a women's centre named for the biblical character who sheltered her sister.

Shortly after she moved to Harkhaven, Dianne's car found the ditch beside a slippery road. She walked to the nearest farm to ask for a tractor to pull her out. Asked inside out of the cold, Dianne noticed the farmer's wife standing hidden and silent behind the wood stove, bruises and beer cans speaking for her.

Years later the chance of a grant to open a women's centre came to Winchester, steered there by WSA's footing in the area; the condition was evidence of grass-roots support. Fifteen people were invited to the founding meeting in the Lion's Club, and a hundred turned up. Dianne served on the shelter's board of directors for several years. Naomi's is rarely empty. Now, when the bruised wife comes out from behind the wood stove, she will have somewhere to go.

18

A LAWFUL
CITIZEN

A sea once covered most of southern Ontario. Whales swam above the present site of the Parliament Buildings in Ottawa. In geographical time, the receding of the sea was a recent event. Lake Huron and Georgian Bay held their ground, and the land between, a limestone graveyard of coral, emerged. A thin, stony soil covered the prodigal landscape, watered by rain lifted by the wind from the lakes.

The Scottish crofters who settled there recognized the land for what it wasn't – much use for crops – and for what it was – good pasture. Calves could arrive from neighbouring Manitoba and swell with the grass and grain that the soil provided. The Grey-Bruce area grows beef. Ontario has more beef farms than Alberta.

There may be a thesis awaiting some graduate student who wants to link terrain and character. Poke a finger into the ancestry and character of the Grey-Bruce cow-calf farmers and you quickly hit rock that won't budge. Canada's first woman MP, Agnes McPhail, left Grey County for Ottawa in 1921, two years after women in most provinces had won the right to vote in federal elections. Nellie McClung, the suffragette leader, grew up there. And it was in the Grey-Bruce that farming first put its shoulder to the eighties and pushed back. Push came when the Grey-Bruce Farmers' Survival Association was formed in an old township hall just south of Owen Sound. Within days, with a strong head of steam building behind it, the association rolled itself into the Canadian Farmers' Survival Association. One of its most visible members was Allen Wilford, a small spark-plug of a man. If our journey into the fields of vision had a seed, it was Allen Wilford. The seed was planted, appropriately for the era, by television.

On February 9, 1981, Wilford sat in the back of a police car. He had been arrested for theft. Shortly before he was arrested, hundreds of farmers had taken over an auction of farm equipment. The proceeds of the auction were to go to the bank that had lent a farmer, John Otto, $200,000. Interest, like a gout, had swelled the money owing until Otto's debt was more than twice what he had borrowed. He had, of course, been unable to make 100 per cent profit on the original borrowing, so he could only manage to feed the voracious interest. The principle would have to wait.

The bank couldn't wait. A receiver (a curious title, since the job involves administering a taking away) was hoping the auction proceeds would go towards the interest – a sale of artefacts to reduce a fiction.

During the Depression a particularly cunning group in the U.S.A., the Farmers' Holiday Movement, revived a device called the Penny Auction. At a perfect Penny Auction, the highest bid for any item was one cent. The bank, hoping for sacks of money, would collect a pocketful.

The Farmers' Survival Association used the same tactic to frustrate the auctioning off of John Otto's farm equipment. The ploy was a success. The auction raised $19.81, rather more than the farmers had intended, due to some overzealous bidding, although the fact that the amount equalled the year 1981 was mystically satisfying. A tractor went for $1.50, a pickup for

$5.00. Once they got the hang of it, the protesting farmers kept prices down to 170 cattle for six cents and a barnful of hay for the same.

The proceedings, while deadly serious, had also a tinge of dream about them. Dollar-fifty tractors confuse the prevailing sense of reality. The police were caught up in the mood, and they arrested Wilford for theft over $200. Wilford, although the architect of the seizure of the auction, hadn't bought anything.

In the police car on the way to jail, Wilford, who had already put his sharp, prominent nose into the law books, decided to go on a hunger strike to establish his right to be arrested only when he had done something wrong, and to advertise his cause. He also wanted the federal government to push through the second reading of the Farmers and Creditors bill, which proposed to give farmers some temporary relief from relentless interest rates.

The hunger strike began in the Stratford jail, and it lasted eight days. The second reading went through, and Allen was acquitted. Mine was one of the many televisions that broadcast the story of the hunger strike. The black humour, the poetry *noir* of a food producer refusing food, caught me. The seed was planted.

Allen Wilford is not a big man. He holds you with his eyes, not his bulk. His eyes carry the faith his mother implanted in him before she died in 1956, when he was seven. She was forty-five when Allen was born. Like many other women, she waited till the Depression had lifted before marrying. "She taught me that life is like a game of solitaire: If you have to cheat at it, why play?"

Allen's father knew the caprice of money. He had worked as a hired hand through the Depression, eaten his share of ground-hogs. A city job in a rubber factory was wrecking his health, and in 1951, when Allen was three, they bought a farm. Calves bought at forty-eight cents that year went out at eight cents. The story was that if you took three calves to market, you wouldn't sell them, and if you looked behind on the way home there would be six. The Wilfords stayed on the farm until 1964, by which time his father had remarried and his health had improved enough to let him work in the city again.

Allen bought his first farm in 1971, at the age of twenty-two. Eventually, by concentrating just on fattening calves, Allen was a successsful farmer. He cleaved to the organic way as much as he could. "The only thing I couldn't get 'round was the chemical you use to clear up warble flies. They come up through the skin in lumps on the cow's back. Spill that stuff on your hands, and you can taste it in your mouth in seconds."

By 1980, he owned 440 acres and leased that many again. Like most of his neighbours, he had a debt load that he could only watch as it grew into absurdity, no matter how hard he worked. Farmers like to say that they work eight hours like everyone else – eight in the morning and eight in the afternoon.

When the banks began to foreclose on his neighbours, Allen sensed that the banks were cheating at life, and he wasn't about to let them. Allen and his fellow farmers in Grey-Bruce forced the banks to rethink. With a series of tactics, such as the Penny Auction and the farm-gate defence, they made the banks negotiate, and they inspired farmers, men and women, all across the country to fight to save their farms – like the MacPhails in Prince Edward Island.

The early eighties for Wilford and the association were very much a campaign, a series of battles and fronts, triumphs and defeats, commandos and commanders. Their uniform — green pants and a plaid jacket — was available at any general store, and their insignia was a red bandanna. Their tanks were the tractors they used to block streets and bank doors. They fought at the home front, at the gates of their neighbours, and some, like Allen, fought away, at international conferences in Ottawa and in town halls throughout the U.S.A. They established lines of communication for farmers in crisis, such as the one Allen set up with money from Willie Nelson's Farm Aid concerts.

They had their casualties. Some were saved. Others are forever lost, sacrificed on barn rafters or on the end of shotguns. Allen took many dead-of-night calls from men with no natural reason left to carry on. They knew him only as a phone number that cared. He never lost one, but perhaps the ones who phoned didn't really want to go. The ones who did went quietly.

"Imagine you are an artist," Allen tells people when they ask how losing a farm feels, "and you have worked your whole life on one canvas. You don't want to sell the canvas. Then someone comes and takes the canvas away. That's how it feels to give your farm to a bank."

Allen could claim some effect on his times, but the times had affected him. Much had happened to Allen Wilford when we finally met, six years after the hunger strike, in May 1987. His marriage had come apart with the strain. He was still living in Grey County, in a modern house near Clarksburg, but he was no longer an active farmer. He was about to become a law student at York University. He had found his mission, which is, as he says, "to screw the banks." The six years he spent as a figurehead of the Farmers' Survival Association had reshaped him.

The years were an education. He became, by promotion in the field, a zealous historian and a warrior economist. He quoted for us a chilling document written in 1945 by an economist at MIT, whose thesis has become the cornerstone of North American farm policy since the war. In summary, it said that "resources" (meaning farmers) should be both forced and attracted out of farming. Commercial farmers would feel the pressure to become more efficient (more chemicals, more equipment, more debt). The remaining farmers would find their incomes so low that they would either go into industry or work off the farm.

Hearing this was like hearing the original shout whose echo has long been in your ears. I'd often heard farmers mention a government paper put out in 1969 that recommended reducing the farm population by two-thirds, using the tactics described by MIT. I got to read it at the headquarters of the National Farmers' Union in Saskatoon. It must be, from the government side, one of the more successful pieces of social engineering.

Allen has the makings of a vengeful lawyer. In the law he has found a weapon that cuts. All conversational roads taken, as we sat outside beside a freshly dug and stocked trout pond, eventually led there.

"It was a judge who helped me convince myself that I should go to law school and certify what I'd already become. He said, after he'd had me in his court, that I should either go into law or politics. In politics you have to convince a whole chamberful of other people to agree with you to make new law. In law you just have to convince one person, the judge, and the new law is made. Like what happened in my own case."

In the summer of 1986, Allen defended himself when the Royal Bank sued him to reclaim his debt, which they had assessed at $420,000. Allen's defence at heart was very simple: He asked the bank, with its constantly shifting, floating rate of interest, to prove the debt. For three days in Owen Sound the bank's three lawyers, flanked by a stack of books and papers the size of a cord of wood, tried to do just that. Judge Galligan, a tall, dark, and handsome man, allowed the bank to include almost everything in its arguments and Allen just about nothing. Then he ruled that the bank couldn't prove the debt, that their floating of the interest rate was illegal, and that they had overcharged Allen by $223,000. It was a historic decision that may end up redistributing millions of dollars out of bank computers and into farmland to irrigate parched farm lives.

The Wilfords' kitchen table was our first farm desk, and the lesson went long into the night. Allen's new family milled around us. He met Gretta at the YMCA, at a talk on how to recognize the assumptions your life is based on. Both of them had abandoned an old set and taken on a new one. Gretta said that on the first night she and Allen went out to dinner she listened to him talk awhile, and then told him, "You should be a lawyer."

We ate well, shared a few beer, and when we began making noises about the Clone Motel, Allen offered us beds for the night in return for a few hours the next morning putting the roof on his new horse barn. We could sleep in the bunks his sons used when they came to visit.

The clean pine ribs of the barn shone in the sun the next day as we nailed two by sixes into place. The rafters rose with easy precision and the first sheets of plywood began to enclose the space and make shade. Allen told of a threat he had once had, after the Penny Auction, to burn down his barn. The next day a barn on the farm next to his caught fire.

I looked past the rafter I was holding to a sky blue enough to be a sea, and realized that a barn is but an inverted ark, grounded in a field. The simple design we were erecting was as old as farming itself. Looking across the fields, other barns hove into view, other members of the fleet. "A little to your left," Allen said, and I pushed the rafter into its true line. The nail went in clean and held it there.

"I've got exams at Christmas, and I come out in April. Then a year's articling." It is two and a half years later. Allen has taken the phone in the kitchen, and at the other end of the line I can picture his cluttered desk with copies of his book, *Farm Gate Defense*, on it, and beyond the windows the trout pond haloed with vegetation and the barn complete and weathered. "The trout are up to a foot and a half now."

Law school has been interesting and hard. "Heh, I'm in some of textbooks we used, on constitutional issues and the Penny Auctions." He has already been advising and researching cases of false farm debt, sparring rounds for the main bout he will soon fight in earnest. "There have been hundreds since my case, lots of settlements." The Royal Bank launched an appeal against that original decision, then dropped it. He is suing them back for malicious prosecution and breach of contract – for $10 million.

Allen also sued the provincial minister of agriculture, again over disputed debt. "I don't know if it was coincidence, but he was fired a week later, while he was out west." A laugh comes down the phone line. I tell him my word for all this, *sue-age*.

In May 1989, Allen and Gretta were married. Two motels were filled with guests from all over the province. Many of them had been alongside Allen in the Farmers' Survival Association, and the rooms were full of the spirit and memory of those days. Someone remembered the time they were on their way back from a Penny Auction. They pulled into a Chinese restaurant, the Canadian kind that advertises Chinese smorgasbord. They ran up a healthy tab, and when it came time to pay, no one had enough on them. They had not taken any money, except for a few cents, to the auction. But the owner let it ride till the next day. He knew he could trust the farmers to pay.

19

THE LAST MASSEY

T he first time I took the controls of a combine, I panicked. It was in a small wheat field, where David figured I could do the least damage. David was a fellow farm hand, younger than me and built like a boxer. He was exuberant with his strength; he could hold a pool cue in his fingers at the thin end and raise it parallel to the ground, his arm straight out. Machinery came naturally to him.

I had parked the grain wagon in the corner and joined him on top of the combine while we waited for its tank to fill. His red hair and freckled face were flecked with straw confetti. His eyes were riveted to just in front of the reel, searching ahead for bumps, rocks, thin growth, reaching out automatically to the various levers that adjusted the height of the reel or its speed. Meanwhile he braked or accelerated, and listened out for the signal that the tank was full, so he could swing out the auger and start pouring the ripe wheat into my truck, all without stopping.

"Here, lad, you try," he shouted to me. He geared the

combine down to a turtle's crawl and climbed out of the little seat at the front of the machine. I took his place. I'd watched him do this as he stitched back and forth across hundreds of acres. No problem.

I made a complete mess of it, instantly, forcing the reel down into the peaty soil and slowing it down until it caressed the wheat stalks without breaking them. Meanwhile, I strayed off course and flushed out a hare that had thought itself safe for another couple of passes. It was like driving a house. I never completely mastered it that summer, but I learned enough to spell David out while he slipped across the border between cut and uncut harvest for a pee break. The combine was a Massey, made in Brantford, Ontario, four thousand miles to the west of the field I first drove it in.

In March of 1988 the Massey Combines Corporation factory in Brantford, Ontario, closed, on a Friday around six o'clock. Management knew it was coming, and the line workers were given what British workers call the DCM (Don't Come in Monday). It had been the headquarters of the combine arm of the company for less than two years. At its height, it was making combines for export to over a hundred countries, ten thousand a year. The year before it closed it had sold less than a thousand. Now no Canadian manufacturer of combines exists.

The first combines were sighted in American and Australian fields a hundred years before the Brantford closure. They combined the previously separate tasks of reaping and threshing. At first, pushed from behind by mules, then driven by steam power, and then pulled by tractor across the evergrowing fields of the prairies, giving them their yearly shave, the combines were ships that harvested the waves themselves. Finally they broke free of the tractor and became self-propelled, the reels huge and voracious, prairie Pac-men.

Daniel Massey was a Yankee, a farmer's son whose family crossed into Canada before the War of 1812. As a specialist in land clearance, he became expert in making machines do the work. Hart Massey, Daniel's son, bought up the patent rights to American farm implements, and the empire was founded, an empire large enough to poach the other empire's slogan and claim that the sun never set on its binders as they reaped a world's harvest. The implements themselves were promoted as rural royalty and given names like "King of the Meadows" and "Queen of the Harvesters." Two generations later they abdicated.

Before we left for the long drive out of Ontario and into the Prairies, I wanted to sit on the last Canadian Massey combine, the last one off the line at Brantford. But the new parent company, Varity Corp., was in no mood for sentimental journalists. No, a gentleman at Varity told me, he was not going to let the receivers tell me which was the last one and to which dealer it might have gone. I thanked him for nothing at all, and he said it had been his pleasure.

The troubles of Massey Combines were unpleasant auguries for our upcoming voyage into the Prairies. The drought there had filled the radio in the Maritime provinces; we listened to farmers, whose cracked lands we would soon visit, talking of stillborn crops and dust plumes behind tractors like airborne avalanches, as the soil withered to dust and deserted on the wind to the next farm. Six thousand farmers in poor, troubled Saskatchewan had applied to the Farm Debt Review Board since the beginning of the year, as many as the other provinces combined. It was going to be a bumper summer for farm failures in the "dirty eighties."

Getting out of Ontario from Ottawa takes two days hard driving, half of it spent skirting Lake Superior, through a corridor of trees. The province lies on its side, like a book that has fallen over. Each small town, Blind River, Wawa (the hitchhikers' graveyard), Marathon, begins pimping itself with billboards stuck in the trees miles out of town. A sign outside White River exhorts us to "Visit the Lake! Take a Swim!" and underneath has been added at a later date the command "Go Shopping!"

Between towns the wildlife make guest appearances: a beaver chewing on a wooden guard rail right at the edge of the road; an elk family crossing the highway in magnificent terror; the almost African sight of a car-killed deer on the roadside with a raven sitting on its flank. On a hill I see the unmistakable outline of a llama, then a herd of them on a llama farm. In Ear Falls, which advertises itself as the Bald Eagle capital of North America, we run out of jokes and stare in silence down the corridor between the trees until, at last, the Trans-Canada breaks free of the hills and we drop down onto the Prairies.

When farmers test the health of their soil, they analyse a handful for the nutrients it enjoys or lacks. In these portraits of Canadian farm families and the land they grow on, we invite you to do the same.

The photographer Joel Meyerowitz says, "Fill up the frame with feelings, energy, discovery and risk, and leave room enough for someone else to get in there." We say, climb in, there's plenty of room.

Top: Charlie and Kevin Powers. Their farm near Logy
Bay, Newfoundland is the most easterly in North America.
Bottom: The crop-eating moose that didn't get away from
Wilf Parsons. Lethbridge, Newfoundland.

Top: Farm hands. Lethbridge, Newfoundland.
Bottom: A farmworker spreading manure while the city
limits of St. John's look on.

Sid Hurry of Prince Edward Island, chair of one of the
Farm Crisis committees.

Betty and Les MacPhail, who fought to keep their Prince
Edward Island potato farm and won. The open book is
Betty's diary of their struggle.

Top: A moment in the marriage of Isabel and Russell Farquharson, fourth generation dairy farmers, Prince Edward Island.
Bottom: An ancient chore. Vance Daurie of Lunenburg, Nova Scotia, who went to court to win the right to farm.

Top: And the day is coming when it will all be real estate.
Bottom: The cemetery on the edge of the village of
Old Barns, Nova Scotia.

Top: The Oultons of Windsor, Nova Scotia. A place where
family and farm become one word.
Bottom: Wayne Oulton prepares another customer's meal.

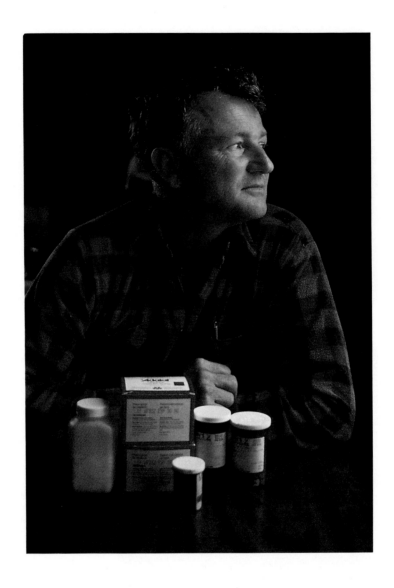

A Nova Scotia farmer, forced into early retirement by ill health, looks off to the ghosts of harvests past. Newport, Nova Scotia.

Top: Ralph Crawford, vegetable farmer turned
bookseller. Maugerville, New Brunswick.
Bottom: Greta and Arthur Day. "Farming? I never did get
to like it." Maugerville, New Brunswick.

Top: The best potato farmer in the valley, who cashed in
his life insurance to buy back his home from the bank.
Perth-Andover, New Brunswick.
Bottom: Some of the McLaughlins. New Brunswick proud.

Top: Luc Turcotte crosses the ramshackle bridge between
two of his chicken coops on the Ile d'Orléans.
Bottom: A Cambodian refugee working in a Quebec field.

Top: The Bergeron brothers of the Lac St-Jean region
call for a pause as a visitor arrives.
Bottom: Cor Rook, the gentle Cobden, Ontario, dairy
farmer. A union man to the tip of his cigar.

Top: Practising for a ploughing match.
Near Algonquin Park, Ontario.
Bottom: At the farm gate. The Ottawa Valley, Ontario.

Top: Allen Wilford, the farmer who went on a hunger
strike in a Stratford, Ontario, jail.

Dustin and Lauren Palsson with their grandparents, David
and Gladys Gislason, Arborg, Manitoba.

Farm partners. Dennis and Wilma Garlick. Roland, Manitoba.

Between jobs. Elm Creek, Manitoba.

Top: We saved you a seat. Minnedosa rodeo, Manitoba.
Bottom: Kid's rodeo. Minnedosa, Manitoba.

Top: Rare meat. A Manitoba bison herd.
Bottom: The Jack's café debating society in session.
Eastend, Saskatchewan.

Top: A gift for the preacher. Ravenscrag, Saskatchewan.
Bottom: At the end of the day. Ravenscrag, Saskatchewan.

Bottom: An early grave. Cypress Hills, Saskatchewan.

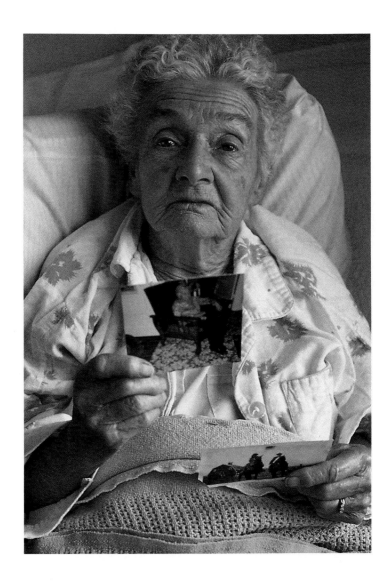

Emmie Phillips tells her side of the story. Eastend, Saskatchewan.

Top: Taking the long way home. Cypress Hills, Alberta.
Bottom: Working off the farm to stay on it. George
Retelbeck, schoolbus driver. Cypress Hills, Alberta.

A busy corner of a National Farmers' Union bulletin
board. Saskatoon, Saskatchewan.

Top: Dinner at Nettie's. Laura, Saskatchewan.
Bottom: Saturday afternoon pool. Retired Doukhobor
farmers, Blaine Lake, Saskatchewan.

Top: Before the bidding starts. Above the stockyards, Clyde, Alberta.
Bottom: Three members of the Whispering Hills Hutterite Brethren
Colony of Athabasca, Alberta.

Hart Highway, central British Columbia.

Top: After the storm. The Torios of Dawson Creek,
British Columbia.
Bottom: Claude, fruit manufacturer. Okanagan Valley,
British Columbia.

Top: Osoyoos, British Columbia.
Bottom: A sign growing in a farm field.
Okanagan Lake highway, British Columbia.

Top: Doing the aerial chores. Ace Elkink, Osoyoos,
British Columbia.
Bottom: Hugh Bradley, landlover. Pelly River ranch, Yukon.

Top: Room to think. Glen Bradley, Pelly River ranch, Yukon.
Bottom: The best manure is the farmer's footprint.
Pelly River ranch, Yukon.

Top: Off to market. Grant Dowdell, on the farm farthest
west. Dawson City, Yukon.
Bottom: A Quebec City schoolgirl answers the question
on her history assignment.

THE
PRAIRIE
FIELDS

20

FLAT OUT

k.d. lang sings "Western stars" as we spot the first working combine of the journey. The headlights of the tireless machine light up a cone of stunted, red-winter wheat in the darkness. The reel of the combine bites into it. The stalks fall invisibly in rows behind like hair to a barbershop floor. The driver, too, is invisible. There is just the cone of wheat, the chewing reel, and the stars in the vast maternal sky.

It is late at night, time to find a bed and breakfast. We are tired of the Clone Motel. A handful of quarters disappears into the pay phone before the Jenkins family of Selkirk promise sanctuary. Now all we have to do is find them.

Country people rarely supply directions; they just give clues. There isn't a Clone Restaurant on every corner to hone in on. The clues get even more vague in the Prairies.

Manitoba has compounded the endless similarity of its landscape by not bothering with street signs or house names. Homes are where they are, and finding them is your business. Addresses in the telephone book are given as directions – 2N, 3E, 1S. The province is laid out on a vast grid, each square of the grid a square mile, or a section. One section is 640 acres. It may also be something in hectares, but the only thing calling them that is government forms. The parcel of land most often referred to is a quarter, a quarter of a section. Two sections and a quarter is called nine quarters. Travelling around the sections is like moving over the surface of a crossword puzzle.

The trick to getting to where you are going is in deciding how far a mile is, and whether that was a driveway or a road you just passed. After a roadside telephone call and some weary swearing, a process of elimination directs us to the gateway of the Jenkins' farm.

The canine doorbells go off; an Alsatian and a Rottweiler. Mrs. Jenkins emerges in her housecoat from a trailer beside a large unfinished log house. She hushes the dogs and points to a single cabin flanked by an outhouse. We fall into our beds like divers into a pool, surfacing hours later to the sound of the dogs saying goodbye to Tom Jenkins, leaving for work in Lower Fort Gary. He is the blacksmith there. Their fields are rented out, although they still stable horses in a huge, white-trimmed hay barn.

Over perogies and bacon and coffee, Pat Jenkins and her son, Matthew, talk at a gentler pace than Maritimers; a function, perhaps, of uninterrupted distance.

Matthew is the fourth generation of Jenkinses on this land. The original farmhouse, built in 1892 and soon to be a century home, stands on the corner, its eyes closed with boards nailed across its window frames. The log house will replace it as the family home.

Once upon a whim, Pat bought a book on log houses. We can do that, she and Tom thought. When the author of the book came to nearby Selkirk, they had gone to the lecture. Now the kids are sleeping on the second floor of the logged whim that has absorbed their lives for a decade. They had thought that it would take them three years to build it; the modern law that dictates that everything takes three times as long and costs three times as much has held true. The house is gorgeous, solid as a fort, a bending of nature into a home, not some city insult to the curve and longevity.

Matthew butts in with an intriguing non sequitur: The well on their land was found by a character named Joe, a dedicated bachelor and a fine drinker. Joe has been called from as far away as California to divine for water, for finding water deep in the ground is Joe's calling.

"The rods he used are in the old house somewhere," says Pat. She takes her son's hand and walks off towards the house, past the cracked earth and the browning grass. The rods are found in a blacksmith's nest of burned-out welding rods and twisted metal scraps.

"I know where the water lies," says Pat, "so you just wander around and see if they work." The rods, shaped like two knitting needles bent into elongated Ls, sit spiritless in Ken's hands. And then the rods become invaded with . . . something. They delicately cross and unfold, like dancers at the end of a minuet, as Ken crosses a patch of ground very much like all the others. "Yes, yes," says Pat, "there is water there. Joe found it, too far from the house to be useful, but yes, that's it."

The rods work, for me, in a balletic variation on the standard crisscross. Only the left rod turns, and it does so anticlockwise, away from the other one. Perhaps this indicates some blockage on the right side of my aura. If that is so, then my left-side aura must be on upside down.

There is, it would seem, a mystic link in all of us to the presence of water. And why shouldn't the link to the land be just as strong? There is irony, though, in this playful search for water in the middle of the worst prairie drought in fifty years. Which means, for most farmers, the worst drought they have ever seen. Ahead of us on the plains of Manitoba and Saskatchewan there are families who have planted whole sections but left the runt-ish, dehydrated crop where it limply stands – unharvested – a framework to hold the snow, if there is any, and thereby get some moisture in the ground.

Others will take off only three or four bushels an acre in fields normally robust enough to give ten times that crop. This won't cover the money they borrowed from the bank to plant it. Their caps will go out again for subsidy, an act that many of them still find embarrassing. Others have grown calluses over their embarrassment. They are all as helpless before the sustained indifference of Nature as their ancestors were before them.

21

FAMILY MATTERS

On her grandparents' sixtieth wedding anniversary, in April 1983, Ruby Reske-Naurocki got the core of her family assembled in one room. A certain style of nose and eyes was repeated around the room, as though it was the fashion that year. Her video camera running, Ruby got her grandfather and grandmother to talk about their lives. Both several years older than the century, the Reskes arrived here in Beausejour, outside Winnipeg, just in time for the Depression – almost as if it had been waiting for them so it could start. The Russia they left behind when they fled first to Poland was still buckling from its recent political earthquake.

Ruby's fine eyes gleam as she watches that video now, five years after the wedding anniversary. She is dressed for the heat wave in faded cutoffs and a halter top that makes it easy for her to nurse her second child, Alexia. The walls of her living room warmly testify to a home founded on faith in marriage and God.

Several fields away, in the deep prairie dark, her husband, Gary, is changing a seized bearing on a swather. It's been a bad couple of days for breakdowns. Yesterday it was the variable speed on the combine, and a new cylinder went into the truck that morning. Sheet lightning is teasing the thirsty crops of corn, wheat, flax, and trefoil as he works.

On the video, Ruby's grandfather is telling his family how this anniversary has felt. His voice comes through the television speakers old and high, but electronics and fifty years haven't made a dent in his strong Russian accent. He turned ten the year Wilbur Wright flew Flyer III. He had retired to a house in town by the time Armstrong stepped onto the infertile fields of the moon. After they had retaken their wedding vows and been royally photographed, they walked out of the church. At the doorway, they turned, and grandfather asked everyone to stand still.

"Look what can happen from two people," he told his wife. Before them were the families of their thirteen children: sixty grand- and great-grandchildren looked back at the first branch of their family that had reached out to the sunlight of the Canadian Prairies.

The Reskes arrived in Canada with a $600 debt and four babies. Ten years later, in 1937, they had their first good crop and the debt was paid off. That year they got $1.50 a bushel for his wheat. Fifty years later, Ruby and Gary got $3.00 for theirs. Their debts, Ruby suspects, will never be paid. It is patriotic in Canada to spend more than you make. Financial institutions depend on it. But to spend more than you will ever make?

On the video Ruby's grandmother is talking about money. She is straight-backed before the camera, looking off into the middle distance. "That is the best life," she says, her voice stronger than her husband's, "when you haven't got too much. Too much is not good. If you haven't got too much, no one can touch you." Ruby asks the founders of her history one final question, for a piece of advice, and Julius Reske, ninety-three years old, replies with a benediction.

"Remember, that is the worst, when you cheat, not to your family, but to your neighbours. Do not cheat, instead do it with good words. That is what I am telling you. Do it with good words." The video ends with Ruby's sister playing "Somewhere My Love" on a Yamaha organ, and then the handwritten credits, all first names only, come up.

There is a clump of two boots being taken off in the hallway. Gary Reske-Naurocki comes through the door. "No, I won't shake your hand," he says, holding up a greasy hand fresh from the bowels of his swather. He is doe-eyed, softly good-looking with flecks of seed in his dark moustache. The digital clock on the VCR reads 10:42 p.m.

Gary and Ruby were high-school sweethearts. They split up briefly when he went to the University of Manitoba to get his agricultural diploma. Ruby went into the University of Winnipeg and came out with a degree in psychology and political science. "I almost married the wrong one," Ruby says, "but we got back together."

One day at university, Gary's class was taken out to listen to a very successful farmer-cum-university professor. This man had 15,000 acres, a strip of land a mile wide and twenty miles long. He told the young farmers lined up before him that in two years he would have doubled that. He had a row of grain bins as long as a city block, and ten combines, all with their number painted on the side to keep them from getting lost. The grain was planted right up to the ditches. The crops were already sold on the futures markets in Chicago and Minneapolis. "Farm by the percentage, not the bushel," was the advice he gave Gary.

When he had his diploma, Gary rented some land and farmed with his father. When his father slowed down, Gary took over running the farm. He bought almost a section and an old fifties Cockshutt combine from his father. The farm was debt and chemical free when Gary bought it.

"Do one thing, and do it big, that's what they taught us at college," says Gary. He had dreams of owning his land and his house at forty. He bought a new tractor, replaced the combine with a slightly newer one, borrowed hard to buy the seed and the fertilizer and pesticide.

At the beginning of the eighties, he and Ruby farmed side by side for a spring, and in December of the same year, they married. They harvested in November that year, a good year for corn. Ruby recalls scraping ice from the combine windshield at two in the morning. But the price was $4.50 a bushel, and they hauled load after load to Gimli.

It was the best of times for love and the worst for money. As Gary and Ruby expanded their operation and their family, the interest rates expanded right along with them. Ruby spent less time in her beloved fields after their first daughter, Natasha, was born, the year they bought the farm outright. Now she is off the fields altogether, a sacrifice she understands but chafes at. She helps where she can, going for parts, raising her daughters to think for themselves, to know how much family matters.

One day, Gary went to a farm auction. The combines and land being auctioned were those of the farmer who had advised him to grow percentages not crops. Before he went broke, he had indeed doubled his farm. Gary found himself standing next to a former employee who told him that the man had gotten so big that one spring he had seeded two quarters of a neighbour's farm before he realized his mistake. A combine had once gone missing for a week.

But prices had skyrocketed and the grain baron had had a lousy crop. He had margined himself on the futures market up to the ditches, and now, like many an entrepreneur before him, he was using the ploy of bankruptcy to save his ass.

The lesson was not lost on Gary. He diversified his crops, trimmed his dreams, and repaired where before he might have bought. He put his part of the world in order and waited to see if the rest of it would do the same. But one dream, he feels now, has left him. Thinking about it, he sighs. "Free of debt," he says, his voice harder than it was a moment ago. The phrase haunts him.

"At one point I did think, sure, that's no problem. Now I don't think so. I really think we will have some debt right up until the time we retire. I think that's being realistic, unfortunately. And I think we're conservative."

"I hate that word," Ruby grins across at her husband.

"Little c," he says, then he offers "rational expenditure" as an alternative.

"Cheap," Ruby tells him with a smile.

As the banks and the times have pushed at them, the Reske-Naurockis have pushed back, Ruby at first guiding Gary's shoulders to the struggle. In 1983, when Ruby saw on the news that a farmer called Allen Wilford had gone on hunger strike in jail, she resolved to act.

They marched outside the legislature in Winnipeg, wearing black arm bands in anticipation of the death of the family farm, and carrying signs that said "Live with One Another, Not Off One Another!" They picketed the local credit union when it moved to foreclose on a local farmer. Some of the picketers wore masks; they had loans themselves and couldn't afford recognition.

When the credit union pressed the foreclosure and tried to auction the farm, Ruby and Gary helped fill the room with farmers chanting "No sale." The auctioneer tried to begin, but you can't sell if there are no bids. Then a young man, a latecomer, made a bid.

"Allen Wilford was there," Ruby recalls, "and he came straight down off the stage and straight across the room. He backed the man up against the wall with his tongue. The bid was withdrawn." But it was a hollow victory. The strain cracked open the farmer's marriage, and two years later they quietly sold the farm.

When the strain begins to tug at Ruby, she replays the video of her grandparents. Seeing it tonight has lightened the strain of the drought, of crops so sparse you can see through them. The months without rain have given Gary no excuse to come in; they have hardly seen each other, except over coffee at eight in the morning, when he comes in as she is waking.

The local newspaper in Beausejour is called the *Manitoba Beaver*. For a brief while, until the paper changed editors, Ruby sent in poems that the editor, a fellow radical, printed. Into a life of facts and figures she wanted to inject the facts of life. She wanted the lines of her poems to strengthen the community of the land that she felt was so besieged. One poem that appeared in the *Beaver* was picked up by the wind and scattered across the fields of Canada. This is the poem:

> My grandparents cleared the land
> Side by side, stump after stump, day after day
> They worked with horse and plow
> They tilled and sowed,
> Watched the clouds and the prices
> And they reaped what they could
> Fed their thirteen children and paid for every acre
> They saw that it was good, and they were thankful.
>
> My parents took over the land
> Side by side, day after day
> They worked with tractor and plow
> They tilled and sowed,
> Watched the clouds and the prices
> And they reaped what they could
> Fed their three children and paid for every acre
> And they thought that it was good
> And they were thankful.
>
> My husband and I seek to take our place
> And farm the land side by side, day after day
> We work with tractors and plows
> We till and sow, watch the clouds, the falling prices
> The high interest rates, the cost of machinery
> Chemical, fertilizer and furl
> And we reap what we can to feed our child
> And make our payments
> And we see that it is not good and we are fearful.

On the way back to the Jenkins's farm from the Reske-Naurocki's, we stop in at the Clone Restaurant for a beer. As I tilt back my head for the last swig, two drunks tumble through the door. We are the only ones in the place. They want, with inebriated generosity, to buy us a drink. It is easier to accept.

They have been, they proudly explain, on the nineteenth hole since lunchtime, which explains their pastel golf shirts. Where have we been? I begin, already bored with them, to compose out loud a summary of our journey. I am granted some cross-eyed attention till I say the words "poor farmers."

"Bullshit," the one nearest me says, covering Ken's glasses with a fine spray. He is a man in his mid-thirties, with a perm and sloppy lips. "The only poor farmer is an honest one," and he waves a limp hand at my misguided bleeding heart. There is no dirt under his fingernails.

22

NEW ICELAND

A thousand and two years before we sailed onto the Prairies and sighted the urban oasis of Winnipeg, Bjarni Herjolfsson, an Icelandic seafarer, sighted the northeast coast of Canada, the first European to do so. He may have turned to a fellow seaman and commented, in Old Norse, that here was land worth settling. The Icelanders had already found Greenland and now, assured of land to the west, used it as a stepping stone to reach the shore of Newfoundland. There they built a small village, had children, and gave Canada its first taste of landed immigration from the east. The village disappeared into history, and Canada settled back to await the French explorers.

Icelanders didn't return to Canada until 1872. A series of calamities, lasting over a century and including volcanic eruptions, epidemics, and starvation had forced some of them to once again leave for the Americas. They sent back word of the promise of free land in Ontario and free transport to it, and boats loaded with hopeful farmers began to travel regularly between Reykjavik and Halifax.

Their hopes, like many hopes before and since, fell into the gap between government promises and reality. The lands they were offered were either barren or clogged with bush. They went farther west, to Manitoba, following yet another offer of reserved land, this time on the shore of Lake Winnipeg.

Loaded onto flatboats, a small colony of optimistic Icelanders set off north from Winnipeg, along the Red River, in 1875. Ken and I, in a dusty blue van, parallel their route as best we can on Highway 9 north into the interlake area between Lakes Winnipeg and Manitoba, into what the settlers called New Iceland.

Life stayed hard for the New Icelanders. Within a year of starting their colony there was an outbreak of smallpox, in the midst of a series of floods. Many of them died and many more retreated back to Winnipeg. But a few hung in, fishing the lakes in winter, and when the crops failed, building schools and gradually turning the odds in their favour. As we pass through Gimli there are still posters up on the walls and telegraph poles advertising *Islendingadagurinn*, the Icelandic Festival from a week earlier, held here annually since 1932.

Another hour's driving through landscape as flat as a chessboard, the lower leaves of the trees dusted beige by the drought, the lake vast and tempting to our right, takes us about as far north as the New Icelanders reached, over a small stone bridge into Arborg.

"Back over the bridge, two miles north and three east," an old man in a garage tells us in an Icelandic accent. He doesn't repeat it, considering it simple enough for anyone to remember. The directions are for the farm of David and Gladys Gislason; David is a descendant of the first New Icelanders. Our question answered, the old man resumes the silence he was working on when we pulled in and cleans our windshield with the precision of someone stripping wallpaper, even stepping back at one point to tilt his head and let the sun highlight any overlooked insect carcasses. He rubs hard at the stubborn thorax of a bee, frees it, and leaves us with a clear view of the world.

"Is that two miles east or three?" Ken asks as we pass the laneway to a turkey farm. Confused as to the exact length of a country mile, we stop at a crossroads and ask. A backtrack into our own dust brings us to a plain white bungalow outnumbered by several barns. The horizon is visible between the gaps in the barns, and I admit to Ken that I feel as if we've been somehow reduced and dropped onto a scale model, a world of levels and right angles. The door of the bungalow opens and a life-sized Gladys Gislason crosses the lawn to greet us. "David is out doing some council business," she says. "He's the Reeve for this township. Stay here and I'll fetch some coffee." We squat down on the grass in the shade of a gigantic four-wheel drive combine.

The Gislasons are continuing proof of the ploy the New Icelanders used to conquer adversity – diversity. By putting their eggs into several baskets, they have survived in a landscape that is intolerant of farmers with one-track minds. Three years earlier these fields were swamped by floods; this year they didn't taste rain until the end of June. Single-crop farmers can be derailed by this sort of climatic roller coaster. David and Gladys have kept their cash flowing by "exploiting" the industry of millions of workers who exhaust themselves to the point of death each summer. The Gislasons grow leaf-cutter bees.

"Because they cut little circles out of leaves," says Gladys, patiently. The cookie-cutter shapes are then used to line the hollows of the hive, creating cylinders almost the exact size of a spent .22 calibre cartridge, rather like tiny hollow cigars, open at one end. In each cylinder the bees store a nectar and pollen mixture to sustain a tiny larva, which is laid there in the fall, sealed in over the winter, and hatches in the spring by eating its way out of house and home.

The leaf-cutter bee and the alfalfa plant have a special relationship. The stamen of the alfalfa flower is bent over. Disturbing this jack-in-the-box mechanism will knock most bees to the ground and discourage further advances. For some reason leaf-cutters aren't daunted by this bee-abuse and the female bees succeed in gathering pollen on the fur on their abdomens and cross-pollinating the alfalfa. (The males are confined to the role of sperm providers.) "They do a beautiful job of it," Gladys says admiringly. "They make a nice plump alfalfa seed. We sell the seed, and we hire out and sell the bees."

When David's grandfather farmed in New Iceland, leaf-cutter bees thrived naturally, but the stripping of the bush and the dominance of grain over forage crops such as alfalfa deprived them of a livelihood and they moved on. Alfalfa is considered "the queen of the forages," stacked with protein; when put in cows, it boosts the quality and quantity of their milk. When the Gislasons began to feel manacled to the dairy herd they had inherited from David's father in the early sixties, they side-stepped into grain. David's wide mind became intrigued by the alfalfa-leaf-cutter affair, and over the last twenty years he has helped lead the interlake area into a worldwide reputation for admirable alfalfa seed and a better class of bee. A quarter of their 900 acres are under alfalfa this year, and they will hatch millions of bees, each year roughly doubling the previous year's battalions.

One of the bees passes close to me as I prop my coffee cup against the wheel of the combine. I regard it with a mixture of respect and caution, and bob my head as it zig-zags close to my ear. Aware now of its biography, I'm reluctant to swat at it; information overcomes prejudice. "It's all right, they don't sting, unless they get caught up in your clothing," Gladys says. "The sting is retractable anyway, not like honey bees. They are more sort of English in temperament; honey bees are more Latin, I suppose." The bee drifts off to a flowering field. A point of mathematics needs clearing up; if the bees increase in number each year, why isn't the place swarming with them? "They die off each year. Their wings literally wear out with the labour." Gladys explains. "At the end of summer they begin to drop, and you can see them littering the fields." Bees surplus to requirement at the beginning of the season are sold in Idaho and Washington.

We have just finished a tour of the paraphernalia that goes with bee-breeding, when David Gislason pulls into the yard. Gladys is still holding an incubation tray as he leans across it and kisses her cheek. They are a handsome couple, twenty-seven years married, a natural partnership in several senses of the phrase. I'm aware, as I have been several times before, of the nobility long-standing farm couples portray. This is not romanticism. There may well be (present company excepted) an equal scattering of the bigotry and cruelty to be found in farmhouses as is hidden behind the front doors of any suburban crescent. It may be that I'm just mislabelling the novelty of meeting people who stay married, appear content, and stay in one place while they do it, but nobility is the word that still comes to mind.

Gladys finishes her year-in-the-life of the Gislason bees. "So then we take them out of the pails in the spring, lay them out on the trays, and raise the temperature. A few days later you can come in and hear them chewing. After around three weeks they hatch. The air is full of small dots heading for the fields, and the cycle begins again."

David has a chore on his mind and accepts our offer of help. "I'm moving some bees from a blossomless field to one with more flowers." As we load large sheets of plywood onto a trailer I have to remind myself that David was born in Canada; he has a strong Icelandic accent, a calm lilt that has the Scandanavian trait of hovering between speech and melody. "I spoke only Icelandic until I was five. My father recited Icelandic poetry when the mood took him. When I was in Iceland for the first time people asked me how long I had been away." The daily newspaper from Saudarkroki, an Icelandic village up near the Arctic circle that was home to David's ancestors, is mailed to him. Reading is almost a sport with Icelanders; five-year-olds there are expected to read for the priest when he visits.

"That's not a normal sunset," David says as its rays strike the windscreen. The sun gloriously concludes its evening performance with a virtuoso display, another in a triumphant summer season. "The day it finally rained, at the end of June, we pulled our chairs up to the living-room window and watched it, with the same enthusiasm we watch the opera in Winnipeg," David says.

A sudden lurch to the side throws some of our load off the trailer. "I was too busy talking," David says. "I forgot that hole." As we untangle the screens he lets us in on the latest hot debate at the local planning committee he sits on as Reeve. "There's a prime piece of land come up for sale, and a car dealer wants to relocate there – put up a service centre and a motel. We met to decide whether to re-zone it industrial. One fellow at the table, not a farmer, couldn't see keeping it for agriculture; farming isn't doing that well, is it? All these handouts. Well, I said, planning is about avoiding conflict. Every time we re-zone and sub-divide, and then sub-divide the sub-division, another city person comes into the country who doesn't understand. And that leads to conflict. I won that one, but I think the writing may be on the wall. In the last provincial election, we lost two rural seats, and Winnipeg gained two. Manitoba for the first time has more urban seats than rural. We are losing our voice." We set off again and silently watch the horizon hide the sun.

There appears to be a bus shelter with a raised floor in the middle of the field we stop in. Its purpose comes clear when we load the large sheets of plywood into it. Each sheet is a man-made hive, with a dense pattern of holes drilled into it, a leaf-cutter housing project. The sheets are arranged in ranks in the shelter, in the same orientation in each field to save confusing the bees; much as we have come to depend on the continental predictability of the Clone Motel. In the morning the bees will awaken in pastures new and, if it is sunny, start to work cross-pollinating a virgin bouquet of alfalfa blossom. "And now, back to the house for ice cream," David announces as the last screen is set in place.

"Icelandic ice cream?"

"No, sorry, just the store-bought."

There is a map of the world pinned above the kitchen table in the Gislason bungalow. "So we can see where the news is coming from," Gladys explains, over the clanking of spoons in bowls. Most news is city news, but the drought has added farmers with furrowed brows to this summer's roster of current affairs. I wonder aloud what impression farmers think city folk have of them.

"Well, a farmer gets up in the morning, jolly as anything, and wanders around the corn all day, enjoying a peculiar lifestyle that most people don't understand, and does it for creative reasons and general enjoyment," David says. "There's always been this stereotype, but it's less true now than it ever was. The margin for error has all but gone." Farmers can't miss the corners of the field any more; they must plough to the edge of the ditch if they want to survive.

"The other impression that lingers," David continues, "is that farmers are unashamed to be propped up by the federal and provincial treasures. Farming seems to be a series of misfortunes, and every time you turn around there is a different reason for public financial support. Well, quite frankly I've been finding it embarrassing lately, the extent to which agriculture has become dependant on public largesse. A lot of us are sensitive to that. We are determined to be independent and successful. That's the reason for diversification." To that end, the Gislasons and seven other farm familes in the area have formed a hive, a company to market and sell their forage seed. They ensure that the company serves them, and not the other way around, by keeping a rein on its growth. It has also bound them together, reawakened their sense of community. They have rediscovered the simple truth that sometimes to expand is be further apart.

On the other side of the table, Ken and Gladys are looking at a book on Prairie farmers, written fifteen years earlier. It begins with a vivid description of a farmer in Landis, Saskatchewan, slaughtering a lamb, and then moves quickly to a prediction worthy of the Book of Revelations, forecasting the almost complete disappearance of the Prairie family farm within a generation.

"Let's call him," Ken says.

"Call who?"

"The farmer in the book. The lamb slaughterer. Let's see if he is still there." David nods his head and smiles at the idea of one bee communicating with another.

Directory Assistance provides the number for Gordon Taylor of Landis, a small town west of Saskatoon, and he answers on the third ring. He has a Santa Claus sort of voice. Oh yes, he still farms, on his own now, and nearly sixty. Grain and some sheep, as organic as he can, with modest equipment. Are many of his neighbours gone? Many, he says, soon to be most of them. "The rabbits here are soon going to die from exhaustion just running from farm to farm." Well, thanks Mr. Taylor, and best wishes. And the same to you, and call me Gordon.

I wander over to the darkened window in the living room, the same window from which David and Gladys watched the rains arrive. A Manitoba half-moon catches the pale alfalfa flowers. A million bees are resting, and tomorrow they will resume the urgent business of collecting nourishment for the next genera-tion, and in so doing, wear out their wings one day closer to failure.

23

CANADIAN OKIE

Steinbeck, in *The Grapes of Wrath*, was a spokesman for the poor and anonymous. He found, in the Okies that he met and reported on, grace under pressure, the grace that comes from chosing to remain graceful when the life you are having could easily turn you mean. And nobody knowing that you have made that choice. We met much of this on the farms we chanced on.

The Garlicks typify this grace. They farm in Roland, Manitoba, birthplace of 4H in Canada, within a day's walk of the Minnesota border. Wilma, Dennis, and their three children seemed to be immune to depression. They reached for a laugh as easily as for a glass of water, and I'd have paid money to sit at their dinner table and just soak in their enjoyment of one another.

I rode a few circuits of a wheat field in the combine with Dennis, perched in the cab beside him. The runtish stalks were barely knee-high in some parts of the field, but Dennis wasn't allowing that to spoil his pleasure in the act of harvesting. Over the roar of the motor I told him a story I had picked up from an Ontario businessman about combining. "I was flying in to Toronto in 1980 from out west," he then told me. "Final approach over Orangeville. Everybody on the other side of the plane from me suddenly burst out laughing. Everyone my side shuffled over and looked out the windows. A farmer in a hay field two thousand feet below us had written, in huge, perfect capital letters: FUCK FARMING."

Later Wilma took us to the elevator with a truck of grain. I had met her only briefly but she was clearly a woman of great inner strength, a worthy successor to Steinbeck's Ma, a woman who had never needed Dianne Harkin's help to show her her place alongside Dennis on the farm.

"I've a friend," Wilma told us as the bone-dry grain poured down into the hopper, "who had a baby in February. She told me yesterday, which was what, mid-July, that the kid has yet to get his head wet." It was a timely reminder that, sunny as the Garlicks were, the rain still hadn't arrived. The whole of the southern Prairies had its thumb out, hoping to hitch a passing rain cloud. Even the weather this year was the same weather as in the pages of *The Grapes of Wrath*.

It isn't surprising, then, that the word Okie pops into mind when we pass a truck in front of a grocery store in Carmen, Manitoba, shortly after leaving the Garlicks'. The load on the back of the truck is the contents of a house, compressed into a loose bale and lashed together with yellow nylon rope. The core of this bale is formed by several mattresses stacked like pancakes. Tonka toys and fans and ironing boards stick to it or hang from it.

Later, as we head on towards Brandon, there it is again, broken down at the roadside. A thin man in cowboy clothes is bent into the engine under the hood, the big heels of his cowboy boots off the ground. A white Ford van is chained to the lame, overburdened truck.

"The carburetor," the thin man says. "It's pouring gas. Where would I find bits for a 350?" He introduces himself with a tip of his hat as Mr. Fehr.

"How far have you got to go?" I ask. "Maybe we can drive you to some help."

"The Pas," he says with a German accent, politely answering the question. The Pas is four hundred miles due north, the last big town before Flin Flon. "I've got a job to go to there on a dairy farm. I worked for a grain farmer here, but the drought . . . Well, anyway, we are leaving Carmen today, for good."

The "for good," echoing a little off the hood, sounds ironic – not much good is happening just now to this man. He admits that he bought this truck especially for the move. It's a lemon, and whoever sold it to him wouldn't argue with that description. Then Fehr turns and says, "Animals are very important to me," and I fall a little in love with him for saying it, for being such a gentle victim, full of grace.

Three kids are cooped up in the truck seat behind him, watching Dad. There are two white-faced boys, one of them with his pants full of ants, and a little girl called Neadie, who has one splendid front tooth sitting in a gap as wide as her smile. His wife is driving the white van that is chained to the truck. She is quietly watching all this in the wing mirror.

"No, thank you," says Mr. Fehr, refusing another offer of help. "I am only going to tow it around to the garage around the corner." The older boy pops his head out of window. "Have a nice day and a nice summer," he says to us with gentle good manners.

We drive a couple of miles west, past two beautiful fields of sunflowers as high as the van windows. Then I pull into a field gateway and stare unfocused at the millions of yellow petals. The Fehrs have dug themselves into my mind. I have the strange sense of having left the movie before it has finished. There is no choice but to go back in.

The Fehr caravan has progressed as far as a garage forecourt. There is a roadside Clone Café alongside the garage. While the owner, a bright, blonde woman, who claims to have the cleanest toilets in Canada, chats on about how much more she is making since she left the farm, we nurse a coffee and spy on the Fehrs.

A mechanic and a couple of engine kibitzers are grappling

with the carb. A new gasket has gone in and the throttle slide has been redrilled. Everyone backs up a step, and Fehr starts the truck; she runs fine and the carb stays dry. Fehr takes this success the same way he took the breakdown, as just another fact.

Fehr and the garage owner begin to settle the cost of the repairs. There is a lot of gesturing, the gestures at odds with each other, a nod versus a shrug, a raised palm versus a shaken head. Then Fehr nods hard, once, and opens up the back of the van and takes something out. He is paying for the bill in kind. The kids are reloaded, the toys on the pile shake in the sun, and the tiny convoy heads north.

"Oh, he was straight about it right away," the garage owner says. He is sitting on an old car seat on the concrete floor of the garage, cheap calendars behind his head. His buddies and his very pregnant wife are alongside, chewing over the Fehrs. "He told me he had a hundred bucks to get him to The Pas, and that was all he had. So I took a vacuum cleaner, an Electrolux, as payment for the hundred for the repairs." The repairs couldn't possibly have cost a hundred dollars. Ten bucks for parts, forty bucks tops for the whole job.

"He can come back and pay me off and take it any time he wants. They've stung me like that before, two or three times before."

"Yah, two or three times before," echoes the wife.

Who he means by "they" isn't clear. If he means travelling farm workers, then he hasn't long to wait before the problem disappears. As the main herd of family farms decreases, then so too do the other species that have helped it survive, and in so doing survived themselves. Itinerant farm workers, like Mr. Fehr and Majella back on the Ile d'Orléans, are an endangered species as well.

"We can buy it back, the vacuum cleaner, and give it back to the Fehrs," Ken says, glad at last of finding some way of helping the Fehrs and, irrationally, of helping all the farmers who have helped us. "And we can beat up an old lady later on," I add reassuringly, "in case we get to feeling too holy."

In the garage, nobody has moved. We promptly rip ourselves

off by offering eighty dollars for the Electrolux instead of asking how much the guy would take. "It's a deal," says the owner,
real fast, confirming that he rooked the Fehrs. He walks over to
the vacuum cleaner, which is piled, an orphaned appliance, in
the corner.

Now the chase is on. Hoping the Fehrs have gone due north,
the speedometer needle glides generously past the legal limit.
There is no sign of them for a good ten miles. I begin to chuckle,
then laugh right out at the thought of being stuck with a yellow
vacuum cleaner for the rest of the journey. A white van suddenly
solidifies out of the asphalt mirage up ahead. Fehr pulls over, no
look of surprise on his face.

The transfer is done quickly, the possibility of embarrassment
and tears speeding things up. "Just send us the, um, sixty bucks
when you can."

"Thank you, I knew he charged us too much," says the older
boy from inside the van. The vacuum goes back to the spot it so
recently left, making the wall of belongings solid again. Fehr
slams the old doors hard so that they catch. The score for the day
drops back, for a moment, to zero, one bad deed cancelled by
one good one, and the two journeys uncross.

24

ELEVATOR MUSIC

T he fields of Canada are the soil of our immigrant history. Those immigrants left foreign homelands and planted themselves in fresh earth. They became a hybrid, adapted to vastness and climate. They stayed, and with hope, stubbornness, endurance, and sometimes cruelty, they rewrote a landscape.

Now there are towns scattered throughout Canada that are mere husks, their seeds gone to the city. It is the modern flux. But these towns are not so much decaying as subsiding, having risen briefly in a world of railroads and kerosene. Now they are finding new levels and people with new reasons to live there.

It is possible for the whole history of some Canadian towns to live in one memory. In southwestern Saskatchewan, near the town of Eastend, there is such a place and such a memory. The town, or to give it its official designation, "disorganized hamlet," is called Ravenscrag.

Three families live within the boundaries of Ravenscrag. Three farm families now work the land around the town that was once worked by many. The cattle yards here were among the biggest in the Prairies, but now the town is so small that, as the locals say, the Welcome To and the Come Again signs are nailed to the same post.

The biggest gathering going on in Ravenscrag when we were there was among the pigeons on the top of the abandoned Pool elevator. Those too came to an end when the elevator was torn down shortly after we left, the last of the three that once formed the town's southern border. Much of the town is heading the same way; the bright sunlight and absence of trees make the desertion all too obvious.

It is not a sad sight. Abandoned buildings gain their own beauty. In Ravenscrag they form the majority, standing among the upstart, freshly painted minority like elders. The boards shed their skin of paint, hold their youthful brown for a briefly regained adolescence, then season from brown to grey. The curve, the true line of nature, invades their rectangles as the nails let go and the sun warps them like old men's spines. Much more is happening beneath the surface of this town than you'd suppose if you just drove through.

One Sunday a month, for example, the small white-board church is as full as it ever was in the heyday of Ravenscrag, before Highway 13 went in and cold-shouldered the town by ten kilometres. The pump organ inhales and exhales the melodies, pursued by the twenty-two-strong congregation and the visiting Anglican minister, Ms. Chapman. The parish is scattered now – but families like the Savilles, seated along the front pew, schooled their children here and continue to pray here.

The Savilles are a fine example of adapting to the subsidence of Prairie towns. Ann and Bill Saville run a bed and breakfast and sell antiques and cowboy gear from the old North West Mounted Police post moved onto their farm by the previous owners seventy years ago. Ann is on a Farm Debt Review Board, a position that keeps her busy in blighted Saskatchewan. She also collects locks of hair of her relatives, which she keeps in a sewing box and calls "hairlooms." Her eldest son, David, and his wife still farm.

Her other son, Jim, a schemer, is moving a heritage home from the Trans-Canada Highway to a coulee on Saville land. It will become a restaurant and farm vacation establishment. The house arrived the day we left, having inched its way past roadside kitchen windows and kids with big eyes. Ann's husband, Bill, a craftsman saddle-maker, is away in the States at a heavy-horse pull. He is one of the few men left in the province who can hitch and drive a team of eight.

Emmie Phillips, whose memory it is that holds almost the whole history of the town, isn't in church today. The screen door of the grocery store in Eastend, pushed open by grocery-filled arms, caught the wind and knocked her flat on her tailbone. She is in the Eastend rest home, waiting for the doctor to tell her if any of her ninety-year-old bones are broken.

Before visiting Emmie, we spend a few minutes behind a cup of coffee in the focal point of the district – Jack's Café. Across the street, the boys in Charlie's Lunch are rolling dice to see who gets the morning breakfast bill. There are skid marks in the dust outside the museum, laid down the night before by some cowboy in a four by four.

Inside the museum, which started out as a dance hall then did some time as the movie house, there are two rows of wood-and-glass display cases. Dinosaur skulls and Polaroid cameras from the fifties are packed in haphazardly, evidence of life spanning millions of years, crammed metal to bone. Eastend proudly calls itself the dinosaur capital of Saskatchewan; there is an annual Dinosaur Days Festival. Leaning up against the stage are three pale blue-and-white bandstands, each announcing the Eastend Rhythm Rascals, the local foot-tappers from the thirties and forties.

A sign in the museum window says Welcome To Saskatchewan; a sign below says Sorry, We're Closed. The waitress in Jack's Café has the keys. In a box just inside the museum door there is a complete set of *Look* magazines covering the Kennedy assassination, twenty-five cents each. We buy them and take them with us to Emmie Phillips.

Emmie is a rancher. She lives just outside Ravenscrag in a

house built by her then husband-to-be for his parents in 1912. On the porch there is a chest, the one she brought with her on the train from Chester, Nova Scotia, in 1923. She was twenty-five and called Emmilie Robinson and she came to be the schoolteacher. Above the chest are the snowshoes she was advised to bring. The school she came to is closed now. The teeter-totter in its schoolyard is tipped to one side by an invisible weight.

In 1980 the two classrooms were full again for the Ravenscrag Homecoming. A thousand people turned up. The mass flushing of the school toilets pumped the well dry, and an abandoned field nearby got some unexpected life poured onto it. The Hutterites brought buns and Emmie donated a sack of potatoes.

Emmie is tough, the kind of tough that had all ninety-five pounds of her up against a steer's backside last year when cattle prods, in male hands, couldn't get it in the truck. Fairly soon after she arrived, Emmie married Aubrey Phillips, a Welshman. The postmistress in Ravenscrag, a matchmaker, introduced them. Aubrey had walked into the area in 1908 to start his first job on a ranch. He took the wrong fork at a break in the trail and would have walked clear into Montana if a NWMP constable hadn't chanced on him and put him straight.

Six years after Aubrey walked in, the steel tracks of the railway rolled past Eastend and on across the Prairies. A railway station was the seed that started the town growing. (A railway engineer named the spot after a Montreal mansion he knew of, owned by a shipping magnate the CPR had bought out. The mansion is now part of McGill University.) The livery barn went up first, then a lumberyard and a grain elevator. The hotel entertained the visiting cattlemen; the town bore the rough with the smooth. The stockyards became among the finest in the province.

We sat by Emmie in the rest-home bed as she hopscotched over the century. She piled stone on stone of bygone details and days that still shook in her memory until she had built a house of oral heritage as worthy of preservation as any fine man's mansion. And every half-hour or so she would pause, inform us that she really had nothing else to say, then plunge on for another half-hour.

Most of Emmie's life has been defined by the buttes to the north and south of Frenchman's Creek, the river that bisects her ranch and the sixty head she still keeps on it. The CPR changed the course of the river from south of her home to the north of it during the First World War, and it has been trying to get back ever since. She has seen the river run dry three times, and camped out more than once on the northern butte when it flooded, taking her geese with it.

The buttes define the space, and time has been a line of arrivals and departures. The mail arriving on Mondays, Wednesdays, and Fridays at the railway station; radio and then the telephones (until the phone lines went in, the Prairies gossiped on barbed-wire telephones, sending messages along the fencing); the storms shouting out that rain was coming; the Indians passing through on their way to a tribal conference in Montana; the wildlife moving in for easy food.

Orders arrived from the Eaton's catalogue, the book club fed the mind, and the Bible school truck arrived just in time to prime flagging souls. Then television came, and soon after that came casual theft and padlocks on the doors. And all the while the hired hands would come and go: Elis, the Métis whose father had harvested the drought on leather knee-pads, and Jim from Seven Persons, Alberta, who planted the poplar sapling at the back that is now a mature tree.

For every arrival there was a departure: The mail back down the line on alternate days. The slates in the schools, that briefly recycled information, and then the school itself. Then the post office, despite a group of concerned citizens sitting themselves down on the steps and going nowhere unless picked up and moved. The Eaton's Catalogue went, the eyes out of Pearson's goose in a hailstorm, and just last year four cows struck by lightning. Twenty years ago Emmie rode her last horse, and lately her eyesight is leaving her. And, one by one, the grain elevators by the railway tracks.

Emmie has no intention of retiring when she mends from this

latest minor setback. Her longevity reminds me of a sheep farmer I knew in England, a man whose first steps were taken on a sheep trail. He and his two brothers herded their sheep in the Yorkshire Dales, until the millionaire whose farm I was working on bought them out and reinstalled them as managers.

His leg broken by a ram and healing badly, the sheep farmer was forced to retire. It was decided that there should be a retirement party on the main farm. We mucked out a barn, made some straw bale bleachers and danced to a slick deejay with a mid-Atlantic accent.

When the time came for speeches, they gave the sheep farmer a clock, a clock for a man whose only times of reference for sixty years had been dawn and dusk, and asked him to say a few words. He was a dour man, and nobody expected any feats of oratory. In fact he only said one line. "If I'd known the job were temporary," he said, "I'd never have taken it."

Here is how the last grain elevator in Ravenscrag was retired, two weeks after we left, at the age of sixty-five. Grain barons far away signed the warrant. The last trucks brought the last grain and filled the bins for the last time, red wheat from a good year kissing the tops of the cedar-sided hoppers. The trains rolled into the siding with empty hoppers and out with them full, bleeding off the crop.

Then the railway men came and tore out the siding. And on a sad, sunny day in the year of the drought, the caterpillar tractors with front-end loaders came and nibbled at the elevator. She fell, and the cameras of the townspeople clicked before the grain dust blurred the collapse from architecture to ruin. The orange-painted wood fell onto the scale until its brass arm bent. The people were moved back, and the foundation was dynamited with thirty-two sticks of dynamite. It was a spectacular retirement.

Two weeks before the elevator was levelled, the northern lights hung clear and full on the last night in Ravenscrag. The evenings were cool and the drought would end soon. Restless, I dressed and walked down to the elevator. The town was moonlit and quiet. Deer crowded the fields and coyotes called to Mother Nature herself.

The door to the weigh scale slid back in arthritic jerks. Inside, the bottom rung of the ladder to the top room caught some window light, but the rest was black and hidden. I climbed slowly up, dislodging kernels of the last harvest with feet I couldn't see in the thickening dark. The pigeons fussed, then panicked as I got nearer. Crossing the room with outstreched hands, I found the door to the outside world and stood out on the gangway, the whole town in its mix of past and present down below.

I asked for ghosts: the remittance men, the section men, the postmistress, and Aubrey Phillips. But the streets remained deserted. Ravenscrag is not a ghost town. Once it was one thing, and it is becoming another. It has sifted out some reasons for growing and is finding others. It is enjoying a brief push against the tide; it was once real estate, but for now it is just plain land.

25

ROAD SIGHTS

Our odyssey has gained the rhythm of a pendulum swinging between two basic sorts of days: days on the farm, and days spent travelling between them. The days between farms run on the windscreen like films. The road, the latest strand of a vast ashphalt web, fills the centre screen. Small moments of drama or comedy, of beauty or pathos, advance and retreat on the sidelines. Once, somewhere in the Prairies, a school bus stopped directly ahead of us. A strong wind was blowing, and the small boy who got off put his back to it and walked backwards up the farm path towards his home. His path wasn't straight, but he adjusted his trim according to where he had been. He walked unerringly up the porch steps and as he did the screen door was opened by a woman's arm in a rolled-up sweatshirt sleeve. The boy went in backwards, and the arm let the door close.

Our eyes search the windscreen for relief as the hours roll on – fish eyes looking for a hook. A half-mile of wire fence with an old work boot stuck upside down on every fence post. A bumper sticker on the back of a geriatric pickup says, "Farmers are serving you – three times a day." We see fat, flat wooden ladies bend over in farmhouse gardens; mailboxes crafted in workshops over the winter – miniature homes, barns: a coach and horses: a haystack – mailbox posts made out of chains welded into a frozen column; someone's initials spelled out in hubcaps on a hillside in letters ten feet tall. (A neighbour of this monument told us that the wind would pry a hubcap loose every now and then and send it zinging down into the valley. You could hear them coming though.)

The backwards boy and the school bus prompted a wish that we could meet and follow a school bus on one the backroads of the Prairies. The wish comes true one afternoon, at a quarter to four, somewhere just shy of Medicine Hat and the Alberta border.

I am map gazing when an almost empty school bus goes past my shoulder and turns up a farm road that eventually slips out of sight on a mildly hilly horizon. The road heads due south towards Montana, passing through the Cypress Hills. The Cypress Hills contain the highest point in Saskatchewan, 1,400 feet. An arrow shot due north from there could travel the full length of the province without hitting anything. "Follow that bus," I order.

We travel five miles, only stopping twice. The maple trees at the side of a house are starting to shift from growth to glory. In a parched field a party of cows are socializing on a small mound. One stands at the top of the mound as if addressing the others. It looks for all the world as if she has forgotten the punch line to a long-winded joke, while the others wait patiently for her to remember.

After dropping three little girls with lunch pails of various colours, the bus hangs back, curious about us following it. The doors swish back and George Retelback admits he and the kids were unsure what we were doing, but he is quick to accept me. George is a stickman with a misleadingly sad, bespectacled face.

"I've been driving a few years," George says. He has a radio voice: unhurried, reassuring, and clear. He has three passengers still to drop off, twelve-year-old Clifford Swadling next and then the older Weise brothers who have two versions of the same face, one a couple of years ahead of the other. They go to school, with four hundred others, mostly farm kids, in Irvine. The Swadlings' is a small operation, just three quarters. The Weise boys have three hundred head.

"I think your dad's come looking for you, Clifford," George calls from the front. Clifford takes this, as he will take most things in his life, in his stride. He begins to talk seriously to his father the moment he leaves the bus. His dad listens just as seriously.

The elder Weise boy isn't sure he likes farming. He can drive the big tractor and work land, sure, but he likes ranching. They hang out in the mall at Medicine Hat, and take their holidays in the U.S.A. He gets his car licence in January; he's been practising for it for six years. As long as the kids can remember, George has been driving the bus, fifteen years without a break and without an accident. He wears a fifteen-year pin in his jacket. Now he stops at the turnaround point and swivels in his chair into a comfortable chatting position.

"They're talking of dropping a bus north of Irvine. South of it, down here, the numbers stay the same, but there's less farm kids, more from town. We passed my farm on the way up. Nine quarters of mixed with fifty head."

Driving the bus is an ideal off-farm job for him. He gets paid a basic rate and mileage on the 176 kilometres a day he drives. He owns the bus, which is new, bought last year for $34,000. The steady money gets him through the bad years like this one, where he has left about half his stunted crops uncut. Now he wants some snow to melt next spring and put some moisture into the ground, a yolk for the winter wheat.

George has three boys, whose ages he can get right to within a year. They are scattered throughout their twenties, the years when the decision must be made – to farm or not to farm. "Two of them would like to, though the middle one is diabetic, makes it difficult. But how do you start boys farming now? Unless you own clear and can say, 'Here, here's a plank off the old block.'

But to go out now and buy land and think you're going to make it – you're not."

"So who the hell is going to farm, George?"

"I dunno. That's a question I often ask myself. Hutterites? Farm kids mostly want to be city kids when they grow up. If we had just one boy, it would be easier. Three makes you have to choose."

The choice makes George leary. The city and the country present a venerable dilemma for all farm kids. In a nearby small town, the mathematics of the numbers of kids in the latest graduating class going into farming was simple: seventy-five take away seventy-five leaves zero.

George has to get back to his farm. He has a Cessna light aircraft, which he may take up tonight before sunset, up above the checkerboard fields. They resemble the game in several ways: pieces moving away from their own territory, taking others out of the game with a leap and the race to victory when only one piece remains, leaving behind one huge, corporate wheat field.

The empty bus pulls away from alongside an empty school-house, closed in 1957, now a storage shed. A legless teacher's desk leans against the porch, and a can of tractor oil sits on the "Warm Morning" wood stove. Inside, underneath the black-board with the Alberta wild rose painted in each corner and its final faded lesson which begins "History – Father Lacombe," sacks of red spring wheat seed have replaced the children.

After two thousand miles of heading west, we turn off the Trans-Canada and head north. The fields gain in health as we move out of Palliser's Triangle, the semi-arid area scientifically surveyed by John Palliser in the late 1850s that sits on the border and points up into Saskatchewan. Palliser considered most land inside the triangle uninhabitable. One hundred and thirty years later it is, as we have seen, becoming uninhabited.

There are fields of flax, flamboyant slabs of blue among the beige grain fields, and dazzling squares of butter-yellow canora.

The sloughs are ringed with salt like drained margarita glasses. One-elevator towns click by as we join the dots along the map up to Biggar, where the waiter in the Clone Restaurant tells us, "Sure, New York is big, but this is Biggar."

A little way past Biggar we pull off the highway to fulfill an invitation to dinner from Nettie Wiebe. Nettie, besides being a vice-president of the National Farmers' Union, has a philosophy degree in ethics from Saskatoon University, where she still gives occasional lectures. She is a Mennonite and a researcher and editor of handbooks for farm women. I had written to her when planning our journey, to establish her as a fixed point in our wanderings. My letter had contained an error in opinion about the role of marketing boards, and she had scolded me in her letter back with irrefutable eloquence.

To reach Nettie's dinner table, we drive through the fading town of Laura. An abandoned elevator leans with Pisa-esque grace towards the derelict church. A rusty speed limit sign hangs upside down on the church porch. It looks like there is a long-standing party in session at a house beside the railway crossing, but it turns out to be the local mechanic with his "you-never-know" collection of rotting vehicles parked on the front lawn. The silent hockey arena has a Danger! sign attached to its disintegrating walls.

The visit with Nettie and her husband, James, is a combination of events. It is, at its simplest, a meal at a farmer's table, food taken with the food makers, Mennonite food at that, Saskatoon berry fritters and honest bread and cold milk. It is a history lesson, told in a Low German accent, the story of the Mennonites and their migration from the wars and purges of the world to Canada, of their refusal to put down the plough and take up the sword, and the persecution pacifism attracts. It is where I first hear the phrase "theology of the land" and have it ring in my ears months later every time I sit down to write. The Mennonite tenet of stewardship of the farm, the idea that the land is a gift from your children that you will one day return to them, becomes my touchstone. The visit is a reaffirmation of the fears and hopes I have for the farm families. The fears are promoted by all the towns like Laura we have passed and by hearing James say that "we may soon be in for another round of thinning," another wave of rural erosion that seems to match, grain for grain, the steady erosion of the soil: The hopes are that spirits like Nettie's are stronger than those of people who believe that the bottom line is a better path to take than the line we have travelled thus far from farm gate to farm gate.

And it is the mid-point of our journey – a caravanserai where we are refreshed and the horses are watered. We gladly retake the road, the Yellowhead, as we climb towards Canada's broad shoulders.

THE
WESTERN
FIELDS

BIG

"Where are you fellas from?"

"Ottawa."

"Well, you are just coming into Canada then."

Canada begins, for Joe Dubiansky, just a little west of Edmonton. Ask Joe if he has been East and he tells you, "No, I've never left Canada." Joe is an auctioneer. He has just finished an hour's selling of cattle, talking dollars and cents nonstop for sixty minutes, a litany of money, a talking ticker-tape in fast forward.

Joe sits back, invites us to do the same, and lights a cigarette. On the hat rack in his office a Stetson and a coffee cup hang on adjacent hooks. He smokes less than a pack a day, to protect his throat. His throat is insured, for a premium of $360 a year, to the value of $500,000, which is, coincidentally, about the amount of money that will change hands at Nillson Bros. livestock auction, which is where we are, on an average day. Nillson Bros. is by far the biggest of the three auction firms Joe works for.

Auctioneering is Joe's off-farm job. About 40 per cent of

family farmers work part time in town, hiring out the skills they use as a matter of course around the farm. Many farm women work double days, teaching or typing in town and transforming back into farmers as they swing through the gate at five-thirty. The percentage of full-time off-farm jobs has been climbing steadily since the forties. Farmers have to go away to stay home. Joe has found an off-farm niche that keeps him among farmers.

Joe fills the chair he is in and rises above it with the bulk of a granite outcrop. His voice is deep and confident, the kind that advertises pickups on the television. Not surprisingly, he has a fondness for heavy horses; the combined weight of himself and the saddle is 350 pounds.

"I've wanted to be an auctioneer since I was six," Joe tells us, "since I went to my first horse sale. When I graduated from school, I said I wanted to be a farmer and an auctioneer, and everybody laughed."

Joe went to Lacombe Auctioneer School in 1978, when he was twenty-five, after years of hanging around and working at auctions, holding things over his head or chasing cattle into and out of the ring. He even tried it once as an untrained novice. He froze. "You realize you are selling a man's possesions gathered all through his life. You don't want some amateur doing that for you."

For the thousand dollars it cost him, Joe was taught some basic law and given the chance to work up his chant. It is Joe's belief that "you can't teach someone to chant, it comes from the inside out." After two months at school, Joe took his chant back to Dap, the small town (population twenty-four) north of Edmonton where he farms, and got it up to speed. He chanted on the tractor, in the car, and, according to his wife, in his sleep. "Did I miss any numbers?" he asked her when she told him about it.

When he works the ring at Nillson Bros., an hour on and an hour off, Joe isn't really aware of what he is saying. He settles into his chair, underneath a huge, anachronistic mural of a buffalo herd on the prairie, bends the gooseneck holding the microphone up to his mouth, cracks open a Coke for lubrication, and opens his lips. The numbers pour out in a healthy stream of ascending cents a pound for the understandably nervous cattle below him. There is an imperceptible slowing down as he negotiates the tricky bend of sixty-six and sixty-seven – "I hate it; it gives everybody trouble" – and then he's back up to express speed.

The crowd is a mixture of the restless and the almost motionless. The still ones are doing the buying. "You get anything from a nod to a wink, to an arm or hand movement, to the guy who just continually stares at you while he's on; when he looks away he's out."

"So, if I swat a fly out there, have I bought a steer?"

"You just damn well might. There's a fella out there now swatting flies, and I've taken his bid twice. Luckily someone bid after him."

The aristocrats of the auction ring are the order buyers, the professional bidders who buy cattle on behalf of the big outfits like Canada Packers, Schultz Cattle Company, Gainer's. They make five dollars an animal bought, and in a market where a million dollars has been dropped in one day, they have become rich men. They dress in the cowboy counterpart of Bay Street lawyers – top-dollar Tony Lama cowboy boots, silk windcheater jackets and tailored jeans, perfect hair, and too-much-an-ounce aftershave.

The smaller farmers sometimes begrudge themselves an order buyer, but, like accountants, the professional buyers make you money even as you pay them. "They can skin, grade, and dress a steer with a glance; they're checking feet for rot and udders for past disease, looking out for pinned-up prolapses and scars. At eighty dollars a visit from the vet, just to stand and look at it, they'll save you right there."

Most cattlemen are part vet, from accumulated experience. Calling in the vet is an economic decision. Joe recalls a time he stuck his arm in one of his pregnant black Angus cows and discovered a dead calf. "I could tell by the smell on my arm. I shot her and saved myself about $350 in vet's fees."

Every job has its bogey; for Joe it's farm bankruptcy sales.

When the auction is brought on by a death or a divorce, the latter a course of action he considers foolish, he can handle it. But a bankruptcy sale is a hard thing to run. "You see the long faces, and you feel for those people. He's standing there looking right at you, and nine times out of ten his wife is in the house, she's looking out the kitchen window with tears as big as horse turds rolling down her cheeks, and there ain't nothing you can do about it. You know that he ain't getting the money, but the more you get for that machinery the less he'll have to settle with the bank when it's all done. So you still try."

As it is with most westerners, it's hard to keep Joe off the topic of horses for more than ten minutes. The abiding object of his affection is King, a twelve-year-old Belgian-Morgan weighing 1,700 pounds, which transports him in regal fashion around the farm.

"He's not a speed king," says Joe, clearly a man in love, "but he's fast enough to run a cow down. Smart. Throw a rope off of him and he knows what to do – and he's big enough to do it. Walks at seven miles an hour, clean feet, no feathers. Ride him nice and he's got a smile on him like a sow sucking on a stick of rhubarb."

He hopes King will still be beneath him when he makes the final payment on his loan – November 8, 1992. The farm will be out of the bank and in the family, largely paid for by the $30,000 or so a year Joe makes from auctioneering. "That, as the man sang, will be the day," Joe says.

Back in the ring for his next shift, Joe tosses a cigarette down into the sawdust. The first batch of the hour, some young steers, pile through the sliding door into view. Steers fetch the highest prices, then heifers, then cows, and finally bulls. The bulls mostly go for baloney, which may be why baloney and bullshit are slang for the same thing. The steers swirl around in a fenced semicircle, and perched above them are Joe and the computer lady.

An enormous man in a blue silk shirt, big enough to teeter-totter with Joe, is leaning with a boot on the bottom rail of the fence, right up by the action. "Cripple in there," he shouts. Joe promises to weed it out, and the handler with the buggy whip separates out the spoiled goods, slides the door open and pops it back into the acres of pens at the rear of the ring.

"Package all right for you now?" Joe asks, and blue-shirt nods. Someone in the audience lets go a cloud of cigarette smoke, and the woman behind waves at it in disgust with her sale sheet. Joe promptly takes her bid, realizes what's happened, and catches my eye with a deadpan worthy of Buster Keaton. I'm busy eavesdropping on the farmer behind, who is telling his friend that he found a rope in the middle of his field that morning. "I didn't know," he says, "if I'd gained a lasso or lost a cow."

27

DOWN IN BLACK AND WHITE

There are some places that, because of their eccentricity, become not tourist traps but journalist traps. Amber Valley, five minutes east of Athabasca, Alberta, is such a place. It was settled by Negroes from the United States just before the end of the first decade of this century. They came to Canada for the same reason that many other of their neighbours in Canada came – to shake off a label that had been stuck to them that was not of their own making.

In 1832 the white American song-and-dance man Thomas Rice used a song about a Negro called Jim Crow in his routine. The name became a synonym for Negro. After the end of the Civil War in 1865, the Constitution was briefly washed clean of colour. But gradually, although defeated in war, racists-for-profit were able to use the laws to maintain segregation, in a series of decisions collectively known as the Jim Crow Acts.

For a brief while, American blacks could escape these laws by riding the sea of wheat on the railway up into the Canadian Prairies. Many of them were members of the Colored Farmers'

Alliance, which actually had more than a million members in 1890. Alarmed at the prospect of a flood of blacks, the federal and provincial Canadian racists dammed the border with acts of their own. The blacks in Amber Valley slipped in just a year or so before these acts brought down the colour bar.

These people are an almost too perfect metaphor for the rural history of Canada. Hutterites, Mennonites, Doukhobors, Negroes, all of them found, in the Canadian Prairies, room enough to isolate themselves for a while, to let their peculiarities flourish. The threat now to these groups is the city. The cities are steadily sucking the vitality out of the countryside. This is not only dehydrating the community of the land, it is choking off history faster than it can be honestly written down. History is not just dates and disasters, it is where we all have been.

"Don't blink or you'll miss it," Doug tells me. Doug owns Doug's Farm Store, on the edge of Athabasca. The store looks very much like a car-parts store, except that everything in it is bigger. And there are no racks of cheap toys for customizing tractors, no Playboy gearshift knobs or scented furry dice. The two farmers, sitting on stools pulled up to the parts counter, both smile in agreement at Doug's estimate of the size of Amber Valley. They have me pegged right off as an easterner. I'm wearing a T-shirt that shows an American Stars and Stripes with one of the stars replaced by a maple leaf and the words NO, EH written underneath.

Amber Valley Community Hall is written quietly on a building set on its own at a crossroads. Valley is a misnomer, it's more of a dip, but its name was probably chosen for spiritual not geographical reasons. On the other side of the crossroads is something we are getting used to – an abandoned schoolhouse. This one was once bright blue.

The dirt road running alongside the hall and off into the rest of northern Alberta goes past a gate with L. MAPP stencilled on its rusty mailbox. A strange element of hunting is creeping into all this as we look out for black farmers, so I suggest pulling in here.

As we drive up a black man shuts the door of a pickup and

walks towards us. Behind him is the now familiar farmyard landscape of grain-managing machinery. A wooden grain bin and its corrugated metal descendant stand side by side, like two generations in a photograph. The grass is long between the machines.

"Well, I've decided not to talk to fellas like you no more," Mapp says. His black face is flecked with grey stubble, and his eyes have plenty of years to them, in contrast to his skin, which is hardly lined at all.

"I have a story to tell," Mapp says emphatically, his chin up a little, "and I'm going to tell it myself. I'm going to hold onto it. I'm the one to tell it."

It emerges that Mapp was bitten by a writer a couple of years earlier. "I told him the true history," Mapp says, starting up again, spearing his finger into his palm, "'cause I've got it. I'm the oldest one living that was born here, born in 1919. I've got maps and papers in the house. My brother, he's eighty-one, twelve years older than me, he was born in the States, and he's still living, and we sat at the table with my wife. She died last year." Mapp pauses, waiting for the memory to subside. "And we got things down the right way. I've got a map of all the families that settled here. I've got the true facts."

Mapp is talking through a tired anger. "That writer fella went off and talked to others. Others is jealous, and when it came out in the magazine, he got things in it that was wrong." The others, envious of Mapp's rank in their history, have perhaps stacked the facts their way. Mapp is wise enough to know that every story has as many versions as it has tellers, and that most of history is gossip, but his version has longevity and love, and that makes it truer than the others.

The previous writer has spilled a mess on Mapp's history. In front of him, Mapp sees only another damned writer, and he says, to close the conversation, "I love history. I loved it in school. If people want to come and get it wrong then, well I'm not going to pass it out any more. I'll wait till my daughter wants to do it, or I'll do it myself."

But Mapp's pride in his lineage bubbles up through his

distrust. He points off down a slope, past the combines and harrows with which he works his six sections, to an abandoned homestead. These are the simple boards he was born within. His father, who died at the age of ninety-two, started his new life as a Canadian on the half-section surrounding it, in 1912. Lester was the third eldest boy of eight children. His mother died when he was two, and his father didn't marry again until the end of the Depression. Father and son built the farm together. A few years ago, Lester went back to the States to visit cousins he had never seen. It was, he says, the first real smile coming to his face – "Wonderful."

Mapp is determined to lay out just enough proof that this amber, wheat-filled valley is something special, not a novelty. I give up throwing in the occasional plea to try and make Mapp hand over his birthright. We shake hands, rough against smooth. Then he goes back to preparing for another harvest. The dust from the van lifts and starts to settle on the Amber Valley Community Hall as we turn right and head back to Athabasca.

28

LIVING TOGETHER

I
n the Clone Motel in Athabasca the boots come off as the television goes on, chewing gum for the eyes. The motel has a satellite dish. To get any one of the eighty channels available, it is necessary first to phone the front desk, where one of the family rotates the dish by holding down a button. The one dish serves all the rooms, so the trick is to be the first to book the next time slot. First call, first channelled.

There is a Hutterite colony nearby. Several times we've heard farmers talk with respect, sometimes flavoured with sour grapes, at the success of the Hutterites as communal farmers, able to weather droughts and top the bidding in land auctions. The colony number is listed in the phone book, which I find strange, as though I were able to dial the past. An older man with a German accent answers just as I am about to give up.

"Well, yes, you can come tomorrow afternoon. I am Eli Gross. You should ask for me." The voice sounds weary. My explanation of our mission is received in silence.

I hang up and call the front desk to book a movie. Ten minutes

later the satelitte dish begins to swivel and the TV screen kaleid-
oscopes, giving us flashes of reality and fiction, rooms and
landscapes. The Hutterites have no television. They do not sit in
their rooms and look out at the world through a television
screen. They are inward looking. Curiosity, I suspect, is their
enemy, the virus that can weaken their chosen isolation. But
their entrenched lack of it may be their strength as farmers. The
city attracts the young and curious. The Valium of television
quickly has me asleep.

When we reach the colony, the noise of a ride-on lawn mower
with a boy on it singing drowns out the radio in the van. The
boy is singing in German as he mows the grass between four
tombstones in a graveyard tucked in the corner of the colony. A
large rock, painted blue, at the entrance declares that this is the
Whispering Hills Hutterite Brethren Colony of Athabasca.
Enter at Your Own Risk is written alongside the name. Blue is
the dominant colour of the colony. Ahead are a gaggle of farm
buildings, breeze-block grey with blue roofs. At the back of the
first one a dead pig is half submerged in mud.

The muddy path leads around to a large hall. The houses all
have their backs to the path. They are small bungalows, more
like austere holiday camp houses, joined by concrete slab paths,
grouped around a plain lawn. Some of the houses have washing
hung at the back, dark scarves pegged to the line like squares
from a chessboard drying out.

The inside of Eli Gross's house, the one nearest the communal
dining hall and kitchens, is bright yellow, and I feel as if I'm
inside a pound of butter. A clock on the wall resembles a sun-
burst. Its tick has only the other walls to bounce off; they are
bare – no art, no cruxifix. "We live," Eli says, "low." The lack of
adornment, the plainness, and the scarcity of the furniture make
it seem as if they had just moved in, their real belongings delayed
somewhere. There is no accumulated history, no family photographs, because there are no cameras.

Eli and his wife, Ester, have lived here since 1962, when they
moved from another colony in Rosebud, Alberta, that had
become overcrowded. Eli had lived in Rosebud since he was

two. He was born in South Dakota. His father was a blacksmith and enough of a doctor to be able to set bones. "I still see him, sweat running down, red-hot iron spitting at him."

Eli and Ester schooled together at Rosebud and married fifty years ago. There is no divorce in Hutterite colonies. Their marriage is uncommon in that they were from the same colony but not related. Finding someone you are not related to can be tricky, so the young women, as Eli says, "marry away" – find spouses in other colonies. "Then we celebrate two days before they go. In winter the unmarried women drive around a lot, visiting."

Eli is recovering from an illness that had put him in Edmonton hospital. His face, round as a clock with a beard running almost from three to nine, is strained. That was why he had sounded weary on the phone. (There are only two phones at the colony; his son has the other one.) Recalling the motel TV, I ask if he had watched one while there. "Maybe ten minutes, when the news was on. Then I wouldn't look at that thing. It just made me feel not good. I would go back to my bed."

Until ten years ago, Eli was the head of the colony in day-to-day matters. He resigned and another man, his eldest son, also Eli, was voted in. He is still the religious head, keeping the communion cup in his house. Communion is taken only at Easter.

"Head" is the nearest word Eli can find to translate the position he holds, but "pivot" might be better. Colony decisions are made as need arises. "We have a meeting and we talk about it, till everyone says his 'yes' word." By "we" he means only the men.

At one such meeting, in the seventies, everyone said yes to putting the colony up for sale. They had had seven years' bad luck, too much rain and too short a growing season, sometimes as little as sixty days. "You can't grow anything in that time, it was all hull, no flour. When you feed pigs, you've got to have something in there. We advertise in the local paper, we could, if someone had wanted to buy, have sold out the colony any day, like that" – and he snaps his fingers. But there were no takers, and the next year things got better.

Using Eli as a historical pivot, I bother him with a row of questions, trying not to sound like an American tourist quizzing a bushman, working back in history then forward from him into the next generations.

"Four students in Tyrol in Switzerland went to school. Two said, 'Infant baptism is no good. You should baptize when you are big, when you know what you promise.' And that was the start of the Hutterite movement. One of those students was called Hutter, which means hat maker. He was burned at the stake. When we baptize someone, we say, 'I baptize you on your belief.'" Eli's soft tone and ancient cut of his suit make it seem as though he is recalling events he attended, although they happened in the sixteenth century.

The perennial religious cycle of schism, persecution, and flight, a cycle as old as Genesis, unfolded for the Hutterites. Moravia to Slovakia, from there to Transylvania, Walachia, the Ukraine, and then the leap to the New World in 1874. They came on the *Harmonia*, the same ship that had brought the Mennonites a year earlier.

In the wheatlands they found themselves in the company of the persecuted, and therefore, for a while, free from it. The Prairies became a bed of European sects transplanted into ground vast enough for them to put down roots that wouldn't tangle with others.

Unlike the Mennonites, the Hutterites have stuck to communal farming. Their colonies, as they did in Europe, take refuge in tradition. The past and present coexist, so that their history is always within easy reach, within sight. All the children learn German as their first language and go to school in the colony. A church service ends each day. Everyone dresses alike. "We're just, let's say, like a police force; we all wear one uniform. No jewellery; a pocket watch, yes, but no wristwatch."

As the future arrives, it is measured against the yardstick of *lüsten für Fleisch*. Television is lust for flesh, or rather it portrays it. Flesh, with its instincts, is the enemy within. Flesh, like phosphorous, is smeared on the pages of modern books, waiting to ignite upon exposure. Only historical and religious books are for their eyes. Music is equally censored. "We sing by the mouth only, no instruments. We sing better than music. The grain tester, he came, when we were in church singing. He listened outside and said,'My you sing lovely.'"

When the future arrived in the shape of the Second World War, the Hutterites would not fight. "This last war, I was in a concentration camp, west of Calgary, for fifty cents a day, cutting down trees to make mine props and timbers for bridges. I think there was five camps, three hundred men in each – Hutterites, Mennonites, Doukhobors – it was just loaded." Eli chuckles, an infectious throaty sound.

The colony recreates the skills it needs in each generation by sending the men to training schools outside the colony. They return and apprentice to the "bigger fellows." "We have a duck man, a chicken man, a hog man." Eli reels them off, and they sound like comic book superheroes. Most of the sixteen men in the colony are mechanics; all can weld. The machinery is impeccably maintained, but they won't hesitate to meet, say the yes word, and buy new machinery if it improves productivity, drawing the money from the bank account in town in the name of the Hutterite Brethren Church of Athabasca.

I wonder if some of the young men come back from school and eventually scratch the itch implanted there and leave the colony. "Not so many if they obey. If someone wants to have their own will, they go. If they think they are working for someone else – they go." It takes me another question to unravel this last bit, by which he means that they have missed the point of the colony and come, resentfully, to suppose that they are working for Eli instead of everyone, including themselves.

Has it become less strict in Eli's lifetime? "Yah," he says, his voice low as though making a confession. "Good times change things. We got up at five with the horses in my young days. Not to work by eight, like now. If you are a good worker and a Christian, you be there!" He pauses, then his voice rises like an uppercut. "Money!" It comes out like a demon in an exorcism. "If you want to see strict, you should go to Woodcrest in New York. You couldn't just walk into their farm like you did here." I quickly thank him for the trouble he is clearly taking, genuinely grateful for his tolerance of my curiosity. The looser reins of this colony work both ways, though. Eli has friends in town he visits every couple of weeks.

Eli has promised to call his son and get him to give us a tour, but the men are in the fields swathing. He gets to his feet as though slowly inflating and pops on a pair of grey slippers. He takes the steps with the same foot first each time and shuffles along the paving stone path. "That is the kitchens. We all eat there together all meals. The women serve the men first, then they eat. The bell is from a ship, we got it in a sale."

The children appear, dressed in smaller sizes of their parents' uniforms. They look fit and thin. The boy from the lawn mower is John, one of Eli's thirty grandchildren from his six sons. The children are drawn to Ken's camera as though it is a kitten. They go off to be snapped.

As we walk towards another of the characterless buildings, the smell of ammonia warns me this is the chicken house. Two men inside are plucking eggs from a conveyor belt coming out of a fowl dungeon. The belt loops around and takes food back into them through a brick-sized hole in the dividing wall. The chickens the far side of the wall are eerily quiet.

The dairy is surgically spotless, almost too clean to be connected to something as mucky as a cow. "Do you use artificial insemination?" I ask.

"The colony stopped us; they said it is no good. The colony in Lethbridge decides how we farm." Not looking before I leap, I ask, "So you don't practise contraception yourselves, then." His face is a complete blank, no stirring of understanding. The concept is as alien to him as twelve-bar blues.

At the schoolhouse, which is also the church hall, the porch serves as the library. I have a secondhand copy in my bag of *The Grapes of Wrath*, which I bought in New Brunswick, and for a moment it is tempting to slip it in between a couple of German spellers. But why? Far from being subversive, I realize, the book would appeal to them. It is a book about wishing to have even the simple things, and about what happens to the hearts of men when they turn away from the land. While I daydream, Eli is shuffling over to Ester who has come out to scold him for tiring himself.

In Ester's kitchen, a plain affair without stove or fridge, we enjoy strong tea and a slice of fruitcake. Eli mentions that some four thousand visitors a year come to the colony. They are used to being a curiosity, a twisted fate for a tribe that has little curiosity for the world outside their own fields of vision. We have stared long enough, time to go.

There is a man working on the innards of a tractor next to where the van is parked. He swings a hammer at a chisel held in his hand against a threaded nut. "Do you have swear words?" I ask.

"No."

"What if you hit your hand with that hammer?"

"I'd say, 'Too bad!'"

"But how do you move things when they get stuck? A couple of good swear words can help unstick things."

"You just think they do," he says, and he hits the end of the chisel. "Here things come unstuck because we push hard enough to make them move."

THE ART OFF
THE WALLS

T he road from Athabasca to the Peace River Valley goes
through the Swan Hills, over the Smokey River, and into
the Birch Hills. The Swan Hills peak out at well over three
thousand feet, and the tiny settlements among them are either
clustered around a native community centre or the cupola of a
Ukrainian church. As we pass the Slave Lake Reservation, two
Indian kids by the side of the road draw a bead on us with
imaginary rifles, and a dog, a veteran tire chewer, races out of the
woods and looks set to chase us clear across the border into
British Columbia.

On the plateau of the Birch Hills the road parallels the railway.
The sun runs along the steel rails like a tethered comet. We pass a
barn that has one face painted entirely with the Maple Leaf flag.
The paint looks old enough to have gone on the barn doors the
year the new flag was chosen, 1965.

All of a sudden the Peace River Valley appears below the hills.
It looks like a piece of the southern Albertan prairie has been
mislaid. The shaved wheat fields, unaffected by the drought, roll

on northward and we pass through them into Dawson Creek, mile zero of the Alaska Highway.

Carl and Joyce Torio, who live to the southwest of Dawson Creek, are the unlike poles that attract. Joyce is an effervescent, thin woman with a shock of short, paprika-and-salt hair that appears to glow from the heat of her personality. Carl is a shy, inward man, with the build of a coal miner, which is something he might have been if his father had not taken the boat from Italy to emigrate to Canada. His true talent is with cattle. He has the kind of eye that will pick out the sick ones almost before they know they are sick themselves.

The Torio home sits among a stand of poplar trees. The hills to the south are collectively known as Bare Mountain. The garden is blushing with tender loving care. Richard Torio, the eldest son, meets us on a three-wheel all-terrain vehicle. His bulk makes it look like a tricycle. An efficient-looking feeding system fills a red barn at the back of the yard. Two venerable horses are in a stable: Cookie, who is twenty-eight, and Duffer, who is a year younger. Both are quarter horses, perhaps with a touch of Arab. The Torios have ridden them for as many miles as you'd find on a secondhand Volkswagen.

Indoors, Joyce Torio is sipping at her coffee at the kitchen table. She has to nurse her caffeine intake since her heart attack. Carl joins us at the table, while Richard lies along the basement steps, his elbows resting on the kitchen floor. Carl is shy, or perhaps just reluctant to unload his memories onto the kitchen table and then have to pack them away again in his head after we have gone. So Joyce starts to tell their tale. When she talks, Joyce is quickly into third gear and travelling. Carl, meanwhile, is still back in first, but they arrive together.

"My family came up from Ponteix, Saskatchewan. Father raised six kids through the thirties," she says. "The drought pushed us all further afield in 1937, into the Peace. We came up in a '36 Chevy truck, ten or more of us. We all slept somewhere on it. I was about eleven. Father was a thrasherman, but it snowed on August 13, so he didn't get any thrashing done, and there he was with us all up here.

"He started to take us back, but my oldest sister and her husband jumped off the truck at Hythe, Alberta. They came back and made their home here. Eventually each one of us came up, first my brother, then my sister to teach school, then me, and finally Mum and Dad bought a farm and farmed out here in South Dawson. I came up in 1944 and met Carl where I was working in the co-op store. We married in '47. Carl has an interesting story about his family."

Carl pauses a moment, runs his tongue over his lips, then looks at his fingernails while he says, "My Dad didn't plan on coming to Canada. Him and his brother thought they were going to South America. The first boat was almost full, so my uncle took that and Dad took the next one. His ticket read Coleman, Alberta, to the coal mines there, but he thought he was still headed for South America. The conductor kicked him off in Coleman, and he did work in the mine.

"He met a Frenchman who told him they should go up to Peace River, the land of opportunity. The Frenchman said they grew tomatoes as big as melons up here. So they walked in here in 1916, from Grand Prairie, which was the end of the steel. There was no Dawson Creek then.

"Dad got a homestead a couple of miles down the road from here, and opened a winter restaurant for the trappers and bachelors. He took his cattle into town with him in the winter. He hauled the first load of groceries into the co-op store when it opened. He had the first bees in Peace River. I was born in 1928, in Pouce Coupe, about five miles from here. I started farming full-time at sixteen.

"The town took a big jump when the army built the Alaska Highway in 1944. It went almost overnight from 500 to 12,000 people. The valley was nicknamed 'Bootshine Valley' because of all the soldiers. I read where it was rated the eighth wonder of the world. Trappers did some of the surveying on snowshoes."

Carl looks up now, and Joyce takes the story from him. "Carl and I started out in his dad's homestead. We'd get snowed in, and I worried about getting the two boys to school. We never did get electricity in there. Carl hooked up a sort of snowplough behind the horses. Sometimes it took a D-8 road-clearer to get us out. When Milton, the eldest, was born, it was February 1949 and we were snowed in. All we had was an old truck to get us to the hospital, so my dad came over with two tractors and pulled us out. I was in labour by then. I got wise and had the next boy in September.

"A couple offered us this place for $10,000 in 1952. Our neighbours thought we were crazy, the price was that high. But the school was only half a mile away. We had built the farm up to about nine quarters. We built the feedlot, and both our daughters were born here."

The traditional areas of expertise on a farm divide roughly into indoors and outdoors – female and male. In any given crisis, of course, anyone can do anything, and they usually do. Carl, like a proud father, mentions the quality of their land: "This is good land, number one and number two soil. Not much hay goes out of the Peace, it's too expensive to truck it. Last year we planted oats and they went over a hundred bushels to the acre. And we got eighty of barley. We've never had what you'd call a crop failure in forty-one years. We were debt free up till about 1976, then we put the feedlot in, and the boys were ready to start farming."

Joyce, the expert with the pencil, begins to explain the way debt can rip through a farm. "Our loan originally was about $165,000, but it wasn't any desperate big loan or anything. It mushroomed and the cattle prices went down, feeders and fat cattle. We bought them at ninety-two cents a pound, and hundreds of pounds of fattening later we sold them at sixty-seven cents. Seventy-five thousand dollars down in one season. We asked the bank and they said, 'Pay off the operating loan, don't worry about the interest.'

"I don't know how they got it up to $400,000 – actually, I lost control of it. They were encouraging us to take more! Nineteen eighty-four we had an excellent year and we put up lots of feed and a thousand head of cattle in this feedlot. It didn't bring us out of it, and 1985 was dry. That finished us. Milton had decided he wanted to go into honey, and that went sour too. In the meantime, the Bank of Montreal decided they weren't going to do business with us any more. Banks give you an umbrella when it's sunny and ask for it back when it rains."

"The banks would like to tell you it was bad management, and with some, maybe it was," Carl says, a little tersely. "But not very many. We started with $500 forty years ago, and built everything from there. No, production costs changed. We bought a new truck, a 1956 International, and it was $3,500 for box, hoist, and everything. Joyce was combining clover seed in 1956 and getting fifty cents a pound for it. It's still fifty cents a pound now, the highest it's been for a few years.

"They built a new bank here, and wanted to get the business, so they put a nice fella in and lend you all the money. They took a lot of business away, big farm accounts. Then, it seems to me, they lent money to Third World countries and decided to collect where they could collect – on farmers. We all had revolving loans, and of course you come to need it every year, and in 1984 they said, 'This year we can't lend, we need more security – a debenture or another quarter of land.' "

Joyce spits out the words "personal guarantees" as though they were a murderer's name, and bangs the table. "Then," Carl says, "they've got it all. We went after a small-business develop-ment bond. If we'd got that bond it would have made all the difference in the world. But our accountant decided we weren't in financial difficulty and wrote a letter to the bank saying we weren't. So we gave them a debenture. The original manager we had was quite a nice guy. He used to come and fish the dugout at the weekend. So then they get a new manager in, spring of 1984. They do that, get a manager in who's a collector. He came to visit in January, and he said, 'What are you going to do about this?' I didn't know what he was talking about because we had just put the thousand head in. He said, 'The bank doesn't want to do business with you any more.' "

The mention of the bank manager almost has Joyce waving her hand to take the story from Carl. "He was a stocky built fella," she says. "He wasn't dynamic. He knew nothing about farming. He thought he was quite sharp with a pencil, type of thing. He called us again into his office, and said it again. Then we started to catch on that they actually didn't want to do business with us. They wanted to close the account. He tried to paint a nice picture. 'A receiver will come in,' he told us, 'and he'll pay you wages and all the bills and run the place. You'll be able to work for them, and be better off than you ever were. And, your neighbours won't even have to know!' About five times, he said that – 'Your neighbours won't have to know.'

"Not wanting to brag, we are well known in town, respected in the community, credit any place in town," Carl says. "We still have. We've been here a lot of years. He must have figured we didn't want our neighbours to know. We finally took our accountant to the bank with us – and he agreed with them! You can imagine the turmoil we're getting in by this time."

Carl is talking with his head down, the calm in his voice draining away. He falls silent and Joyce bangs a fist down and says: "We knew by God that we weren't going to leave here. We thought we could work with the bank. We had no intentions of just walking down the road with our suitcase. We went to our MP next, asked him for help. He said, 'Well, you're old-timers here, done a lot for the community. You deserve to rest and go on welfare.' Now then we were mad! Don't think the Irish didn't come out in me then. The lawyer in Dawson Creek, who we've known since he was born, tried to tell us the same thing. He said, 'They've got you tied up like a Christmas goose.' He kept saying this goose thing."

Carl moves his hand a little closer to Joyce and says quietly, "We knew this was happening down East, but not up here. Farmers are real bad for not telling each other. They are proud and won't tell each other they are in trouble. Some had gone quietly around here, we found out. We weren't going to go quietly."

Pride. We met another farmer in Dawson who was leaving farming. A clever man, he had invented a bushel of reasons why it was a smart thing to do. Built them up for us like a house of cards. The pain at the back of his voice called his logic liar. Ken asked him next day, as he was combining his final crop, for a picture. "No," he said, "I don't want to be in your book as the asshole who got out of farming."

Carl picks up the story again. "I phoned everyone I could think off, including a guy in Kamloops working for the receiver as manager for a couple of ranchers. He said, 'Well, there is a guy shaking the rafters down here called Larry Whalley.' So I called Larry.

"A week later a farmer thirty miles west of here, who was in trouble with another bank, was due to have an auction. He had decided to sell. We didn't know him well, but we had talked back and forth because of our situations. The bank moved in before the sale, and seized their stuff without any notice. A dirty thing to do. They came in with the bailiffs. That morning I said to Joyce we should go out and visit those people, but we better phone first. The wife answered the phone, crying, and she said, 'Joe White is out here with tow trucks taking everything away.' We jumped in the car and went out. Here he was all right, driving the combine away.

"Larry Whalley was in Nanaimo. He came right up when we phoned, sat in that chair there and phoned the head of the Toronto-Dominion Bank in Vancouver. By God, in an hour he had the manager here phoning back. That's when we decided to get organized up here."

Joyce manages to smile as she recalls the next act in the drama: "We picketed the bank. It was also graduation day. The high-school kids were all running around the streets, and they came and banged on the bank windows. The bank gave the farmer his stuff back.

"Then Larry sat down with us and we figured out a proposal to our bank. Two months later they sent a demand letter saying they wanted everything, right now. All the interest figured out. Wouldn't talk to us. The cattle weren't financed through the bank, and we were doing some custom feeding, so we paid off everybody we owed money to when we sold them."

"July 1, 1985, I was haying. The banker came out with the receiver. He said, 'Can we go inside?' and he introduced me. Joyce served them all coffee. The receiver said he was going back to Prince George, and he'd be back up Tuesday and he'd make arrangements for our wages and the utilities.

"Tuesday he never did show up. Larry Whalley was still here, so he knew we were going to fight. Suddenly he showed up in September, after Larry had gone, while I was weighing some cattle for some other people. Right in front of them he says he wants to take down the serial numbers of some of the equipment, and some photographs. 'I'm too busy, I said. Come back Wednesday.'

"Wednesday, Allen Watson, the head of the Farm Crisis Committee, came with a few neighbours. He's an awfully excellent man. The TV people were hid in the living room. The receiver didn't come. I called the bank and they said he had gone back to Prince George, surprised he didn't let us know. So we said to the TV people, 'We're going in!' They said, 'Give us time and we'll go and set up.'

"We went straight in, TV camera behind us. It was all confused, for the bank. They wanted to kick Allen out, so he opened an account while we were in the office on our own. We came out and told the TV that the bank had said we could keep our car. All we were asking was that we could buy the place back for the same as they had had an offer on it – fifty cents on the dollar."

Carl steps in. "They had sold hundreds of farms that way. Our logic was, why not sell it to the farmer already on the farm? Leave us farmers on the farm. That was our logic. We weren't just fighting for ourselves, remember that, we were fighting for all the farmers.

"We went to another lawyer, but they all eat out of the same dish in a small town. They didn't want to make no noise with the banks. That's okay. A friend kept coming to us, told us, 'For God's sake go to this lawyer in Prince George.' For some reason we held back. I suppose we were awful, awful scared. We hadn't slept. Finally we let him help us. The lawyer looked through our papers and said there was a lot of things he could do. The bank decided they would talk to us now.

"It was terrible what they done to us that day. Really terrible.

They sat here, four bankers, including the president of the bank from Calgary. I offered them coffee and they wouldn't take it. We had an agricultural consultant with us who was on our side, or supposed to be, and they sat here and just ridiculed us, something terrible. One of them pointed at that picture [a landscape] and said, 'We can have that picture right off the wall.'

"He pointed his finger in my face and said he wouldn't talk to us. 'I want a statutory declaration,' he said. We didn't even know what that means. 'Absolutely no more talking,' he said. 'We're done.' "

Carl's face shows not anger but pain. The story continues building like a thundercloud. Carl steps out of the sentence he has begun. Joyce carries on.

"Still by Christmas they hadn't done anything. Except they hired a security guard and put him at the end of the road here, just before Christmas. They took every number of every vehicle that come into our yard and every vehicle that left. Larry was here and he just couldn't stand it. Then they sent the sheriff, and we locked the shed and hid our equipment. He come again, and all we had in the garage was the one tractor and outfit we were feeding cattle with. Carl let him in there.

"'Where's the rest of your equipment?' he said. 'I've got it,' Carl said, 'but I lend it to my neighbours and they don't bring it back.' We had a fantastic lot of support from neighbours and the newspaper, and we knew if we backed down, they'd roll over everybody else like a steamroller."

"How far were you willing to go?" I ask. Carl answers with a flash of lightning.

"I was willing to go out of here in a box. We had to keep fighting for the sake of all the people backing us and the others in trouble." Carl, for the first time, looks me directly in the eye, the light of history in his eyes. Joyce has a different but equally powerful light in hers.

"At times, sure, one of us would say, 'That's it. Let's pack it in,' " she says. "But every time we'd say that, I would think. . . . I'm going to cry" – and the rain breaks free of Joyce's fiery eyes and falls onto her cheeks – "I would think of his dad walking in here, and I thought if he had guts enough to walk in here, then we've got guts enough to fight for it. Every damn time when I got that way, that's what I'd say. And my dad, too."

"It damned near killed Mom," Richard, who is still leaning on the basement steps, says. "She had a heart attack." I look over at Carl when Richard says this. He is crying. The sadness of all the scarred fields behind us, and these wounded fields around us now, spills out of my eyes too. Joyce finds her voice first.

"This went to April 1986, and they'd never done anything. And I had a heart attack. Two weeks intensive care." Joyce turns to Carl and quietly says, "This isn't good for me, right now."

Carl collects the tears from his cheeks in a handkerchief with Joyce's initials on it. "Larry was still here, and he put it over the news, her heart attack. So right away then they settled with us. They gave us a chance to stay here. Farm Credit came up with $100,000 and we raised the rest, selling property and equipment. Our land is down from 1,500 acres to 240, and we rent the rest. So we settled with them for $160,000. Plus we had paid them more than $50,000 in interest every year for a lot of years. Over $700,000 over the years. When it boils right down to it, we didn't owe them a damn thing."

"And ever since then, I guess, God's been good because we've hung on," Joyce says, "and we've never had to borrow one cent of operating. We bank at the credit union. Our payments are $12,000 a year, and both years we've paid them ahead. Walking down the street, people would say, 'Good for you. Keep fighting!' I go to our dentist, he says, 'Boy, you've got a lot of guts, you guys. Keep fighting.'

"But you know, when this was over and settled back, I gave this place over to God. I had to or I wouldn't have made it. I said, 'It's yours God, you do with it what you want.' I said, 'Now I'm through with it and I'm not going to let it get to me again.' I don't feel bad towards the Bank of Montreal, no regrets towards them, and even that little dink [the bank manager] that sat out here, we shook hands with him."

Carl has been adding salt tears to his reopened wounds. As

Joyce says this, he catches two tears on the corner of his smile. It moves him to a defence of farming, to his motive for it.

"When you're a mixed farmer and raise animals, you have feel for things – it isn't dollars and cents. Well, it is in a way, but. . . . How will I explain that? Sure you have to have dollars to buy, but that isn't what's important – to us anyway. It's all the other things. It's a life."

Carl turns his head to the land beyond the window. He is not embarrassed by his tears. I fill the air with nonsense about two photographs we had talked over in the van. One would be of a desk in a field, the other of an office in Ottawa, filled with soil and planted with corn. Joyce has moved to the kitchen counter and offers us fresh peaches and ice cream. Carl turns his head back and with all the glory of a simple man reporting a truth, his quiet voice stumbling and failing towards the end, says, "I don't know how many cows here have given birth to calves, but if a cow is calving now, it's still just as exciting as the first one we ever had."

Joyce is busy distracting herself with bowls and spoons, but she hears Carl and says, soothingly, "Yes, our roots are terrible deep here."

Carl is not quite finished. Not quite. "You know, it'll be October soon, time for weaning the calves off the cows. There is nothing nicer than the smell of a bunch of calves, there is a different smell about them. There is a smell about everything about farming. You get a handful of soil and you can smell it."

"Carl can tell if something will grow, just by smelling it."

30

IN SIGHT

On the first hill south out of Fort St. John, a sign stuck to a tree at the head of a rutted path reads Fantasy Acres. The Fantasy has literally worn off, white letters peeling away from a blue background. But around the corner, on the downside of the hill, the landscape is indeed fantastic. A conjunction of valleys competes in beauty, farms bordered by rivers that take paths of their own choosing. A black bear on a bridle path, scooping water from a puddle into his jaws, briefly allows us to enjoy his curiosity before he moves back into the forest.

With clear vision I look from a high point down onto a farm, then slowly raise my line of sight past water, forest, and hillside into a monochrome sky. An unseen, discomforting, habitual hum inside me is noticed even as it fades – the hum of cloistered city life. My thoughts expand to fill the natural space available. Why?

The answer lies, for me, in the architecture of the two landscapes – the rural and the urban. The city allows only one architect, the human being, to dictate its content. Cities are exercises in restricted vision, the triumph of height over width, the animate caged by the inanimate. Trees are held captive by sidewalks; parks have straight edges; the sky runs in strips parallel to the streets.

In the countryside, species and materials that the narrow-minded city can only dream of all contribute to the architecture of the landscape. They range from the almost invisble to the overwhelming, from a grub to a tornado. They are incapable of repetition.

Farmers know themselves to be only one element at work in an infinite list. They may be forced, more and more, to contrive roofless factories, to subvert, amplify, or circumvent nature, but they can only tame the mystery of what they do. The mystery is growth, and when they, too, arch their eyes to the horizon, the abundance of the mystery reappears.

We drive on down the backbone of British Columbia, pausing on each of the vertebrae to talk with strangers who quickly assure themselves of perches in our memories. In Williams Lake we are in cowboy country, and I am reminded of the story of Howard Johnston and Doc Bell, as told to us by a skinny cowboy called Donny Watson.

"Howard Johnston was the same tall as me, but not so heavy-set; wore a hat so as he'd throw a shadow. He came up from the States on a fast horse and never went back. He was sixty when we started partnering together. Never learned to drive a vehicle. If it didn't have a rope handle, he didn't know what it was for.

"When we were riding for Doc Bell, Doc Bell came into our cow camp one time. He drove right in in his pickup. There was a wheelbarrow and a shovel in back of the pickup. Doc, he unloaded them. Johnston says, 'Doc, what's that wheelbarrow and shovel for?' And Doc, he says, 'Well, Howard, I thought when you weren't riding maybe you could haul the horse manure away from the barn there.' And Johnston says, 'Better take her back to town, Doc. I don't know one damn thing about machinery.'"

On through 150-Mile House, 100-Mile House, 70-Mile House, and a chance encounter with Albert, the ex-army sergeant on the reservation near Cache Creek, a Second World War veteran Shuswap Indian. Outside a dilapidated church, with its walls pulled together by a huge steel bolt with nuts the size of paving stones at each end, he asks me to put my hand on the lump of shrapnel in his back.

Heading for Salmon Arm we cross the Thompson River to find the ghost town of Walhachin, advertised as such on an information sign on the highway. One of the supposed ghosts, Charlie the postmaster, invites us in for homemade red wine with his family. Walhachin was a boomtown at the turn of the century. A wooden flume brought water into the valley from the hills, and the English settlers transformed it into a fruit garden. The First World War pulled the men back to Europe, and while they were there a storm tore the flume away from the hillside.

The town has gently slid towards, but never quite reached, oblivion ever since. When Charlie dies, the post office will close. As we leave he gives us a photocopy of the *Walhachin Times*, dated March 21, 1912. The pages thrive with activity. In Situations Wanted this appeal appears: "Wanted – By Widow. Anywhere in Canada. Good milker, butter maker, thoroughly understand incubator system, have raised ten out of twelve. Practical vegetable producer." And under Lost, someone is looking for "Black Cat, pink spots on eye, last seen wending its way towards store. Please return to cottage."

At Shuswap Lake we turn right and head for the American border down the Okanagan Valley. Okanagan Lake is a magnetic turquoise, but it is not strong enough to distract us from the scores of For Sale signs at the entrances to fruit orchards. In the regiments of fruit trees behind the signs we catch a glimpse of an occasional peach picker, held aloft by a hydraulically raised platform. "The only guy making money around here," Ken says, "is the guy selling For Sale signs." Near Osoyoos we switch from counting the orchards for sale to counting those that aren't – it's less work.

The end of Main Street in Osoyoos is the Canadian-American border, the forty-ninth parallel. From the garage, opposite the Clone Motel, a huge Canadian flag stands out in the southerly breeze. The edge of the flag nearest the border has torn away and extends in a tatty red streamer towards America.

31

BIG FRUIT

There's an old song in which a lover tells her true love not to go under the apple tree with anybody else but her. The lovers would have a hard time going under the apple tree in front of us any way other than horizontal.

The apple trees of a modern orchard are stunted, two-dimensional bushes. They are designer trees, customized to fit the reach of a picker with both feet on the ground. Eve, the inventor of apple picking, would have found little cover for her new-found nudity in these orchards. The branches extend sideways but not forward or back, so that the trees can be packed in like books on a shelf. The branches are held apart by nailed sticks, tied to the ground to slow down their upward growth. There is an air of the torture chamber about the place.

The apples on the tree nearest us are perfect giants. All the apples on all the trees in the row are perfect giants. They are the size of grapefruits, burnished red, the colour of a Mountie's jacket. A dusting of white powder hides their glow. To pluck one off I just have to reach forward and tug down. Wiping the powder off on my jeans, I bite into it. It doesn't taste like an apple. It tastes more like a white, wet fibre into which some trace of essence of apple has been injected. And these are a good crop, better than last year when it was so hot the apples cooked on the trees.

"They're for export, these," Claude tells me, "to the Japanese. For display. They like bowls of big perfect fruit on their tables."

Claude isn't sure what we are doing here. He can't get his head around the idea of anybody being interested in his job. It's just his job. Sure, there are worse places in the world to make a living than the Okanagan Valley, but he is here because his father came here from Portugal in the fifties, one of the several waves of immigrants to the valley from Old World fruitlands.

The first wave into the Okanagan consisted of Hungarians and Germans after the Second World War. The government, anxious to develop the valley, invited the Portuguese to join the flow and relieve the new labour shortage. The architecture of the houses, and indeed the landscape outside the orchards, resembles the land they left. Claude is up around forty, small and swarthy with a solid black moustache.

"It's all changed dramatically, though, in the last eight years. My father planted forty by forty (the distance in feet between trees and between rows of trees). Now its twelve by five, high density. We've developed a root stock that lets us do away with ladders."

So why all the For Sale signs along the road? Claude reveals that perhaps half of these are being put on the market by speculators caught with their assets down. "Land prices around here climbed to $35,000 an acre. Then they crashed and came straight backwards. Now it's down to $15,000, less. Some of them I wouldn't give $2,000. They just raped it, took off what they could and put nothing back into the land." The land they leave is barren; only a plough and extended convalescence can help it again bear fruit.

Claude puts quite a deal of work into the land. His yearly cycle begins in February with pruning. By mid-March he's planting, through to the end of April. "That's when we spray with oil, to prevent San José scale, spots that get on most fruit. If you want to export and they've got scale – forget it."

The honey bee army flies in around May Day; imported pollinating mercenaries. Adjacent rows of trees, which will bear red and green apples, are waiting, and the bees set to work. They fly like loom shuttles between the rows, feet laden with pollen, to produce the hybrids. Then comes a dose of pesticides for worms. Claude registers the by now familiar loathing for spraying, and yet admits that "we are spraying more than we ever have."

Next comes blossom time: the blooms ripple down the valley like petticoats, and the orchards are coated in false snow when the blossom falls. The blossom is culled with a chemical that burns it off, to allow the chosen few buds to develop to their inflated size. Thinning, watering, and then the cherry harvesting army arrives in mid-June and sets up camp for a couple of weeks, then leaves and works its way north up the valley. They retrace their steps to harvest the "cots" (apricots), peaches, plums, prunes, and finally the apples. Claude started picking his McIntoshes the day before, the last day of August.

After the final apple is off the tree, in mid-October, there is sprinkler maintenance, some gardening. The back hoe will come in and plough out all ten-year-old trees, and new ones – most likely a New! Improved! strain – take up residence. Deciding which apple best suits the ground that will feed it is a science; deciding which apple will be fashionable is clairvoyance. When you're investing $20,000 an acre to replant, you hope you get both right.

The Europeans have been growing fruit this way for twenty years, the Americans ten, planting up to two thousand trees per acre and taking apples off the trees shortly after their second birthday. "We started planting this way," Claude says, "last October."

The five- and ten-acre family orchard has all but disappeared from the Okanagan Valley. A family could manage to pick a parcel that size, but the inevitable takeovers, of little fleas by bigger fleas, has brought about farms like Claude's, forty-five acres that next year will be out of soft fruits altogether and exclusively into apples.

The top-of-the-line apple is the B.C. Extra Fancy. That's an apple that is 98 per cent red – the perfect specimen. From there apple status descends in redness through Extra Fancy, Fancy, Common, to C-grade. Beauty in apples is skin-deep, since there is no difference in taste between a Common and an Extra Fancy. The Commons, less forced in their growth, are sometimes actually sweeter. Apples are also rated on size – thirty-six, forty-eight, fifty-six – according to how many apples will fit in the standard forty-pound box. For a single apple with the right vital statistics and the perfect complexion, the Japanese will pay ten dollars. They make gifts of them. "The Taiwanese, on the other hand, prefer the striped, red-green apples," Claude says. "They'll pay top dollar for those."

Even fruit, it seems, has come to reflect the era of style over content. Claude prefers the smaller, sweeter apple. A worm hole is an endorsement from the worm, but no bruises or drillings must mar the perfection of the modern North American apple.

We drive back to the house from the cramped fields, the American border dead ahead. It has been free and open for fruit trade as long as Claude can remember. This means that the Americans set the price of our apples simply by setting their own. Trucks with U.S. plates will sometimes come up with a load of apples, sell them, and return with a full load of a different variety, playing both ends against the middle to make a buck, indifferent to whether there is a queen or a president on the buck being made.

The unfettered trade allows shopkeepers with dirty aprons to pass off U.S. apples as Canadian, simply by putting them in a Canadian box – which is why those little, edible stickers declaring the apple you are about to chew to be Canadian have appeared in the last year or so. Some of those stickers will find their way to Ontario.

"The chances are actually more likely you'll eat one of my apples there than in Vancouver," Claude says with a chuckle.

"The good stuff goes there, where the money is. The garbage? Oh, Alabama, somewhere like that."

Claude's youngest son comes into the kitchen backwards. Without taking his eyes off the television, he takes the lid off the cookie jar and snakes his arm inside. Two months ago he couldn't reach in, but now he can hook them with two fingers. Cookie in place, he heads back towards the screen.

Before Claude, now an eternally busy man (he had his golf handicap down to seven, once upon a time), gets back to the sprinkler rearranging we have interrupted, he runs us over to the co-operative storage and packing house that the growers share. They own it and govern it with a board of directors elected annually. It's a quiet day, the rollers, box makers, label stickers, and packing machines are all catching their breath. A forklift truck, the driver with a hat reading "Canada's Plum Crazy," ferries some apricots into the controlled atmosphere warehouse, a chamber of 1 per cent oxygen that puts the not quite ripe fruit into suspended animation till next March, when winter-weary Canadians will pay anything to sink their teeth into "fresh" fruit.

Back in the field, Claude reties a few branches into bondage and props up a sagging branch, barely three years old and obese with fruit. Claude's orchards, unlike those of many of his neighbours, will not be going up for sale. He has seen the future in time to grab hold of it and survive, by teaching Mother Nature the tricks of the production line.

A dog appears and wants to play fetch. He retrieves an apple and spits it out at my feet. "He'll do that all day," Claude warns me. I throw it again and it goes into a neighbour's field. "Let's go over there," Claude says.

Over there, the trees have grown unfetterd. They are tall, almost voluptuous as the evening sun casts their ample shadows into Claude's adolescent orchard. We can stand in the shade of these domes of green, with their apples spaced among the branches like Christmas tree baubles. But they are inefficient and so their days are numbered. And then where will the lovers go?

32

EAGLE'S-EYE VIEW

In the summer of 1973, I was handmaiden to a select band of ten Aberdeen Angus bulls. Every day they were brushed from nose to tail with a pig's-hairbrush till their coats shone like onyx, the parting exactly following the line of their spines. Their tails were combed, the hairy pom-pom at the end freed of knots. Their feet were blackened with shoe polish and buffed to an army shine. They were fed twice a day with buckets of warm mash mixed with lecithin and seaweed. Even the tuft of hair encasing their majestic testicles got the treatment.

They were the thousand-pound prima donnas of the barnyard, and in two months, when they were a year old, they were due to travel up to Perth, Scotland, for the annual Aberdeen Angus show, perhaps to become champion bulls and return, bright rosettes pinned to their halters, to a life of selected breeding.

This reminiscence of pampered show cattle has been prompted by an altogether different class of bull standing half a mile away on the eastern slope of Elkink Valley. It is a Hereford, serene and implacable, his reddish flanks blending with the rusty grazing ground beneath him, his white patches rendered a dusty beige by the clouds his massive feet raise as he wanders, unbrushed and self-sufficient, through his domain.

To reach Elkink Valley, we travelled two hills and a vale beyond Osoyoos. The road to the ranch house runs halfway up the side of the valley which has the outline of a baking tin, wide and flat at the bottom. There is a trout pond dug into the valley floor, with a fence around it and a sign on the gate saying Fisher Persons Keep Out. Next to that is a shallow lake stocked with smallmouth bass and perch. The end of the valley is dammed by a mountain, Chapaka, which has golden and bald eagles nesting in its outcrops.

Some people have comets named after them. Others have their names grafted into the Latin titles of plants and insects. Ace Elkink has given his name to a valley. The cattle ranch that Ace and his family work is 30,000 acres, one-third owned, two-thirds leased, including the valley and the range lands either side. Walking the fence of the Elkink family farm, at four miles an hour, would take ten hours.

For part of the walk, you could have one foot in the United States and one in Canada. Several of the Elkink herd of Hereford cattle defect, unwittingly, to the States each year. There is an annual roundup on the Elkink ranch, by horse and twin-seater light aircraft, to repatriate the lost tribe.

Ace is unsaddling a horse as we pull into the farmyard. He drops the saddle onto the hitching rail and silences a tubular wind chime with one hand while he shakes ours with the other and catches our names. I wonder how far you'd have to push a pin into his palm before he'd feel it, it's so callused. The shadow from his straw hat hides his face, then he turns to finish a little business with his eldest son, Jody, and displays a well-sculpted profile, slow-cooked by sun and wind. "We should corral them colts, so we can cut that one out and start halter breaking it; find out if it's smart enough to keep. Maybe a kid's horse if she's quiet enough. We'll use the mare, they'll follow her down."

While father and son go through this ranching equivalent of an interoffice memo, a frustrated young bull limps back and forth across a pen just up the hill bordered by a white rail fence. There are battle scratches on his hip. "Probably been in a fight trying to jump his place in the pecker order," Ace says. "He'll be back out in a day or so. Come on in for coffee." The cow dogs follow us to the door. A well-bleached steer skull sits on the grass by the door where the pink flamingo would go on an urban lawn. Two satellite dishes sit cross-eyed on the bungalow roof, one pointing to the States and one towards Vancouver, two hundred miles due west.

Ace's wife, Rose, a Similkameen Indian, whose father has been chief of the reserve next door for nearly forty years, is unloading groceries into the kitchen cupboards. We gather at one end of the dining table. "Dad bought the place in 1967. We've about doubled it since then. You come down the Ricter Pass to get here, and the Ricters had the land originally. There's some abandoned houses and a schoolhouse up on the hills back here, emptied out in the Depression. It's getting as dry now as it did then. There's streams dry this year I ain't seen dry before."

Elkink Valley sits in a climatic warp, a bald patch surrounded by districts that enjoy a higher rainfall. This is semi-arid land, more like New Mexico than the mind's-eye image of British Columbia. Rattlers, bull snakes, and scorpions live out on the hills. "A bull snake's like a rattler without the rattle, and not poisonous," Ace explains. "But meaner. A rattler'll run around you. You run around a bull snake."

The Elkink operation, in its simplest terms, involves two crops – beef and grass. The latter goes into the former, in the form of scrub grass or hay or silage, and when enough has gone in, you sell the beef. If you're lucky, the beef fetches more per pound at the livestock exchange than the cost of the grass you had to put in to grow the pound of flesh. Reproduction supplies you with the raw material on the beef side, castration speeds up the fattening process, and irrigation promotes the grassy side of the equation.

Man and nature combine to make things a lot more complicated than that, on a grand scale. Ace has around a thousand head ranging out in the summer, most of them Herefords, with some longhorns and Brahman bulls mixed in. Each bull will run

with around twenty cows, and they maintain tenure by producing a favourable ratio of bull-calf winners to losers. Otherwise
they go for sausage meat.

The herd can stay out on the range until after Christmas,
when they will start coming down of their own accord to the
winter valley pasture when the hills get slippery with snow.
"They'll start hanging the fence after that, wanting to come
home, but we won't bring 'em inside till we have to," Ace says.
In a mild year the temperature will rarely dip below freezing for
more than a couple of weeks, so the herd may stay out right
through till spring.

Some time around March 1, just before the sunflowers start to
bloom on the hillsides, the cows will begin to calf out, between
620 and 650 calves born in an average year. They are branded
right away with the Elkink insignia, an E with a lazy E – an E on
its back with its legs in the air – right next to it. A branding iron
is still used, but these days it is heated with a propane torch. The
calves are castrated at the same time, their testicles collected,
cooked, and served as Rocky Mountain oysters.

For the first two months of their lives, the calves are vulnera-
ble to coyotes, eagles, and rustlers. "If you see coyotes in bun-
ches of three," Ace says, rhyming them with "shoots," "you're
going to end up with some trouble, because they are smart.
There is one animal that will never go extinct." Controlled
hunting keeps the coyotes manageable. I have visions of fabu-
lous eagles carrying off calves to mountain nests, but they slash
and dine on the spot, swooping down with one talon extended
and zipping open the calves along the belly, returning later to
feast on the liver. The rustlers were a problem – "We lost twenty
head one year" – but the district cattleman formed a neighbour-
hood watch called Vandalert that keeps the numbers down to
one or two head lost in a bad year.

The calves that do make it through, which is the vast majority
of them, will bulk up 500 pounds heavier by fall. Most of those
will go through to the second year, which guarantees a tenderer
meat. A select few, the friskier ones, the kickers and buckers,
will get to postpone their appointment with a dinner plate by

going on the road and appearing in rodeos. Even if the price of beef is good that year, you can get hit sideways by fashions in nutrition or interprovincial dumping of stock at a dime under the lowest possible price you had decided you could live with.

While the herd is ranging on the summer pasture, Ace will get three or four cuts of hay off the four hundred acres he has under seed. Irrigation is a constant chore. "Let's go down in the valley and I'll show you," he says, and we move from the kitchen-table classroom out into the field.

Sitting three across on the pickup seat, Ace points us down into the valley, past his Maule airplane with a bull's head logo on the stabilizer. The plane is a winged tractor, a tool that has converted the two days it used to take to survey the herd into a morning's overhead surveillance. Roundup has been reduced from a week to a day. "I'll fly while the boys are riding, signal to them if they miss some. It's great for finding stragglers when they come in for winter. We might have two groups five miles apart that would take a day's riding to spot."

Alongside the plane, a field of alfalfa is almost tall enough for a third cut. The crop is enjoying some artificial rain from a pivot, a sort of radio tower laid on its side, with sprinklers along its length. The whole thing is mounted on wheels and rotated at the centre by a motor. Maintaining these pivots is a short-straw job, but like the airplane, each pivot is worth a hired man. I can't see it moving until I focus on one end and watch it click forward like a minute hand on a wall clock. The well feeding the pivot is nearby, two hundred feet deep and pumping out water at the rate of a million glasses of water an hour. "Listen, you can hear it sucking on air," Ace says, pointing down into the hole. "I haven't heard it do that in fifteen years. We'll need some snow this year to fill up the water table."

Like the calves, the crops face a wildlife problem – marauding deer. "If you come down here in the late fall and shine a spotlight across this field, it'll light up clear across with eyes, like coming into Vancouver in the middle of the night." Ace and his men have counted 400 deer working their way across a field. They shave the top off the field, one mouthful and on to the next plant. "You don't notice till you realize the field is shrinking instead of growing. You can lose a whole cut, so you have to buy in." On a ranch this size that can mean spending $40,000 on an extra hundred tons of hay you'd planned on making yourself. A cull, either natural or man-made, is the only thing Ace can see that will solve the problem.

There is a bale of hay alongside the old custom house that Ace has converted to a bunkhouse. In keeping with the larger-than-life feel this whole visit has had, this bale is enormous, shaped, appropriately, like a truck-sized loaf of bread. Ace guesses its weight at three tons. The hay is compacted in the collector wagon as it is mown, and popped out the back when it is fully grown. It can be picked up and put down by a forklift arrangement, and the same machine can hack off a piece in the winter for feed as easy as toast in the toaster. I still have a vestigial set of calluses halfway up my fingers from handling countless old-fashioned bales twenty years ago, and less than fond memories of kicking the rats away as they tumbled from rain-soaked bales being hoisted onto a flatbed wagon. These modern bales are clearly the best thing since sliced bread.

Ace glances at his watch and realizes he'll have to take off soon if he is to make an environmental committee meeting of the British Columbian Cattleman's Association in Williams Lake. Ace sets his hat a little forward as we drive into the noonday sun and steers the pickup along the well-worn path in his valley back to the ranch house. A repeat of the handshakes beneath the wind chimes, and he is off to fuel up for the trip. A longhorn bull on the hillside, busy sniffing out the chances for romance with a reluctant Hereford cow, doesn't even look up from his work as we drive out of the valley.

33

FARTHER STILL
TO GO

Through the windows of the British Columbia Land Commission office on the outskirts of Vancouver, I can just see the mountains, too beautiful, the ultimate city back wall. I drag my eyes off the view and focus on a map showing the Queen Charlotte Islands, which is spread on the table. I'm searching for the farm farthest west.

The map shows the land in British Columbia designated as agricultural; more accurately, land capable of being used for agriculture. In 1981 the provincial government locked in its farmland, present and potential, setting up a legal fence that the developers would find too hard to climb. About 2 per cent of B.C. is farmland, including Ace Elkink's 30,000 acres. The fence held them out till June 1988, when a paragraph was tacked onto the regulations that allowed golf courses, and made their allowance a political decision. Environmentalists are now not sure how much longer the fence will hold.

When we started west from Newfoundland, we agreed to

leave the discovery of the farm farthest west till we got over to the left coast. Tracking it was going to be half the fun, and the idea of knowing exactly where we would end up three months before we got there seemed like opening your biggest present a week before Christmas.

The CBC, twenty years earlier, supposedly had linked Canada's two most separated farmers by radio and broadcast the conversation. Our choice of farmer farthest east differed from theirs (we'd used land rather than farmhouse as the marker), and they'd pegged the farm farthest west on Vancouver Island.

This is, by my reckoning, dead wrong, since the whole of the Queen Charlottes are west of the island, parked between the 130- and 135-degree lines of longitude. And there is a farm there, both according to the maps and the agricultural rep we'd phoned in Smithers, who told us it had been there seventy years and belonged to a family called Richardson.

This is great news since the Queen Charlottes are high on my list of bits of Canada to get to. Their southern islands were our newest national park, covered in part by rain forest, toured by whales. As I walk out of the Land Commission office, I have visions of myself stroking a humpback – and then the vision fades and I take two steps back. In the foyer a large map of Canada in its splendid entirety hangs on the wall. The Yukon is clearly to the west of the Queen Charlotte Islands. But do they farm up there?

Outside, we head for the nearest phone booth and dial directory assistance in Whitehorse. Is there, I wonder, a Yukon Department of Agriculture? Yes, there is. I dial the number, tracing its route in my mind as it speeds up to the satellite and bounces down into a phone on a desk in the Yukon capital.

"Hello, Department of Renewable Resources."

"Are there, um, farms up there? Full-time farms?"

"I hope so. I'm looking at a map with about thirty of them marked on it."

Whitehorse is as far north from Vancouver as the Mexican border is south of it. A round-trip up there and back down to the Trans–Canada would take two weeks, and it is already Labour Day. We are dressed for a drought, not a snowstorm. There is only one thing to do: drop back to Ottawa, wait eight months, and then punt.

THE
NORTHERN
FIELDS

34

RUNNING OUT
OF CANADA

U nmolested is the best word to describe the Yukon. Vast parts of it look back at you with an ancient, innocent stare. We urban Vikings, shod in Reeboks and in search of fresh real estate, haven't got to it yet, but we will. There are not yet thirty thousand people living in half a million square acres. That's not enough people to fill a Rolling Stones concert. Most of them wouldn't bother to go.

The department of agriculture in the Yukon is called the Department of Renewable Resources. It is a tiny outfit, but it is still too much bureacracy for most of the farmers who live north of Whitehorse. They came to the Yukon to have as little as possible between them and the sky. They wish to do something timeless and simple, and to be left in peace to do it. Not one of the farmers we met there had a television.

In the offices of the Department of Renewable Resources in Whitehorse, Art Hutchinson runs his finger over a map of the Yukon. He is going through the list of contenders for the farm

233

farthest west, the bookend to the Powers brothers' dairy farm 3,500 miles east of us.

"Well, there's a priest up at Old Crow who grows his own," Art says, thinking out loud. "If there is anybody at Beaver Creek, it would be them, but I ain't heard of nobody there. No, it's around Dawson. Peter Horsnell had a crop in last year the other side of the Yukon River from Dawson, which would put him westerer, whatever, than the Pelly River Ranch. I don't know if he put any seed in this year, but I'd start with him. But, if I were you, I'd stop in and visit Hugh Bradley at the Pelly on the way up. No finer place to be in the whole world. Special."

Wild roses line the Klondike Highway as we pull out of Whitehorse. First chance we get, at Lake Laberge, we pull off. A sign nailed to a small scrub poplar on the road down to the lake reads Tax Returns Completed, despite the fact there isn't a house in sight, let alone a taxpayer. From the lakeshore the view is stunningly prehistoric. Looking into the view reflected in the water is like looking up at the restored Sistine Chapel ceiling. It is hard to believe that six hours up the highway there are farmers for whom this sort of graceful scenery is commonplace.

"About that thick," says Hugh Bradley. He is describing the depth the ice will sometimes get to on his windows in the Yukon winter twilight. He is pointing to the base knuckle on his thumb, holding the thumb up – two inches. "Insulation," he calls it. A very efficient Yukon stove (a forty-five-gallon drum with feet welded on and a fourteen-inch door cut into the front) provides the central heating. Hugh has worked the Pelly River Ranch for thirty-five years. We have been here about an hour, and I have already decided never to forget this farm.

The Pelly River Ranch is thirty miles due west of Pelly Crossing, a rather forlorn Indian settlement tacked to the side of the Klondike Highway halfway between Whitehorse and Dawson City. The dirt road connecting the ranch and the crossing runs along a perch on the river's valley wall.

The road was getting a spring-cleaning when we turned onto

it. A wall of dirt across the road had us snookered after we had barely gone a mile. Hours of delay seemed inevitable. The wall was silent and tall, until it began to rumble, and over it came a huge yellow bulldozer. The Indian driving it noted us, lit a cigarette, backed up, and in three passes had reduced the wall to level road. His nod as we passed was almost imperceptible.

Twisting like a child's squiggle, gophers popping up like furry pistons, the track tried its best to parallel the Pelly River on the river's last few miles before it joins the Yukon River at Fort Selkirk, once the biggest town in the Yukon. River and road finally came together at the farm gate of the Pelly River Ranch.

There was an ancient vintage tractor parked by the gate, fencing materials piled on the back of it, when we pulled up. Hugh Bradley was nearby, erecting a fallen fence that runs into the river. Taking up the second hammer, we wandered down, introduced ourselves, and began to help. Hugh accepted all this as though we had just returned from lunch break.

"The cows will walk around the end if it's not out into the water," Hugh explained. Physically, he resembles the fence posts, tapering balm of Gilead poplar trunks, being lifted into place. He is weathered to a hard satin glow of health, all the bark long removed, his age as hard to guess as a tree's, hair just a touch longer than a brush cut, and wire-frame glasses.

"That's a 1942 2-N Ford," Hugh said when Ken inevitably asked about the vintage of the tractor. There is a Band-Aid, a joke, stuck to the cowling. "My dad bought it in Alberta in 1945." It has worn out the pant seats of three generations of Bradleys.

The fence restored to a stable geometry, Hugh escorted us on the tractor to the cabin whose winter insulation he has just explained. The path to the cabin along the riverbank is second generation. The first one went into the river when they lost thirty feet of bank in one year. "It's settled down since then."

With the same absence of fuss that went into the fence repair, and without asking us, Hugh makes us lunch and answers a couple more winter questions. Tea is served in a pot with a lid that was once the top of a Magic Baking Powder tin.

"Do you have a source of income in the winter?"

"Same one as the rest of the year," Hugh says, putting a pan of soup and three mugs on the table. "Farming. Trapping is part of farming."

"Ever get snowed in?"

"Depends how you look at it. The rest of the world gets snowed out. There was an emergency one year, 1977, meant we had to go to Pelly Crossing. Took ten days."

Settling onto a tree-stump stool, the sink, the cupboards, and wood stove all within easy reach, Hugh sketches out the ranch's biography. The title to the land the cabin stands on was first issued in 1901, when Edmonton was still considered the capital of the Territories. Hugh and his brother Dick came and worked it with two other men in the spring of 1954. They had visited the farm as students at an experimental station at Haines Junction, southwest of here on the Alaskan border.

When the two men dropped out of the partnership a couple of seasons later, Hugh and Dick Bradley carried on. Dick married and had a son, Glen. Hugh remained single. Glen grew to a fine size, did a stretch in the forces, saw some of the rest of the world, then made a prodigal return to the ranch.

Dick's health recently deserted him and he has moved into Whitehorse. The big, thin-walled house that Glen grew up in now stands empty, a stone's throw from the cabin. The chicken barn, the stables, and an assortment of log outbuildings, most of them with roofs that double as shelves, lie between the two homes, neither of which has bothered with electricity.

Glen and Hugh run the farm now from this pint-sized cabin, with the quart of belongings in it, which Hugh has lived in for all those thirty-five years. Everything in it is two steps from the door, as far back as it needs to be. Clothes are racked over the bunk beds, giving the cosy impression of a burrrow.

It takes me two cups of tea to realize that Hugh and the cabin share the same trait – both are utterly without pretence. I've been tainted by too many homes that are putting on an act. Words such as spacious, tidy, tasteful, elegant are relative terms. There are no Joneses here to set the pace. A pan, a chair, a picture have a home as long as they fulfil their function. While they do they are left in peace. Same with people. Hugh passes no judgements on other people's different solutions to living.

But the cabin is not where Hugh and Glen live. They live outdoors. They live in an outdoors as marvellous as anywhere in Canada. "I like to read when I have the time. I don't usually have the time. I spend as little time in the house as possible."

"You've never wanted TV, all the toys?"

"First thing I like to learn about any TV I meet is how to turn the son of a bitch off."

The cabin door opens and in comes Glen, Hugh's nephew, his head ducked to get his hat through without taking it off. Glen is a storm to Hugh's tree. He is big enough to take your best shot, shake his jowls, and ask you why you did that. His hat, bandanna, jeans, and boots are a second skin.

"Let's have some music," Glen decides after the handshakes. "Some horse music, not that hippy thump thump stuff. You fellas get enough to eat?" Unlike Hugh, you can see a little clearer what Glen is thinking. You soon find out anyway; he likes to say what he thinks, and hopes you'll do the same. No pretence. He is river of opinions, all of them fast over the rocks, most of them hugging the right shore. He enjoys a little rough and tumble in the conversation, but he shares his uncle's unconscious hospitality.

"Glen, why do all the books have the same cover?"

"Uncle Hugh makes a white paper jacket for them when they turn up, so as we don't have to wash our hands to read 'em." The radio phone chirps up and Glen chats with a woman who wants to sell one of the horses she stables at the ranch. Most of the horses the Bradleys stable belong to guides; Glen reckons that "they make more profit than them cows for one twenty-fifth of the labour."

The doorway to the Bradleys' cabin is capped like a country church entrance. When Hugh steps out there in the morning, to stretch and smoke his first hand-rolled cigarette of the day, he is in a world of beauty. The Pelly River is his doormat, its current too strong for even the Ranch's horses to swim against. The last steamer went down the Yukon River, five miles west, in the late fifties, the steamboat *Keno* on its way to a berth in Dawson.

"We could hear them when we first got here," Hugh says. "We were going to go down and watch, but we never did get her done."

Behind him are the flat fields of the ranch's half-section that he has title to. The soil has never been desecrated with pesticides or chemical fertilizers – it doesn't need them. A sample taken from the potato patch got the official comment "Wow!" in the space on the analysis form reserved for Nutrients Required. "We let the worms and the bugs take their share," Hugh says. "There's plenty for everyone."

The base for this fertile soil was laid some fourteen thousand years ago when the last glacier to inch down this way stopped just about here, dumped its load, and reversed. The river has added the rest. Honest management has kept the soil young.

Hugh leases another thousand or so acres in the hills, and the cattle graze on those. In the evening they come down to sleep in the corral. The fifty-odd Herefords thrive, as do Hugh and Glen, on the food that grows around them. Since a bull arrived in 1974 to take over the procreative duties, the stock has got lean and smaller. His successors have maintained the tradition.

The front and back of Hugh's point of view are the mountains. A high basalt ridge forces a bend in the river to the west. To the north there is a dormant volcano, last active about a hundred years ago. The Indians have stories of a world filled with smoke and fire. There is a child's grave in the foothills, the only one on the farm, dug before Hugh and Dick arrived.

The talk carries on over to the potato patch that needs weeding of lamb's foot and horsetail. Going into the patch I notice that every gate on the farm has a different, and equally efficient, way of locking. Same problem, different solutions. Hugh flicks the weeds out with a hoe, while I pull with my hands. An hour or so later, we settle down in front of the cabin table, behind a meal of homegrown pickled beef and vegetables from the garden.

The food consumed, Hugh settles back, legs crossed, elbow

on his upper knee, cigarette in his fingers, and hands the conversation over to Glen, who is keen to lay out his endorsement of a plan for dividing North America down the middle and making two new countries out of the split.

"Here's how it goes," Glen explains. "The East gets Ottawa, New York, Washington, Quebec." He converts the tabletop to a map. Ottawa is the pickled-beef jar. "The West is the Rockies, the wheatlands, the oil, California." It makes as much sense, or lack of it, as the horizontal division that history has glued on halfway up the continent. I must be getting tired. I remember you have to choose when to go to bed in a northern summer.

"You can sleep over at Dick's place," Hugh says, "if you want. Beds already made up. Take your pick." After the cosiness of the cabin, the half a dozen rooms of Dick's two-storey house seem overstocked with space.

Morning brings rain and a sore back from yesterday's weeding. Wiping a cold-water wash from my face, I see Hugh in the small weather station, surrounded by a white-picket fence, where he has been recording the daily vagaries of the climate since June 4, 1954. The sun has burned a trail almost all the way round the clock on the graph paper.

We take the cattle herd down to the river for a drink, passing Glen on his way to tether a horse. He pauses long enough to inform me, accurately, that I look like ten pounds of shit in a five-pound sack. "What do you call that bull, Hugh?" I ask, hoping for a clue to something in the choice of name.

"Bull," Hugh replies.

Over a bucket of eggs that need cleaning and scraping, Hugh and I do a roll call of the visitors that have come by air, by road, and by river to the ranch in the eighteen hours since we arrived. The Bradleys fill a visitor's book a year, near enough. "I'm sure we'd notice if there was three or four days when we didn't see somebody."

Shortly after we arrived the day before, a helicopter came in from the nearby resource management office to restock its fuel depot; two separate boatloads of Indians tied up, and one of them, John Roger Alfred, a professional guide, helped Glen break in his new horse; the relief nurse came in from Pelly Crossing, and recognized her first customer among the Indians. "His eye had been knocked out by a bar-room bottle," she told us. She asked after a cow that had been chewed by a wolf, leaving a hole in its haunch you could put your foot in. Hugh had pointed her out, limping and with a resplendent scab, but otherwise recovered.

Towards what would have been dusk back to the south, three guys from a geological survey, all beards and boots, had stopped awhile then headed downriver. Watching them go, Hugh recalled the young German boaters who had parked their raft at the farm one spring. Needing to make some repairs, they asked Hugh for a hand. He said he'd be glad to help them when it got dark. "When will it get dark?" they asked. "August," said Hugh.

Last, and least, there came Amos the American and his wife who called him "Daddy." As each visitor arrived, Glen would call "company" and head for the stove, ready to whip out a meal and coffee. No one, until Amos arrived, had managed to miss out on both.

Amos, a well-fed elderly man, was on a mission. He was, so he claimed, the frontman for a multi-million-dollar scheme to put a tourist-bearing railway in from Fort Nelson all the way to Cordova. The line on his map went right through the Pellys' ranch, and he was glad to offer Hugh and Glen shares in this rich vein of dollars. "Figures can't lie, but liars can figure," was Hugh's only comment on all this.

Hugh shared a log with him by the river and let Amos slowly deflate. When Glen came over to offer the latest guests coffee, Hugh shook his head in a silent no. Amos didn't see the shake, but Momma did. "Come on, Daddy, we'd better go," she whispered, taking Amos's arm. They went back down the thirty miles through raw nature, visions of tourists and trains dancing in their heads.

"So what do you think, Phil, did you get what you came for?" Hugh asks me. We are down to the last egg apiece. It is time to go, something I haven't the least desire to do. The Bradleys' ranch, to me, is everything a farm hopes to be: a livelihood made in beauty, a palette for the urge to grow food, and a massage for the aches the urge brings.

"I did, Hugh, and I think everyone does who comes here."

"Well, there was one guy that didn't," Hugh says, taking his knife to some stubborn chicken shit. "He didn't take to the air." The air on the Pelly River Ranch is sweet enough to put in your coffee. "Said he was going back to California where he could see what he was breathing."

35

GETTING WARMER

Dawson City is an overnight success that lost its top billing, played the smaller clubs for a while, and is now making a comeback, heavily made-up to disguise the wear and tear. "The Tijuana of the North," Glen Bradley called it. Gamblers drop or pick up a few hundred bucks a night in Diamond Tooth Gertie's and do tricks with the ten-dollar chips for tourists, while underage Indians slip into a tavern and slip out again with a brown bag, headed for a motel room. There is a weird-looking mongrel dog on every corner, an endless circus parade of recreation vehicles lumbering down Front Street, and in the background the steady click of hammers as tourism bankrolls the rebuilding of the town.

Dawson City is named after George Dawson, the first geologist up there. Dawson predicted that somewhere beneath his feet there was gold. There was.

Gold attracts flesh. Ten years after the Klondike gold rush began in 1897, when a handful of prospectors and natives lived here, more than thirty thousand men had sardined their way into Dawson. (The gold rush was a boy's club. Women were there mainly as service depots.) Not many struck it rich, but not many starved to death. They were fed by pioneering farmers, many of them men who had first come looking for gold and had seen a steadier profit in vegetables.

Nicholas Fax, who came as a child to Canada from Luxembourg in 1876, hopped between farming and prospecting in boomtown Dawson. In the first year of the new century, on an island in the Klondike River, he made $15,000 selling his garden produce to restaurants. Looking to turn cabbages into gold, he went mining and lost $5,000 in ten months. Realizing he was in financial free fall, he bought land again, called it the Klondike Garden, grew potatoes, and had four good crops in seven years.

When the gold rush hunger died down, the Klondike farmers left their homesteads. The land, only briefly disturbed, reverted to bush. The town root cellar out at Bear Creek gradually filled with permafrost and Canada did its growing elsewhere. It grew enough, in half a century, to drive some people back into the Klondike, people looking for fresh starts. Some of them were farmers.

"I thought I was going to Dawson Creek in British Columbia." Joan Kerr laughs at her former self, the one who transferred twenty years ago from a Vancouver Island bank to its Dawson City branch. "I realized when I started heading north from Whitehorse on what we used to call the Vomit Comet that I'd got it wrong. I had a wool dress and a fur coat on. It was 110 degrees when I got off here." That incarnation of Joan Kerr is a long way behind her. She is now in her mid–forties, a stocky woman of tested confidence. Twenty years of Yukon farming have tempered her.

Joan worked the bank for a while, dealing with the miners in the early seventies who still walked in with nuggets of gold in coffee jars. Thursdays she would go with a mobile bank out to an isolated asbestos mine. Then she met George, a red-haired bush pilot and a man without fear. They took their love across the Klondike River and reopened an old homestead.

"We felt there was going to be a colossal depression again, and the only place to be was on the land," Joan says. "For the first five years out there we were completely self-sufficient." The only legacies from the gold rush were a hay barn, a woodshed, and a cabin on seventy acres. They cleared the land by hand until they could afford a secondhand caterpillar and went shopping, very carefully, in Edmonton for used implements. (Road freight from Edmonton is four thousand dollars a truckload. That sticks about twenty cents a pound on food. To all intents and purposes, Dawson City is a tiny importing nation.)

The Kerrs learned their farming from books and from the land itself. They peeled back the outer layers, the other careers, and found that at the core they were growers. Ten years after they broke ground, they grew more than they could eat and opened a roadside stand. The roadside stand graduated into town as a farmer's market, then moved next door as a grocery store that sells local and imported produce.

Rejecting the reins of civilization, as the Kerrs did, bends you back into situations your great-grandmother could have faced. Dawson City is guaranteed six weeks of sixty-below weather in the winter. At that temperature, there is hardly enough oxygen to light a match, and if you drop your car keys, you don't take your glove off to pick them up.

On such a day, Joan took her toddling son Graham, well wrapped and on his sled, over to the root cellar. The dog came too. She sat Graham outside at the head of the cellar steps and closed the door against the frost. When she realized that she couldn't get the door – jammed at an angle – open, Joan began to tear at it with the desire for freedom of a trapped wolf. It took forty-five minutes for her flesh to conquer the wood. Her arms, shoulders, and back would be black-and-blue by that night. Graham hadn't moved.

The farm has a satellite dish and electricity now, but still no running water. Nothing is taken for granted. There is an earned satisfaction in flicking the barn light switch with a free hand that used to have a lantern in it. The Kerrs have fast forwarded the history of the twentieth century, going from bush to thirty-six television channels in one generation. The kids found the world in books, and are both A students. They take nothing for granted.

For love to stay love, it has to be tested and to triumph. That's how it renews itself. Joan and George have stayed in love. "You have to have a really good respect for one another, you have to understand each other a lot. You have to know what's important in your partner's life as much as in your life – because it's really hard. It's hard work. There's not very many rewards that you can see. I think the most satisfying part of it is that you sit down to a meal and everything on that table has come from your land. You feel rich when you have a full root cellar, and your back porch is full of canned goods and your freezers are full of vegetables.

"A farmer is a unique person. They're not like anybody else. They have the love of the land, and they have a desire to produce for the people. That's what drives them on, just to see the ground produce. It's the best lifestyle that you will ever come across."

There is, Joan believes, richness enough in the river valleys for the northern Yukoners to feed themselves.

"There isn't anything that you put in the ground here that won't grow," she says. "We've grown tobacco and smoked it. Our potatoes you can eat like apples – they are that sweet."

Growing the food isn't a problem; getting to the other side of winter is. A storage unit would help, and some government seed money to build it. Mentioning government to the northern Yukon farmers, however, is like spilling coffee in their laps. Government is bureaucracy, and bureaucracy is two dead-weights tied to their ankles, one down in Whitehorse and one way down and to the east in Ottawa. Joan Kerr has had a title claim for 160 acres hopscotching its way around Ottawa desks for eight years. Money that could build the storage centre walls disappears like melting snow into government subsidized schemes on the sandy soils around Whitehorse. The biggest cause of erosion on Joan Kerr's farm, she figures, is the steady flow of soil samples south down to Whitehorse to tell her what she already knows – anything grows.

A north-south split in any territorial mentality is, of course, historic. The Yukon, sitting on the shelf of the sixtieth parallel, is so far north that the idea that it has a south seems flamboyant. But the disease of rules has nudged ten thousand Canadians, such as the Kerrs, north of Whitehorse up there into the pristine air. It was the disease of rules, we supposed, that drove the farmer farthest west, whom we have yet to find, into the uninfected North.

36

WHO'S ON FIRST?

T
he owner of the bed and breakfast we stayed at in Dawson had the scoop on the contender for the farmer farthest west, Peter Horsnell. It seemed that Horsnell, a man in his fifties, had got out of farming and bought a gas station. He had sold his stake to Joe Feller. Feller was a gold miner, who farmed a little on the side. Whether Feller had planted anything this year remained to be seen. The notion of the farm farthest west being a hobby farm for a gold miner gave me no joy. Journey's end, it would seem, was to be a myopic field of vision.

Peter Horsnell had moved onto a few acres just behind Dawson. Driving past the city dump to get there, an oddity caught the corner of Ken's eye. Turning into the dump, the oddity resolved itself into two bears, one of them a grizzly bear. The power of its arms and claws was being expended on a cardboard box. A grizzly was on the wildlife checklist I'd compiled for the journey, but sighting it in a dump somehow added to the depression brought on by the straggly end our voyage was having.

Peter Horsnell proved refreshing for two reasons. The first was the man himself. His slightly hangdog features and Jack Benny delivery put a topping of laughter on his entrepreneurial philosophy. He spoke at about the pace a horse walks, as befits a man originally from Caribou country, south of Williams Lake. His expositions were complemented with neat, geometric doodles; he was a planner, a maker of theories, all of which, if left alone, he knew he could make work.

He and his wife, Gwen, came into the Yukon, not without coincidence, the year Trudeau was elected. In 1980 Horsnell moved to the other side of the river from Dawson, and started his farming business. He grew hay for his cows and beloved horses, slaughtered his own calves, and planned for a line of vegetables, "Arctic Boy Produce," which would contribute to Dawson's self–sufficiency.

Though he won't quite say why, the disease of rules, in the shape of an NDP government, seems to have forced his sale of the O.K. Barn to Joe Feller in 1987. Blocked expansion, and the governmental countering of his wishes for a storage unit in Dawson with plans for an elk farm, drove him back across the river and into the more lucrative sale of fossil fuels at the Gas Shack. Putting the fourth side on a doodled box, he keeps his eyes down and says, with resigned irritation, "Of course nothing can succeed of a development nature unless your government decrees or wishes thou shalt succeed."

And then, with rapid sweeps of his pencil, he builds towards his historical summation of Canadian agriculture, using the Yukon as a microcosm. The Yukon's population is a thousandth of the country as a whole. What, to his mind, is happening there is "just a historical past being enacted in a new era, a new place at a later time in history. The twist is that here the rules and regulations are coming before the fact; Catch-22, the chicken and the egg, the horse and the cart." He looks up from this barbed strand of axioms and notices his wife saddled up and trotting off for an evening ride. Wistfully he pushes his theory to its peak.

"Agriculture being that, and given the history of man, well I mean, look at the Prairies," he says. I'm confused. "You grow the product, can't dispense it, so then the government steps in and you're screwed, glued, and tattooed."

There being nowhere to go after that, I ask him if he knew that he and Gwen were the farmers farthest west in Canada. "Stuff like that doesn't turn my crank," he says. But under his indifference there must be an annoyance at a farm they planted that didn't bear fruit. "No, it worked. There is something there now for someone else to carry on." And his eyes harden with pride for a moment before settling back to reflect his wry grin.

Though he shrugged it off, he is intrigued enough by the notion of the farm farthest west to say suddenly, "Actually, I guess, as a vegetable farmer, Grant Dowdell would be farther due west. He is what we call a truck cropper. He brings his produce upriver by boat. He lives on an island, and he turns out a heck of a nice product. I would say that family knows the value of real hard work."

"So you would call him a farmer?"

"Oh, no qualms about it. He produces and sells produce. It's a damn hard tough go, but they've wrassled a beautiful living out of it." And then Peter Horsnell gives his ultimate accolade: "I'd say Grant knows what he is doing."

A rhythm in the distance resolves itself into the hooves of his wife's horse coming back up the drive. Horsnell puts down his pencil and looks out the window at the vegetable garden.

"It's the first year there's ever been a crop in that soil," he says.

"Would you keep farming if you won a million bucks in a lottery?" I ask him.

"Sure I would," he says. "I'd keep on farming till it was all gone."

37

EXPOSING THE ROOTS

With a push the sky blue boat begins shoving its nose against the swift, muddy Yukon River. The rain falling onto the river disappears into it without pockmarks. Dawson City falls behind, partially hidden by the levee built after the flood in 1979.

"There is more rampant sex in that town than you can shake a stick at," a tired looking Eric Stretch tells us out of nowhere. Eric is taking us, for twenty bucks, upriver to the Dowdells' island farm. Upriver on the Yukon means we are heading south. At a bend in the river half an hour ahead we will begin heading almost due west. The occasional bit of driftwood rushes past, flowing north to Alaska. There is still mist in the side valleys.

We enter a channel between two islands, and Eric throttles back the outboard. The river is too low to reach the dock in front of us at the island's corner. Further up the channel the engine grounds and cuts out; we drift off, restart, and make it to the steep bank. We scramble out, and Eric waves and carries on towards the small gold claim he has farther upriver.

A path runs through the poplars. The Dowdells have a radio phone, which they only turn on between six and nine at night – they have no idea what time we'll be arriving. We have already met them the night before at a barbecue, among a crowd of Yukoners around an iron pot filled with stew hung over a damp fire. Grant and I traded licks on guitars while a dog team of huskies whined in the background. He learned he is on Canada's most westerly farm at the end of a slow blues, and he seemed pleased with the idea. "Is that right?" he had said, and aimed a cat's grin into the fire, the grin lifting his glasses. His wife, Karen, all eyes and a chattering smile, laughed with pleasure at their title – "not a bad distinction, is it!" – and tells her three children. "Is that right?" the oldest boy Jon said, with the same staring softness as his father. They left the party early, the light still strong at eleven-thirty.

The trail breaks clear of the poplars into a glen – and there it is. The path to it alongside an unplanted field begins with a kid's tricycle and some toys on the ground beside it. The house catches and charms the eye. It is octagonal, made of thick logs and flanked by a stacked woodpile and a new greenhouse of plastic and wood. Regiments of young plants stand in one field. Market gardening is done mainly by hand, which seems to dictate neatness, closer attention to detail. The feeling comes on that somehow we have arrived at the roots of farming.

"Grant's not well," Karen says cheerfully as we walk through the door. He is upstairs in their house; upstairs is a three-quarter octagon reached by plain wood steps rising to separate the kitchen from the living room. Stephen Hawking's *A Brief History of Time* is half read on a chair in front of the piano. The home feels like a well-appointed cottage, oiled not varnished wood, pelts scattered about, including a grizzly on the bed, and a black bear, a beaver, some fox, and a couple of lynx on the walls, big windows, earth colours. It is as comfortable as a dream come true.

"August 25, take away seven, ten years ago. That's how I remember when we moved into the house. Daniel was born a week after we moved in." Karen came up to Dawson from

Prince George in the mid-seventies to teach, and took guitar lessons from Grant. Grant had come from Toronto five years earlier as a twenty-one-year-old Baha'i. He was working as a janitor in the school. He took her to visit the island he had leased and was clearing.

"He just kind of drove around in his boat till he found a good spot," Karen says. "He chose this one because it was high, with a really good stand of spruce." The following summer they came up, and for three summers after that they lived in a log-sided tent.

Grant made the hole for the basement of the house with dynamite, blowing apart the fibre mat and shovelling it out. He set out to cut enough twenty-six-foot logs for a four-sided house, realized the island didn't have that many twenty-six-foot straight trees, so he halved them in true lengths and went with an octagon.

"He is methodical," Karen says of her husband, "and he believes that you can really learn a lot yourself, if you want to." A friend of Grant's at the barbecue had summed him up for us – "Grant considers the Sears Catalogue to be propaganda."

Husband is a word with a variety of meanings. It started as Old Norse – *husbondi*. *Hus* was house, and *bondi* was someone who had a household. For a while the word could also mean a farmer, a husbandman, or a manager of an estate. Husbandry still means farming as a skill or art. In the way Karen describes Grant, he seems to incorporate all these meanings. "Too well!" she says with a laugh when Grant's management is praised. Laura Dowdell, who is five and ridiculously cute, sums it all up by pronouncing that "the vegetables get big."

Karen has taught the children from Grade One. She has been their only teacher, although they correspond with a Mrs. P. Mrs. P.'s notes with little praises like "This is very good work!" are pinned above the boys' new beds, which Grant made as his winter project. The children are without competitors, a blessing or a curse depending which side of the school fence you are on, but they gain self-discipline. This last winter the boys have become old enough to swing an axe and make firewood for the furnace, the first of the series of adult chores they are growing towards.

Laura, who is practising her skill in chattering, interrupts to show her latest work of art. "This is Storm, the dog, and he's going to get that vulture. He's a very good hunting dog of mine. Those are two trees and this is my cabin. There is a bed in the cabin." As Laura concludes her explanation, her father's thin, tall frame slowly comes down the stairs. Grant lies on the sofa by the guitar and the sheet music. (Fresh guitar strings are ordered from New Brunswick every couple of years.) He bought a generator, a massive old English one, primarily to be able to play classical records. Yes, he tried a Walkman once on the hour's journey by dog sled into town. "I was kind of disgusted with it. I felt like I was in a movie, like someone should be narrating it."

Through the fog of his influenza, Grant describes the transformation of the island into a home and a working farm. The first small garden was some beans, peas, and radishes. "That was a lot of rows ago," Grant says. There is now an extended family of crops, including the flowers they grow for Parks Canada. His customers include friends and friendly restaurants. In mid-June he begins going back and forth with produce in the boat he built himself. His cucumbers were once declared by Tim, the river cop who checks that nets are lifted when fish quotas have been reached, and who doesn't consider vegetables food, to be "the best I have ever hated!"

This year the wooden frames of the two greenhouses were replaced with galvanized steel. A water tower, a miniature version of the familiar landmark of rural towns, gravity-feeds the young plants, each one individually served. The soil is not naturally healthy, and while he won't use pesticides he has no qualms about fertilizer. "It's nitrogen whether it comes out of a bag or a cow," he says. "The danger is that you can end up with a pure mineral soil. I don't have room for the animals to make the twenty tons an acre of manure required to keep the soil organically rich, so I use bag fertilizer and I plough back clover or barley." He will soon have cleared enough of the island's sixteen acres to allow him to leave some land in fallow rotation.

Like many other Canadian farmers, Grant works off the farm – he traps. In an area thirty miles along and thirty miles back from the other side of the river, which he patrols by dog sled, his lines capture mostly lynx, some fox, and the occasional bigger carnivore. In summer they also net around six hundred dog salmon.

There are no qualms about trapping, no contest of matter over mind. "Whenever trappers get together," Karen says, "the thing they talk most about is the quickest way to kill the animals."

"In my well-considered opinion," Grant adds, "a well-managed trapline makes an ethically and environmentally sound contribution to wildlife management" – a statement he has had many hours to consider in the winter months.

The hours and days spent in the snowy hills have to some degree reprimitivized Grant's senses. He can catch the smell of a skidoo on the trail long after it has gone by. The smell of your own urine that greets your nose, reawakened in the Yukon air, is pungent enough to make you question your health. It makes me realize the symphony of scents the huskies must tune into as they pull Grant along the trap lines.

The various trapping seasons begin in November and end by mid-March. That leaves a month's breather before the household switches gears from the carnivorous to the vegetarian, and the Yukon turns its face to the sun for three frost-free months before turning away again.

On the boat ride here with Eric, we had passed several islands. I wonder if there are regrets about the choice of this particular island. There are none. "It's good flat land, lots of water, good transport access," Grant says. "I'm convinced this is about the warmest spot on the Yukon. It's low, and the water acts as an insulation barrier in the fall. There's no permafrost here." There was some bureaucratic testing of the Dowdells' desire to make a go of it in their first few years here. The lease was extended out like a tether on a training horse. Finally, about five years ago, the Dowdells were able to cut the rein and claim clear title to their island.

A large-scale map comes out, all seriousness aside, to help locate the farthest west point of the fields of vision, the absolute edge of our journey. It is at 139°W 64°N, and it is a garbage pile. The irony gets a laugh, but the dig in my romantic ribs knocks a hunch into place.

"It's an article of faith, with you, being here?" I ask Grant.

"In a way I suppose. Living on an island, for one thing, you have to have a certain amount of faith. It's humbling – when you stop to think about it."

I imagine that Grant does stop to think about it, perhaps as he looks back along a row he is harvesting to the home and family he and Karen have reared, but he prefers planting and nourishing his philosphy to simply recounting it. The article of faith, however, is not self-sufficiency.

"I don't think of it in those terms. I'm part of a market economy. I don't work for wages, and that's as self-sufficient as I care to be."

Grant no longer cleaves to the Baha'i faith, but there are vestiges of it in him. As we all do, he has with the years become his own second cousin, related to the man he once was but no longer completely him. He defines the Baha'i faith as accepting the notion of progressive revelation; "the mind can only take so much divine dispensation at one time." So there is not one prophet but a series of prophets, each adding an insight, a further clue to the divine plan for us.

An island in the Yukon River is a fine, uncluttered laboratory to undergo personal progressive revelation. The results are admirable, and are admired by his many friends. (Asked if he owed anyone money, he replied, "Not that I know of." A visitor behind us said quietly, "His friends owe him." She didn't mean money.)

Before we leave, hitching a ride back with some friends who had come Sunday visiting, Jon takes me to the site of the tent his parents lived in those first two summers. The walls are still there, and a board for a shelf stretches empty between two trees. A treehouse overlooks it now, and Jon comes here to read. His favourite books are stacked inside: *World of Wonders*, printed in 1914, and an equally old series, *The Rain People*, *The Leaf People*, and *The Cloud People*.

"Will you be *The Farm People* when you grow to a man?"

"I think I'll find an island of my own." He unfolds a map he and his brother have drawn of the island. The scale at the top reads "About One Mile."

When he was digging their well, Grant went down seventeen feet, and there he found driftwood. In the years he has plied the river he has seen other islands begin to form on other embryonic piles of driftwood. "The piles trap silt. Then willows appear, and maybe ten years later some poplar. It can all get swept away in a night, or it can grow into an island." And the island can accept the weight of a family, a family that can find itself wanting and then leave, or like the Dowdells, feed from the island and stay.

On the journey back up the river to Dawson City, a piece of driftwood with ears moves magically at right angles to the current – a young moose crossing the river. It reaches the shore and climbs the steep cliff with a camel-like run. Hunched like a chilled sparrow on the boat seat, I let my mind's eye eclipse the view before me. The fields of Canada line up ahead in a vast long, narrow quilt, squares of grain and flower and dirt, ribbed or flat or broken. Here at its edge, the truth of Canada is clear: It is a vastness, not some scattering of urban dots linked by asphalt and airline corridors. The cities may be where most of us live, but the farms are what we most live on, from Logy Bay to the Yukon River.

EPILOGUE

38

BACK IN TIME

Back in Ottawa, I let out the breath I had taken in the Yukon and inhaled some urban chemicals. For a few days the traffic lights seemed vindictive, brash mimics of the fall leaves. The architecture was alien and the whole city surged as though it were the site of an overattended convention of pushy strangers. Fashion seemed mere camouflage. A few movies, some faraway cuisine, and banking at three in the morning, and I was repatriated.

A piece of string laid along a Canadian map revealed we had made a journey of some 30,000 kilometres. Traced on a map, the trip was no more than a skate blade's scratch on an ocean of ice. Canada's most abundant resource is its size. The frantic gregariousness of its city centres becomes absurd when measured against this. Having travelled to the edges of Canadian agriculture, I wanted now to travel down through its history, to its origin.

The first broken ground in Canada, and its first tiller, are hidden in unwritten history. A proto-Iroquois, perhaps. The history of Indian farming remains unwritten. The European seizure of the wilderness and its subversion from land to field dates from Louis Hébert, a Paris apothecary turned farmer.

Hébert's training as an apothecary helped get him his ticket on board an expedition ship leaving for L'Acadie (now Nova Scotia) in 1604. He had inherited money from his father, so it was a sense of adventure that brought him here. The journey took two months. The colonists wintered at Ile St-Croix, Hébert dividing his time between healing scurvy sufferers and growing food. In the spring of 1605, the colony moved to Port-Royal. Hébert's love of the land is noted by a contemporary, and he studied the medicinal properties of native plants. The colony was recalled to France, with some regret on Hébert's part, following an Indian attack.

He was back in Port-Royal by the winter of 1610, this time as the husband of Marie Rollet. Marie was the first European woman to step onto New France and she has taken on a folk role with the women of Quebec. Hébert tended his garden and turned his attentions to the illnesses of the local Indians. This time an attack by Americans – Virginians – forced him back to France.

His third return wasn't so easy. The Company of Merchants had staked their claim in New France in furs. Farms pushed the fur animals further away and men like Hébert rattled their profits by trading directly with the Indians. Hébert reached high and got King Louis XIII to have a regal word with the company. The company agreed to take Hébert on as a paid apothecary, with three years' support and ten arpents of land. (The arpent and the acre cover roughly the same ground. Some older Quebec farmers still talk in arpents.) Hébert sold off all his French holdings and prepared to leave.

The company pulled a late move and tried to go back on the agreement. Hébert added Samuel Champlain and the Récollet priests to his corner, but the company gained ground, and a new contract was struck, one a McCain or a Cargill would be proud of. Hébert this time got five arpents. In return, he agreed not to trade with the Indians and to sell any extra food grown to the company – at a price set by the company.

Hébert and three other families were given land near the Fort of Quebec on the shores of the St. Lawrence. Hébert, Marie, and their three children made a home, in 1617, on the cliff above the fort. He had spent a year out of the last twelve in boats on the Atlantic. He lived ten more years on the land.

The Héberts planted wheat in their fields and cabbage, lettuce, parsley, sorrel, and rape in their garden. Champlain writes of the farm as being full and fruitful. The soil was rich, fertilized by ash from the stove. After three years he had extra food for trade. The eldest Hébert daughter took the first marriage vows in Canada when at fifteen she married Guillaume Couillard. Louis started a second farm for his son-in-law on the banks of the St. Charles River.

To the company, Hébert was setting a dangerous precedent. His success as a farmer was attractive to other *colons*. Like any trading company would, they feared self-sufficiency in their customers. They hassled the colony, thereby forcing them to unite and appeal to the king. The agricultural lobby won, and the company was dissolved.

Hébert carried in his heart the classic twin motives of the Christian colonist: to broaden the rule of his king and to deliver Indian souls to salvation by first routing them to Catholicism. Louis and Marie learned to speak to them in their own language; Marie opened a school to teach them catechism. Louis became important, filling in for Champlain while the explorer was at work. Near the end of January in 1927, Louis Hébert died a truly Canadian death: He slipped on ice and never recovered from the fall. Three months later the plough he had ordered from France arrived. It started a furrow three hundred years long.

Before leaving for Quebec City to visit Hébert's monument, I wrote to the Powers brothers in Newfoundland and the Dowdells in the Yukon. Could they, I asked, send me a sample of soil from their farms? I intended, in gratitude, to mix them together and bury them on the site of Canada's oldest family farm, a sort of space-time finale to our odyssey. I might even say a few words.

The replies came quickly back, as did two little Ziploc bags of dirt. Both families had gone to farthest corners of their farms to collect the samples. The easterly soil was reddish, the westerly grey. I transferred some of each sample to empty film containers, and put them into the fingers of the winter gloves I'd packed as insurance against a Quebec November.

Rain, the farmer's blessing, is falling on Quebec City's narrow streets and grey buildings when we arrive. A tourist map of the old part of the city guides us to the seminary, which now stands where the Hébert family once lived.

We find Louis Hébert's monument in Montmorency Park. The triangular park is wedged between the rear wall of the seminary, the cliffs, and another venerable building housing the offices of Parks Canada and a post office. There is an exhibition in the Parks Canada portion on the origins of Quebec gastronomy.

The monument is in the corner of the park nearest the Rue Hébert, a thin street dividing at the Galerie de Louis Hébert into two equally thin streets. The park has had a glamorous history. Hébert shares the park with Cartier, who stands in an opposite corner pointing towards the post office, and there is a rock in the third corner; a plaque on the rock explains that between 1850 and 1866 the capital of the province of Canada and the legislature trogged back and forth diplomatically between Toronto and Quebec. The first time the members of the legislature met on the site of Hébert's farm was 235 years after his death. The park was also the site of the famous Quebec Conference in 1864, where the process of putting a federal string around the separate packages of Canada began.

Directly in front of the monument are the rear gates of the seminary. Hébert, cast in bronze, stands atop a truncated obelisk. The bronze has aged to a dark green, the green of moss on barnwood. Hébert is looking northwest over the land he broke with a hoe. He is standing in a wheatfield, a small sickle in his right hand and in his left a short sheaf he has just cut. He wears a cummerbund and a loose rough-spun shirt. His pose is triumphant. He is looking, as all farmers do at least ten times a day, above the fields and into the sky.

Below the sheaf of wheat in his left hand, perhaps too far below, is Marie Rollet. Her dates reveal that she lived twenty-two years after Louis' fatal fall on the ice. She wears a full dress and a lace cap. She is seated with her three children, two girls and a boy. The boy is the youngest. She is looking pensive, as though pausing in reading to them from the book in her lap. The pages are blank, but it is probably the Bible because the youngest daughter is praying. The boy is offering his oldest sister a flower, and she is holding a mop.

On the other side of the monument stands the oldest girl's husband-to-be, Guillaume Couillard. He died the year the Turcotte family settled just down the river. His right hand rests on the plough that arrived after Louis' death. He is more smartly dressed than his in-laws, as though posed for a Sunday portrait.

Hébert has his back to the river and the town of Levis on the opposite shore. Guarding his back are several cannon. He stands as he lived, between God and the wide-open spaces.

There is a small wedge of grass and a maple tree on the mound supporting the monument. I dig a hole the size of a fist with a penknife, and Ken lines up a shot. The two soils from the two ends of our journey fill the hole, red on grey. I pause a moment, waiting for the game of touch football in the seminary car park to die down so I can say something for posterity, and we are suddenly invaded by a gang of schoolgirls, clipboards in hand, on a fact-finding mission of the city's monuments. They agree to pose in a line beneath a plaque on the statue listing the first immigrant colonialists. A moment's stillness, then energy reinvades them. As they rush off, I pick up a maple seed and add it to the soil. The earth is packed back into place.

39

SINCE THEN

Betty and Wilf Parsons' farm in Lethbridge, Newfound-land, is still up for sale. They had two very dry summers in a row and no abatement in the moose problem. Their son Donny, who went off to work in a factory in Ontario, came back home before the end of the year, having shot a nail through three fingers. He didn't go back.

The Lings, the organic farmers on Prince Edward Island, continue to get yields the equal of their neighbours'. Last year their only chemical use was to spot-spray some tenacious potato aphids at a cost of less than a dollar an acre. Their cattle, fed on organic crops, have gained a tasty reputation that spreads as far as Nova Scotia. Edith uses a mixture of the Selkirk and Acadia milling wheats they grow to grind her own flour and bake bread. The soil of their farm continues to deepen in colour. It's now a chocolate brown.

★   ★   ★

On May 13, 1990, Les McPhail, the valiant Charlottetown potato farmer who, with his wife Betty, rescued the farm from the bank in 1985, went into hospital with blood-pressure problems and died of a stroke. He was fifty-nine. Betty says that Les's final harvest was the best they had had since they came there. She carries on by "having a farm family around."

Vance Daurie, the man who gave his name to the Nova Scotian act protecting a farmer's right to use his land to produce food, and a pig's right to smell, is still in business, with a calf-cow operation. He is still busy getting the rocks out of his field. He wrote to me with great sympathy about the Sullivan case. Terry Sullivan was a New Brunswick pig farmer, who in the summer of 1990 probably took his own life after years of struggle and harassment. "It seems a cruel thing when lawyers and the public can drive a man over the edge," Vance writes. "I know they can because I was once a victim to the same kind of punishment."

Darrell McLaughlin, the New Brunswick potato farmer, has switched from taking a law degree to a master's degree in sociology, with a special interest in rural societies. He figured that since he'd been doing it most of his adult life anyway, he might as well make a profession out of it.

Cor Rook, the chairperson of the Farm Crisis Committee who farmed in the Ottawa Valley, died on May 1, 1989, of an aneurysm. Mrs. Rook continues to farm, with hired help, maintaining their dairy herd at thirty head. The farmer Cor spoke to on the phone the night we visited him eventually lost his farm.

★   ★   ★

Dianne Harkin, the founder of Women for Survival in Agriculture, has a new focus. She is studying the natural healing arts, and will become a therapist and a lecturer. Her husband, Dan, has retired from Agriculture Canada and they have taken up ballroom dancing. They continue to grow crops and enjoy their three granddaughters. Their door remains open to guests and whatever new challenge lies ahead.

The firm that bought the Massey Combine technology did nothing with it for two years, and then sold it to the Western Combine syndicate of Guelph. They have started production. The new 8570 models will carry, like retired colonels clinging to their rank, the Massey-Ferguson name and the three-triangle logo, and be sold through Massey-Ferguson Ltd., whose headquarters is in Des Moines.

Ruby Reske-Naurocki, the young farmer-poet in Beausejour, Manitoba, wrote to say that her grandparents, who had emigrated to Canada from Russia just in time for the Depression, both died peacefully within a year of our visit. Her grandfather died in October 1988, two days before he was due to go into a personal-care home, and her grandmother died nine months later, in their original homestead, surrounded by her family.

Almost blind, a little smaller and sharp as ever, Emmie Phillips has semiretired and moved into Eastend from her farmhouse in Ravenscrag, Saskatchewan. She visits the church at Ravenscrag every other Sunday, where she can hear, over the sound of the pump organ, the horses and cattle grazing by the school she once taught in. Her great-nephew, Dave Saville, because of the Gulf crisis and low prices, has returned to using horses, a team of four Belgians, to pull the hay wagon.

★   ★   ★

George Retelback is still driving the school bus in Irvine, Alberta, population three hundred. "I can't afford to retire," he says. None of his three sons has taken up farming. In October 1989 the school burned down, the same school George attended forty-five years ago. There is no decision yet whether to rebuild or to deploy the children elsewhere.

The Torios in Dawson Creek are still farming – very much so. They have made every annual payment to the Farm Credit ahead of time. Carl's gift with animals has allowed them to cover the risk on their own cattle by doing custom feeding of other people's cattle, six hundred head this year, and a profit has been made every year since they beat off the bank raid. They have even managed to invest a little in a nest egg. Carl and Joyce have returned to good health.

The deer problem in Elkink Valley in southern British Columbia took care of itself. A disease called EHD, a fatal form of internal haemorrhage, culled the herd the year after we visited. The dry spell has continued for three years, and Ace is still hoping for snow. The herd has held steady, and the eagles continue to enjoy calf's liver as part of their diet.

The Dowdells on their island in the Yukon River have ordered a mower for the tractor and will see how much hay the island can produce. If it looks good, they will do some fencing and buy a horse or two; they hope that the southern end of the horses will provide organic fertilizer and allow them to wean themselves off the chemical brand.

A Note about the Photographs

Most of the colour photographs in the book were shot on Kodachrome 64 Professional film, but for a few shots taken in poor weather or where the natural light was dim, I used Kodachrome 200 film. On a couple of shots, when I wanted a 6 x 7 cm, not a 35 mm, transparency, I used Fujichrome RPD.

For most of the photographs I used a Leica reflex body and a variety of lenses from 19 mm (wide angle) to 350 mm (telephoto), including my favourites, the 24 mm Elmarit and the 90 mm Summicron. Only rarely did I supplement natural light with flash.

The fifty-five colour and five black and white images which made up the final selection were reproduced as 4 x 5 inch duplicate transparencies on Kodak Ektachrome duplicating film prior to scanning.

Ken Ginn